The Information Commons Handbook

Donald Robert Beagle

With contributions by Donald Russell Bailey and Barbara Tierney

NEAL-SCHUMAN PUBLISHERS, INC.

NEW YORK   LONDON

Published by Neal-Schuman Publishers, Inc.
100 William St., Suite 2004
New York, NY 10038

Printed and bound in the United States of America.

The paper used in this publication meets the minimum requirements of American National Standard for Information Sciences – Permanence of Paper for Printed Library Materials, ANSI Z39.48-1992.

ISBN-13: 978-1-55570-562-6
ISBN-10: 1-55570-562-6

This book is dedicated to Lucy and Will Talbert.

Contents

Foreword

They hang the man and flog the woman
That steal the goose from off the common.
But let the greater villain loose
That steals the common from the goose.
　　　　　　　　　　—Folk poem, circa 1764

I have been enthralled with the concept of the "commons" ever since I read David Bollier's excellent work *Silent Theft*, and his annual updates on the state of the American commons. I've never forgotten the old poem above from this work. Personally, I am also enthralled with technology. My career has been based on and enhanced by it. I believe in technology's power to transform. I also believe in the power of libraries to transform—learners, researchers, society, and more. However, I worry deeply that we may have remained in a techno-centered approach for too long; it's time to return to a user-centered approach that uses technology in the service of our clients. If we don't, we run the risk of being too similar to the Googles, Yahoo!s and MSNs of the world and losing our fundamental positioning in the minds of our users: information coaching, information fluency training, and improving the quality of questions. We risk losing our key and important market differentiators.

Therefore, I was thrilled when Don Beagle asked me to write the foreword to this book. It is the right book at the right time. The core concept of the commons is essential to the long-term health of libraries and the transformations that libraries are undergoing now. This book presents a great framework to discuss the transition of libraries through this next phase of global change. Libraries have been through a period of dramatic technological change that has resulted in an era of a strong focus on technology—and too often to the detriment of the users. As librarians learned about and wrangled with the massive potential of these new technologies in the service of their users, they sometimes neglected to ask themselves the basic question: *What is the best environment for communities, culture, learning, and research?* To be fair, libraries weren't at the present stage where we can integrate many new technologies in the service of the users more seamlessly, more easily, and better than ever before. The Web 2.0 trends are working to the library's benefit.

The evolution of libraries is at a tipping point. Librarians can either continue on the path of technocracy or debate and implement the next generation of libraries in a new way that combines the best of past traditions with the opportunities presented by new technologies reimagined in the service of society. This book is a major contribution to this effort, following in the steps of Scott Bennett's *Libraries Designed for Learning*.

Just as railroads, airplanes and interstate highways changed the patterns of travel in the world, technology and the Internet have changed the patterns of learning, research, and discovery, as well as the underlying staffing, rules, services, collections, and tools that support this essential effort. And each change has had untold unintended consequences—both good and bad. It's up to those who consider these trends strategically to ensure that the good outweighs the bad. Librarians need to reimagine a world of libraries that takes advantage of the best of the new while ensuring that the human touch remains.

Don and his contributors have wisely provided the first steps in this book. Too many projects of this nature—whether they are called computer commons, reference commons, research commons, information commons, or learning commons—start by talking about space, wiring needs, lighting, staff requirements, and the like. It is a leader's role to ensure that the bigger picture is addressed and discussed first. Don's approaches, outlined here and supported by an international range of examples in all types of libraries, are imbued with the wisdom of experience. Start with the user! Start with the strategic vision and goals of your enterprise. Test your assumptions and engage the community. Step up to being political; don't shy away from it. These are just some of the key concepts that will come through as you read this book. Here they are not just platitudes. They are supported by the key management and strategic prioritization techniques and methodologies that will allow you to traverse a successful path with your commons initiative. This book's detailed examples of the best ways to make key decisions, and how to ensure that they are successful, are its great strength. Don has provided simple, yet sophisticated tools that will empower your teams for many years to come.

Libraries are social organizations. Yes, there is the need to manage cold inventories of objects and ever-changing technologies, and to ensure the preservation of these assets, but this book reminds us of the absolute need to keep our eye on the real goal. Too many library projects forget the 90 percent rule: spend 90 percent of your time in planning and the rest of work will flow like a river. Too many library strategic processes fail to align the process first with the institutional and community goals and the needs of users and learners. Librarians leap to answering the assorted who, what, where, and when questions instead of starting with the why and the how, trying too often to *manage* in this difficult age instead of *leading* through to a grand *vision*. Information and Learning Commons initiatives provide a great opportunity to be both visionary and real. They provide the opportunity to re-create the central role libraries play in community and learning institutions—but modified for the new millennium.

The Information Commons success stories that accompany this book are excellent. They cover virtually every type and size of library and have been sourced from major libraries in the United States, Canada, and around the world. They make the process real and give confidence that others have trod this path before. Throughout the narrative of this work, there is a cornucopia of learning from other professionals who have pioneered the commons and share their experiences. You will find a range of early adopters and innovators who are sharing their key insights with us, but with the benefit of 20/20 hindsight. You can walk in their footsteps and benefit from their bruises and war wounds.

The great strength of this book is that it brings together, for the first time, all of the strategic issues inherent in a commons-style initiative. You will find the tools and critical thinking needed to embark on your own major project. Don ensures that you will stay focused on the needs of your users and the context in which you are operating. He also doesn't shy away from taking a stance and sharing an informed opinion. You are provided with tools and insights to bring along your management and staff in the process. The ongoing focus on managing the subtle political context of these projects is a strength of each chapter. You are endowed with tried-and-true strategic planning techniques, including the development of robust scenarios to test your ideas and creative insights.

By following this work and learning from the author's wise approaches, you will enhance your chances of success. You will leap over the old days of shackled service desks operating in traditional chimneys of circulation, reference, research, ILL, copying, reserves, etc., into a world where service triumphs in a dynamic and user-empowering way. You will have a foundation for growth. You will have built a foundation for better relationships with your boards, management, trustees, and partners.

Don has resisted the easy way out. Others might take a prescriptive approach, but that's just not good enough. It would create the illusion of dynamism and yet remain sound and fury. In this book, Don has pushed for encouraging the best process that will lay a foundation for not just a successful Information Commons but for a bright future for your library, its patrons, and its host institution and community. And he's right. We won't find the future with half measures.

Enjoy. Learn. Grow.

Stephen Abram
Vice President, Innovation, SirsiDynix
Stephen's Lighthouse Blog
President-elect, SLA
Past President, Canadian Library Association
Past President, Ontario Library Association

References

Bollier, David. *Silent Theft: The Private Plunder of our Common Wealth*. New York: Routledge, 2002.
———http://www.bollier.org
On The Commons Blog. http://www.onthecommons.org/
Understanding the Commons. http://www.friendsofthecommons.org/understanding/index.html
Bennett, Scott. *Libraries Designed for Learning*. CLIR, 2003.
  http://www.clir.org/PUBS/abstract/pub122abst.html

List of Figures

Preface

Throughout much of the last century, people shared a collective understanding of the way information was organized and accessed. Change seemed continuous but controlled. The computer age initiated by the electronic revolution of the 1980s and 1990s transformed this relatively stable process of development, splintering it through the refractive lenses of new paradigms and possibilities. As it did so, it redefined how, where, and why people used information. These radical changes brought about a new vision of knowledge and forever transformed the ways we learn.

In the past, the "commons" was a city or township's open civic space, at once market and meeting ground. Even as the ways in which we interact with one another have changed, the need for such a mutually accessible locale has not vanished outright. Its newest form is that of the "Information Commons," an umbrella concept describing the physical, virtual, and cultural environment for new learning communities of students, teachers, scholars, and researchers. As a new model for service delivery, it is not about technology per se, but how an organization reshapes itself around people using technology in pursuit of learning.

The Information Commons Handbook is a practical guide to this new terrain, designed to map a wide range of vantage points. It covers the history and theory behind the Information Commons, the need to create innovative spaces to house it, and the best ways to further tomorrow's ever expanding world of knowledge. It is designed to help chart the ongoing transformation of libraries into innovative arenas for learning, research, and instructional support

The Lay of the Land

To better understand the different levels of an Information Commons, imagine a newly settled community of pioneers building a village.

- The *physical commons* is the village itself, composed of the best raw materials available and erected through collaborative effort. In the Information Commons, this entails innovatively designed workspaces offering complete access to the widest possible range of resources.
- The *virtual commons* reflects the way ideas and specialized knowledge moves through the community, making possible the environment they are constructing together. Today this network of information is equated with the way the endeavor coexists in cyberspace, the panoply of digital sources now available.

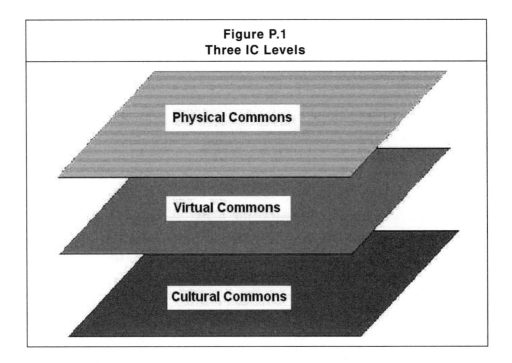

Figure P.1
Three IC Levels

Physical Commons

Virtual Commons

Cultural Commons

- The *cultural commons* represents both the shared views that ground the pioneers' efforts and the new understandings that arise from their individual and cooperative labors. In today's learning environments, the development of such shared assumptions and understandings is a crucial step toward the creation of a space where group process can shape knowledge in ways that parallel the large-scale evolution of knowledge in the workplace and culture around us.

This book uses various metaphors and diagrams to describe and visualize aspects of the three levels. The simplest description is shown in Figure P.1.

Libraries and Information Commons

Professionals everywhere have the exciting task of turning these transformative ideas into practical realities. *The Information Commons Handbook* recognizes that every public and private institution must transform itself to meet the demands of the last quarter century. Even so, no organization has changed more than the library. Libraries have always gathered, stored, and organized information, acting as the prime cultural repository of knowledge. Likewise, librarians have always possessed a passionate interest in finding ways to best serve the needs of learners. Yet where the path to meeting these goals was once a straight one, we are now called upon to enact new strategies and systems. This handbook focuses on how these changes affect libraries, their users, and their facilities. How do we design, build, and implement the best spaces to serve users? Consider a few scenarios that reflect library life today:

1. a large state university creates a space with hundreds of workstations that provide data services for reference, media production, and research;

2. a midsize private college designs a novel floor plan in an otherwise traditional library that highlights a single bank of powerful workstations;
3. a small liberal arts college implements an electronic resources facility to align the library with new learning priorities in a college-wide curriculum redesign;
4. a public library opens a "Virtual Village," extending traditional services and making them available to both in-person and remote users;
5. a public school library system sponsors an online "Learning Community" growing out of an IBM Reinventing Education Grant.

Each of these situations is indicative of the transformations libraries are undergoing. All are examples of the "information commons" concept at work.

A good Informations Commons brings together researchers, instructors, students, teachers, and users, equipping them with the technology (computers, projectors, Internet access) and furnishings (workstations, conference rooms and classrooms, print stations) to meet the goals they set for themselves. The concept is versatile, working equally well in libraries of all types, serving both large and small populations, and responding to the needs of all user demographics.

The following example illustrates the change from the old concept of libraries to the new notion of the Information Commons. Compare yesterday's idea of a "reference desk with a computer lab" to the services and facilities offered at The Toronto Public Library.

The Information Commons at the Toronto Public Library offers users access to a variety of cutting-edge resources.

1. *The "Information Connections" Electronic Reading Room* provides a direct connection to the library's various databases, the Virtual Reference Library, and the Internet. It is an area of approximately 80 computers with full Web access.
2. *The Centre for People with Disabilities* provides adaptive technology that gives all users equal access to library electronic information and collections.
3. *The Personal Computing Centre* provides access to computers with a variety of office software applications for business presentations and report preparation, plus educational and recreation software.
4. *The Digital Design Studio* provides public access to cutting-edge software and computer equipment for applications such as Web design, image scanning and editing, and publishing.

Information and Learning

True Information Commons do more than provide access to computers. Much more important, they are designed to facilitate interaction and serendipitous learning. Regardless of their scope, all true examples of the Information Commons share this orientation, emphasizing technologies that lead students and faculty on converging paths of learning and scholarship. These supportive learning environments are often mobilized in tandem with the learning initiatives of other academic units. Indeed, they are most meaningful when aligned with cooperatively defined educational goals. This fusion of ideas, people, and energy has raised the bar, changing not just the way we gather information, but also the way we learn. How, then, might we define an Information Commons? Based upon research presented in the next chapter, the author will suggest that an Information Commons can be defined as *a cluster of network access points and associated IT tools situated in the context of physical, digital, human, and social resources organized in support of learning.* Though all ICs, by this definition, are supportive learning environments, when the physical, digital, human, and social resources supporting the IC are *organized in collaboration with learning initiatives sponsored by other academic units, or aligned with learning outcomes defined through a co-operative process*, the IC has passed a phase transition to what might more accurately be called a *Learning Commons* or a *Collaboration Center.* Figure P-2 illustrates how physical, digital, and social resources support access to the physical, virtual, and cultural commons re-spectively. Human resources are viewed as the key resource supporting access to and use of all three levels.

For those who question the validity of remaking yesterday's "library with a computer lab" into today's Information Commons and tomorrow's Learning Commons, I ask that you consider a parallel scenario. If an information commons is just an *array* of electronic equip-ment gathered in one space, would you also call a modern library a mere warehouse for books? One of the fundamental purposes of this book is to show how an Information Com-mons can be made into something more than a mere row of workstations.

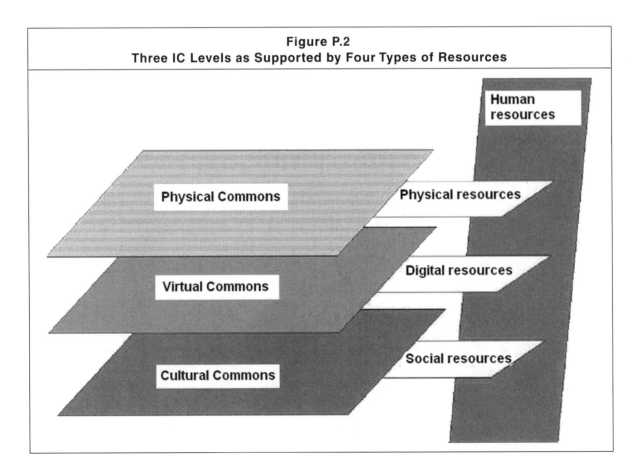

Figure P.2
Three IC Levels as Supported by Four Types of Resources

Human resources

Physical Commons

Physical resources

Virtual Commons

Digital resources

Cultural Commons

Social resources

Audience and Scope

The Information Commons Handbook explores the ongoing conversion of traditional libraries into innovative environments for learning, research, and instructional support. The topic is not technology per se, but how organizations can put technology to use in the pursuit of learning. While the ideas, discussions, and instructions will be relevant to any institution grappling with these issues, the spotlight is focused firmly on how the Information Commons concept can be put to service in libraries.

I wrote this book for a variety of audiences. It will interest

- academic, public, and school librarians involved in the assessment or upgrading of their organization's publicly accessible electronic resources;
- administrators seeking to understand how libraries must redefine themselves as they balance technological opportunities and fiscal responsibilities;
- faculty who teach and research in campus libraries who want to explore the concepts and practical implications of these changes; and
- students and faculty in graduate programs of library and information science who wish to further examine this emerging trend.

The Information Commons Handbook contains essential material for those institutions that have already built an Information Commons, as well as the many more still taking a cautious "watch, consider, and wait" approach.

Organization

The Information Commons Handbook explores the subject in three parts.

- Part I, "How the Information Commons Can Transform Knowledge and Information," explores how theory and practice have merged to create this new way to view the basics of learning. Chapter 1, "Exploring the Physical, Virtual, and Cultural Manifestations of the Information Commons," and Chapter 2, "How the Information Commons Evolved from Novel Concept to Remarkable Reality," discuss the emergence of this novel approach to learning. Chapter 3, "Information Commons, Information Literacy, and the Learning Commons," discusses how the different strands of information literacy, pedagogy, and technology can be interwoven in pursuit of learning.
- Part II, "Designing and Building the Physical Commons," walks administrators and their planning teams through the stages of developing a new space using a structured template. Chapter 4, "Strategic Planning I: Discovering Needs through Surveys and Focus Groups," and Chapter 5, "Strategic Planning II: Preparing Scenario-Building Techniques and Projecting the Future Commons," introduce how to set the groundwork of a project. Chapter 6, "Tactical Planning: Managing the Conversation and Drafting the Project Documentation," shows how to get the job done.
- Part III, "Making Vision Reality," provides guidance on how to improve existing spaces and launch new ones. It includes Chapter 7, "Information Commons and the Public Library: Special Considerations," Chapter 8, "Implementing an Information Commons,

Growing a Learning Commons," Chapter 9, "Assessing the Success to Enhance Space and Improve Service," and Chapter 10, "Balancing User Community Needs with Intellectual Property Rights to Create Practical Public Policies," discussing how user needs can be better understood through ethnographic research, and how user communities might reshape "public domain" discussions about intellectual property, copyright, and freedom of expression.

- Finally, the "What's on the CD-ROM" compiles several real-worlds scenarios included on the disk. The five North American institutions presented in this format reflect the diversity of schools that have recently embraced the Information Commons model. They include a large university, small university, community college, secondary school, and public library. The stories feature photo tours, background information, planning documents, and interviews with the directors of the facilities. As an added bonus, the CD-ROM also contains tours of several international Information Commons.

The Information Commons Handbook is designed to illuminate how recent changes in technology and the ways people use it have led to more than an advance in knowledge through a leap in skills and abilities. This exciting era offers nothing less than a fresh new way for all information institutions to reimagine their goals, mission, and purpose. I hope it will inform, instruct, and even inspire information professionals to imagine original ways to make the future real.

Acknowledgments

I first want to thank Barbara Tierney of UNC-Charlotte and Russ Bailey of Providence College for their vital contributions to this book. Barbara has invested the same energy, intelligence, and commitment to quality in compiling the content for the CD and bibliography that she brings to her position as Information Commons Desk Coordinator. Russ has authored the important chapter on IC assessment for this volume, but his professional contributions to this topic go well beyond the covers of a book to include his vital work organizing and moderating several important conference events on ICs at ALA and ACRL, as well as with his own presentations that have reached an international audience. Together, Barbara and Russ have provided priceless encouragement, support, and active assistance throughout this book's development.

I want to thank Stephen Abram, Vice President for Innovation at SIRSI/Dynix, for the kind and supportive words he has offered in several of his own conference speeches and presentations in describing my ongoing research projects. I also want to thank Christine Gläser of Carl von Ossietzky Universität, and Jens Lazarus of Hochschule Merseburg (FH), Bibliothek for their kindness and hospitality when attending my lecture for Deutscher Bibliothetkartag 2005 at Heinrich-Heine-Universität in Düsseldorf. Several key concepts in this book grew out of that presentation and subsequent discussions with Christine and Jens. Closer to home, thanks are also due to Dean de la Motte, now Vice President for Academic Affairs at Salve Regina College. In his former role as Academic Dean at Belmont Abbey College, Dean was an unwavering supporter of the library and a paragon of collegiality, academic integrity, and good humor. I also want to give special thanks to the following people for providing excerpts and giving us permission to use material: Susan Beatty, Don Buckley, Alec Couchman, Dr. Andreas Degkwitz, Heather Gordon, Paul Hagner, Joel Heikes, Marjorie Heins, Shelly K. Hughes, Sandra Keys, Nancy Kranich, David Leighton, Russ Martinelli, Gina Midlik, Hester Mountifield, Nathalie Noini, Frank Odasz, Melanie Remy, Lori Van Rooijen [Larkspur Associates], Jeremy J. Shapiro, Marilyn Von Seggern, Lizbeth Wilson, Nancy K. Young, Diane Graves, James Duncan, Grant Pair, Rich Rosenthal, Sallie Ives, and Jim Waddell.

And great thanks are also due to Michael G. Kelley, Development Editor at Neal-Schuman Publishers, Inc. Michael's patience, expertise, and professional insights have been crucial factors in helping to guide this volume from concept to completion.

Donald Beagle

What's on the CD-ROM?

Overview by Barbara Tierney

Success Story 1: Community College IC:
Brookdale Community College
Lyncroft, New Jersey

Success Story 2: Secondary School IC
Charlotte Latin School
Charlotte, North Carolina

Success Story 3: Large University IC
Colorado State University
Colorado Springs, Colorado

Success Story 4: Small University IC
Elon University
Elon, North Carolina

Success Story 5: Public Library IC
Toronto Public Library
Toronto, Canada

Success Story 6: International Academic IC
University of Calgary,
Calgary, Alberta, Canada

Success Story 7: International Academic IC
University of Auckland,
Auckland, New Zealand

Success Story 8: International Academic IC
Brandenburg Technical University of Cottbus,
Cottbus, Germany

Success Story 9: International Academic IC
University of the Sunshine Coast
Queensland, Australia

Success Story 10: Research University IC
University of North Carolina–Charlotte

I

How the Information Commons Can Transform Knowledge and Information

In Part I, Chapter 1 examines the physical, virtual, and cultural levels of the Information Commons, culminating in some recent research into student learning modalities that may impact the IC's future configuration. Then, Chapter 2 reviews the origins of the IC concept in the microcomputing and Internet developments of the 1980s and 1990s. Early proposals to establish ICs in two community colleges and two universities are discussed, together with their implications for traditional libraries and subsequent ICs. Chapter 3 discusses the convergence of the IC pattern of service delivery with developing models of Information Literacy, and looks at innovations in pedagogy and academic technology that now offer a pathway toward a phased evolution from Information Commons to Learning Commons.

1

Exploring the Physical, Virtual, and Cultural Manifestations of the Information Commons

The past two decades have seen the emergence of the Information Commons (IC) as a new model for service delivery in academic, public, and school libraries, reflecting the pervasive and ongoing impact of information technology. The bootstrapping dynamics of the knowledge explosion and the IT revolution have forced a wide range of organizations in the private and public sectors to reposition, restructure, or reinvent themselves. One could hardly expect the library to be an exception, as it has always been both knowledge-intensive and technology-dependent. In fact, the typical library of the twentieth century reflected a traditional model largely intact since the time when an earlier technological revolution—*printing*—transformed it from even older archival and scriptorium models built around collections of clay tablets, papyrus scrolls, and illuminated manuscripts.[1]

The IC first appeared in the early 1990s under various labels, such as *Information Arcade, Media Union,* and *Virtual Village,* but the term most frequently and generically applied continues to be *Information Commons* (IC). The popularity of this term remains somewhat problematic, however, as it has come to be used by various interest groups on at least three distinct but interrelated levels. For clarity, these three levels will be introduced here as the Physical Commons, the Virtual Commons, and the Cultural Commons. For the student learning to navigate these three interdependent levels, they can be visualized as the sort of surrounding environments shown in Figure 1.1.

Physical Commons

In its most precise and prevalent current usage, and the primary focus of this book, the phrase *Information Commons* is used to denote a new type of physical facility or section of a library specifically designed to organize workspace and service delivery around an integrated digital environment and the technology that supports it. As such, the physical commons is designed to incorporate a cluster of access points to this digital arena, along with

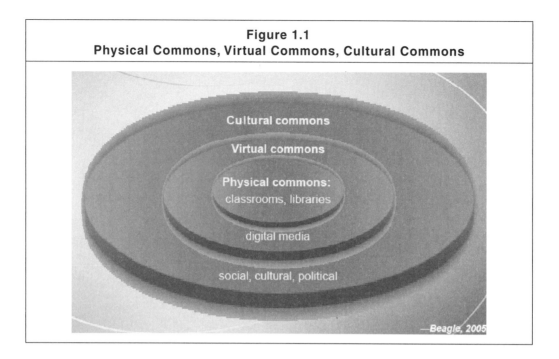

Figure 1.1
Physical Commons, Virtual Commons, Cultural Commons

Cultural commons

Virtual commons

Physical commons:
classrooms, libraries

digital media

social, cultural, political

—Beagle, 2005

tools and trained staff to help users navigate its environment, query its resources, process and interpret its content, create their own knowledge, and package, publish, or present their creations. It also provides the framework for services based on artifacts, printed books, and tangible publication containers. The Information Commons as a physical facility may exist as a department or floor of a large academic library, such as the Information Commons in the Leavy Library at the University of Southern California (USC), or as a stand-alone dedicated building as in the case of the University of Michigan's Duderstadt Center. As these spaces have evolved, some institutions have begun applying variant terms to describe more targeted second-generation academic library ICs, such as *Learning Commons*, *Research Commons*, and *Collaboration Center*.

Virtual Commons

On a second, broader level, the term information commons has denoted a pervasive online environment in which a wide variety of electronic resources and services can be accessed through a single graphical user interface (GUI) and potentially searched in parallel with a single search engine from any networked workstation. In her prescient article "Revolution in the Library," historian Gertrude Himmelfarb described the early manifestation of this online environment from the scholar's perspective: "It is not only the library catalogue that is computerized; the computer can call up a variety of other catalogues, indices, data bases, CD-ROMs, the Internet, as well as books, journals, newspapers, archives, even manuscript collections..."[2] And, one should add, subsequent years have seen the infusion of audio and video media, aggregated databases, course management systems, learning objects, hypertext writing spaces, geographic information systems, video-gaming content, virtual reality simulations, blogs, wikis, cognitive tools, and collaborative work-group software. It is broadly accurate to describe the virtual commons as a single entity transcending institutional and political boundaries, accessed by many physical ICs on campuses scattered around the world. However, local gateways to the virtual commons are most often currently organized around subsets of commercial online services with access gated by proprietary licensing and, in some cases, consortial portals. Each physical IC serves as a window to a specific subset of virtual IC resources, so that the boundaries and topography of the virtual commons appear somewhat different when viewed through the lens (or desktop) of each individual physical commons. On some campuses, the virtual IC is planned and "branded" primarily as a localized resource, and appears to be more central to collaborative library and IT planning than does a physical commons.[3] A variant on the virtual commons has also appeared in cases where multiple institutions create a shared pool of proprietary resources for specialized disciplinary research, such as the *South Carolina Biomedical Research Information Commons* (BRIC), meant to facilitate data sharing among South Carolina biomedical researchers.[4]

Cultural Commons

On the third and broadest level, the term Information Commons is also now being used as a label for the entire social and cultural arena of free speech, shared knowledge, and creative expression in the digital age, as contained within the surrounding envelope of laws, regulations, commercial practices, and popular traditions (some have also called this the "creative commons" and the "social commons"). David Bollier has described this arena as "...a robust public 'media space' of commercial, amateur and fringe expression," and he makes the case for using IC as a label for this broad and diffuse arena because it: "...helps us talk more cogently about constitutional and cultural norms that are increasingly threatened in the new digital environment...the 'information commons' is not a trendy buzzword, but a useful socio-political concept for understanding the American 'ecosystem' of creativity and information in the digital age."[5] The Information Commons Working Group of the American Library Association (ALA) has added: "We might understand the commons as a 'place' or 'space,' but we should also understand the commons as a collection of processes for meeting the information needs of our societies.... For example, some elements of the commons are embodied in ideas such as fair use and public domain."[6,7] In this sense, the broad legal and cultural envelope of the cultural commons both supports and extends beyond what this book refers to as the physical commons and the virtual commons.

Figure 1.2
Working Definitions of the Three IC Levels

Physical Commons: sections, floors, or departments within libraries, or in facilities apart from libraries, providing workspace, service delivery, and access points to the Virtual Commons, along with tangible tools and resources.

Virtual Commons: an electronic continuum of knowledge media conveyed via the WWW, and associated online productivity tools to help users identify, retrieve, process, synthesize, and generate knowledge.

Cultural Commons: the social, political, legal, regulatory, and economic envelope surrounding creative expression, public speech, popular and academic publishing, and scholarly inquiry.

None of these three levels can be completely understood in isolation, because of their inter-dependencies. This book will focus our discussion on the concept and development of the physical IC's service delivery model and technology platform on hundreds of campuses across the United States and Canada and around the world. This review, however, will also secondarily reflect on how virtual and cultural ICs may increasingly shape (and be shaped by) future trends in knowledge growth, learning, and scholarly communication. And Chapter 3 will specifically discuss how certain aspects of learning theory and information literacy may be reinterpreted by way of the three levels. Only within the interdependencies of all three levels can one arrive at an adequate understanding of how the knowledge explosion and attendant IT revolution is likely to transform higher education and learning in the future.

Research Summaries

By the definition of an Information Commons presented in this book, students will learn to navigate the three IC levels by the ways in which the attendant physical, digital, human, and social resources are selected, structured, and interpreted. This definition is not arbitrary, but is based upon a careful review of pertinent research, three examples of which will be very briefly mentioned here. In their early survey of how reference specialists might apply a problem-solving model to assist students and promote information competencies, Eisenberg and Cotrell noted that *information synthesis* was a critical step in problem-solving competency. Yet, library reference workstations used for data retrieval at that time typically lacked key *digital resources* for synthesis activities. The authors concluded:

> ...one of the areas normally thought to promote these competencies—the library—is, in fact, not providing resources for major stages of the model: synthesis tools...schools who wish to emphasize all aspects of information literacy may choose to create an **information commons**. [emphasis added][8]

Other research soon showed, however, that simply plunking down a computer lab in the reference room to provide these digital resources (or synthesis tools) failed to properly address the underlying problem. In a focus group study of students' information-seeking behaviors, conducted in a library that hosted such a basic computer lab (but not, by our definition, an Information Commons) Young and Von Seggern found that while the search and retrieval skills employed by librarians matched in certain respects students' conceptions of a "dream information machine," they also found that the library reference desk failed to provide the scope of *human resources* needed to support the broader range of needs of students working in new online environments:

> Undergraduates revealed that they perceived no difference between the computer labs...and the library itself...the library staff is assumed to know how to help...with questions about software programs. This confusion is [a] source of frustration for users...Adoption of the **information commons model,**...could be an effective step in reducing frustration [emphasis added].[9]

Clearly, some organizational structure beyond the generic "computer lab in the reference room" was needed. But how to characterize or define that structure? A definition may be found in the research of Mark Warschauer, who studied "problematical examples of community technology projects" and analyzed the reasons certain projects had failed. He concluded that the failures were largely due to the tendency to simply plunk down computer labs and network connections in public access settings with no meaningful context and organization of broadly supportive resources, including *social resources*. He summarized the problem and categorized all the critical resources as follows:

> Access to ICT [information & communications technology] for the promotion of social inclusion cannot rest on the provision of devices or conduits alone. Rather, it must entail the engagement of a range of resources.... They can be labeled (1) Physical Resources, (2) Digital Resources, (3) Human Resources, and (4) Social Resources.[10]

What Warschauer found for broadly-based community ICT literacy initiatives also appears to be true for the microcosm of library-hosted or campus-hosted technology learning centers. Warschauer's conclusion, and four-part categorization of resources, forms the basis of the IC definition offered earlier and indeed, the underlying premise of this book. But a random or arbitrary selection of resources from the four categories is still not sufficient. Under this book's definition, one should strive to select resources from all four categories that will support:

- the learning styles and modalities of students;
- the pedagogical goals of faculty;
- the disciplinary content of the curriculum; and
- the social identity of the hosting institution.

Moreover, for the IC to reach its potential, it is not enough to simply *select* these four types of resources. They must then be organized and *interpreted* for the user in meaningful ways. Figure 1.3 relates the physical, virtual, and cultural IC levels to Warschauer's four categories of ICT support resources. It represents an annotated version of the schematic shown in Figure P.2 of the Preface. The human resource component occupies column three of all the rows of Figure 1.3 because human agents (librarians, technology support assistants, media specialists) are necessary to interpret the physical, digital, and social resources, and to facilitate student and faculty interaction with *all three* IC levels.

A skeptic might remark at this point that the three research examples mentioned above were well and good for their time, but all three shared the underlying reference point of the physical computer lab as a baseline service model. Might not the current proliferation of new wireless devices render this whole discussion, and the physical commons itself, outmoded? After all, increased remote access to digital journals certainly caused a decline in print journal use within physical libraries. Perhaps ICs have represented a temporary bridge between an old world of physical libraries and a brave new world of pure wireless roaming and detached academic cocooning that will soon lead to "the deserted Commons." Perhaps over the next decade, NetGen students totally accustomed to wireless access will want to evacuate physical campuses altogether, and migrate toward pure e-learning.

The best current research on student learning styles, expectations, and preferences indicates something quite different. In surveys of students' reactions to online learning experiences, the Research Initiative for Teaching Effectiveness (RITE) reports that student levels of satisfaction and engagement with pure online learning declines significantly by generational

Figure 1.3 Relating the IC Levels to ICT Support Resources		
Level of Information Commons interpreted by resources	**Specific examples of these types of resources to be assembled and organized**	**Human resources needed to create and support each level**
Physical Commons	**Physical Resources:** *Hardware:* Workstations, Peripherals, IT tools, etc. *Furnishings:* Pods, clusters, carrels, etc. *Spaces:* Commons floor spaces, group study rooms, staff work areas, consultation offices, production studios, etc. *Traditional Library:* print collections, archives, artifacts, tangible media formats, etc.	**Human Resources:** Librarians Architects Facility design & construction consultants Interior designers Furniture selectors Systems designers Network specialists IT support assistants
Virtual Commons	**Digital Resources:** *Web environment:* Portals, Web sites, interfaces *Digital Library:* databases, e-books, search engines *E-learning:* learning objects, CMS/VLE, *Online tools:* search engines, productivity software applications, multimedia resources, etc.	**Human Resources:** Reference Librarians Software support staff Academic Faculty Peer tutors and coaches Data retrieval and manipulation specialists Media specialists
Cultural Commons	**Social Resources:** Learning groups, Study teams, Communities of scholarship, Communities of practise, Research collaboratives, Academic skills programs, Writing workshops, Faculty coaching projects, Teaching centers, Peer tutorial programs, etc.	**Human Resources:** Reference Librarians Academic Faculty Mentors Copyright specialists Assessment and Accreditation Teams Visiting Scholars Researchers

groups from Boomers (born 1946–1964), to Generation X (born 1965–1980), to NetGen (born 1981–1994).[11] While the numbers correlate with age, they also reflect an inverse correlation between levels of exposure to technology since birth and levels of satisfaction with pure e-learning experiences. The best evidence indicates that academic detachment and cocooning is far less attractive to entering freshmen than to mature students and faculty. This may also forebode a danger of library managers (often themselves over 50 years of age) projecting their own online learning preferences upon their expectations of entering NetGen freshmen.

One also must factor in looming changes in pedagogy among many faculty. Malcolm Brown, Director of Academic Computing at Dartmouth College, comments: "A shift in the teaching and learning paradigm is well under way from a transmission paradigm to a constructivist paradigm . . . the constructivist theory implies that learning is best served when it is **contextual** (taking into account the student's understanding), **active** (engaging students in learning activities that use analysis, debate, and criticism), and **social** (using discussions, direct interactions with experts and peers, and team-based projects)."[12] Nor will NetGen students be well-served if we attempt to facilitate all such contextual, active, and social engagement via technology. Reflecting on research showing NetGen student preferences for interpersonal interactions, Carrie Windham of North Carolina State University observes, "The constant glow of a computer screen and the cacophony of clicking keys has only left the Net Generation longing for more face-to-face interaction . . ."[13]

This is also reinforced by pedagogical best practices spotlighted by the National Survey of Student Engagement (NSSE). In a study done for the NSSE Institute for Effective Educational Practice, Jillian Kinzie highlighted the importance of emphasizing ". . . active and collaborative learning, structured group presentations, peer evaluations, and meetings outside of class . . ."[14] In another NSSE-based study, "Technology and Student Engagement," Thomas F. Nelson Laird reports in general ". . . higher levels of IT use for educational purposes are associated with higher levels of engagement with effective educational practices," and more specifically: "Of those students who report that their faculty frequently use technology in class, 59% indicate that they frequently work in groups outside of class (compared with 41%)."[15]

The data suggest that young mobile learners will still want and need to find a central welcoming location on campus where human help, IT tools, online knowledge resources, and well-selected physical knowledge containers (yes, books) are aggregated, and where fellow students assemble, sometimes for individual research, sometimes for structured out-of-class group learning activities *assigned by faculty*. The physical commons will not likely be abandoned so long as one understands that an IC is much more than a computer lab in a library, *and designs and equips it accordingly*, to encourage and support active, contextual, and social learning styles and pedagogies. As students embrace new technologies, of course, ICs will be challenged to maintain their edge, and to move beyond basic productivity software and entry-level tools to exploit the academic potential of student-owned devices. In his article "Going Nomadic: Mobile Learning in Higher Education," Bryan Alexander, codirector of the Center for Educational Technology at Middlebury College, points to the IC's suitability:

> What does a campus look like when students are accustomed to reaching the Internet from wherever they stand, stroll, or lounge? We may be seeing . . . rising interest in new learning spaces such as **information commons,** where wireless, mobile connectivity admits the full informatic range of the Internet into any niche or conversation.[16] [emphasis added]

The definition of IC already advanced in the Preface should not be read to imply that a physical commons must somehow become moribund or inert, with chairs aligned in neat rows, with workspaces arrayed in drab cubicles. Nor should it be oversized in expectation that multitudes will migrate en masse to its doors. This book envisions a flexible, reconfigurable space that is sized to a reasonable subpopulation of students and equipped with group learning spaces as appropriate to a likely level of faculty utilization. The chapters that follow discuss how this cluster of network access points and associated IT tools can inhabit a physical space that both accommodates and facilitates mobile learners, while providing a stimulating physical environment that harbors a rich and varied array of resources for student exploration, and that incorporates the informatic range of the Internet into social interaction and group process learning.

Endnotes

[1] But some of these early libraries, such as the famous Library of Alexandria, also anticipated certain collaborative and integrative activities of modern "teaching libraries."

[2] Himmelfarb, Gertrude. 1977. "Revolution in the Library." *The American Scholar.* 66 no. 2, (Spring): 197–204.

[3] Jones, Barbara. "The Library and Information Technology Services: Creating the Information Commons Together," Wesleyan University. Available: http://www.wesleyan.edu/wesleyanplanning/essays/meertsjones.htt

[4] "South Carolina Biomedical Information Commons." South Carolina Biomedical Research Infrastructure Network, Available: http://brin.sc.edu/GrantBioinfo.asp

[5] Bollier, David. "Why We Must Talk About the Information Commons," *The Information Commons, New Technology, and the Future of Libraries.* (June 2002). Available: http://www.info-commons.org/arch/1/bollier.html

[6] Information Commons Working Group, "To Support the Information Commons: Principles for an Effective Information Commons," American Library Association. Available: http://www.info-commons.org/arch/1/icwg.html

[7] Krannich, Nancy. "The Information Commons: A Public Policy Report," Free Expression Policy Project. Available: http://www.fepproject.org/policyreports/infocommons.II.html

[8] Janet R. Cottrell and Michael B. Eisenberg. 2001. "Applying an Information Problem Solving Model to Academic Reference Work: Findings and Implications," *College and Research Libraries* (62)4. 345.

[9] Nancy J. Young and Marilyn Von Seggern, "General Information Seeking in Changing Times: A Focus Group Study," Reference & User Services Quarterly Vol. 41 No. 2 (Winter 2001), 159–169.

[10] Warschauer, Mark. 2002. "Reconceptualizing the Digital Divide." *First Monday*, 7 no. 7 (July), Available: http://www.firstmonday.org/issues/issue7_7/warschauer/index.html

[11] Hartman, Joel, Patsy Moskal, and Chuck Dzubian, "Preparing the Academy of Today for the Learner of Tomorrow," in *Educating the Net Generation*, edited by Diana G. Oblinger and James R. Oblinger. EDUCAUSE (2005). Available: http://www.educause.edu/educatingthenetgen/

[12] Brown, Malcolm. "Learning Spaces," in *Educating the Net Generation*, edited by Diana G. Oblinger and James R. Oblinger. EDUCAUSE (2005). Available: http://www.educause.edu/educatingthenetgen/

[13] Windham, Carrie. "The Student's Perspective," in *Educating the Net Generation*, edited by Diana G. Oblinger and James R. Oblinger. EDUCAUSE (2005). Available: http://www.educause.edu/educatingthenetgen/

[14] Kinzie, Jillian. "Promoting Student Success: DEEP Lessons for Teaching and Learning," National Survey of Student Engagement (October 2005) Available: http://nsse.iub.edu/pdf/conference_presentations/2005/POD2005_kinzie.pdf

[15] Laird, Thomas F. Nelson. "Technology and Student Engagement: Lessons Learned from the National Survey of Student Engagement (NSSE)," National Survey of Student Engagement (April 2005). Available: http://nsse.iub.edu/pdf/conference_presentations/2005/tech_and_stu_engagement.pdf

[16] Alexander, Bryan . "Going Nomadic: Mobile Learning in Higher Education," 2004. *EDUCAUSE Review*, 39 no. 5 (September/October). Available: http://www.educause.edu/pub/er/erm04/erm0451.asp?bhcp=1

2

How the Information Commons Evolved from Novel Concept to Remarkable Reality

Librarie-keepers ought to become Agents for the advancement of universal
Learning... his work then is to bee a Factor and Trader for helps to Learning...
— John Drury, 1650

Background

As noted earlier, the prevailing model of the Information Commons is already well established, but how, where, and when did it actually originate? Early efforts to create this model began taking shape in the mid-1980s, and grew directly out of the underlying parallel dynamics of the knowledge explosion and the IT revolution, and within the context of broad historical definitions of a "commons" already being discussed by social theorists of the day. A full description of those dynamics is beyond the scope of this book, but the table in Figure 2.1 provides some very basic IT chronology.

During the mid-1980s, the time of early microcomputer market penetration designated "c" in Figure 2.1, a small group of authors and researchers began to associate the new technology of networked personal computers with the old concept of a cultural or societal commons. In his 1985 book *The Knowledge Executive*, Harlan Cleveland contrasted the stand-alone personal computer (PC), which itself tended to be a type of data enclosure or container, with networked PCs linked via global telecommunications forming a new type of online commons:

> The noosphere of knowledge that is power, this accessible resource, has many of the characteristics of a commons...In earlier times sharing arrangements for a common resource were customary, for example in tribal ownership and nomadic practices.... The older commons, such as those for sheep and cattle, have disappeared through enclosure.... The idea of commons has now been revived in a big way, as the basis for worldwide cooperation in the environments that...belong to noone or everyone (deep ocean, Antarctica, outer space)...For the management of an **information**

Figure 2.1
IT Chronology in Brief
a. 1950–1964: Period of early commercial mainframe computing dominated by general numerical tabulation, inventory control, and accounting applications. Federal government and defense applications.
b. 1965–1980: Period of increasing minicomputer market penetration highlighted the rise of specialized design and manufacturing applications such as CAD/CAM and early transaction processing. State and large metropolitan government applications. Early library applications included COM (Computer Output Microform) catalogs, followed by real-time OPACs based on command-line interfaces running on greenscreen terminals.
c. 1981–1995: Period of microcomputer market penetration highlighted by the appearance of office productivity and desktop publishing applications, multimedia technologies, and growth of retail-level transaction processing. Computer technology for local government programs, with applications such as tax mapping and GIS. By end of this period, library OPACs had begun the transition from command-line to Windows interfaces.
d. 1996–Present: Period of client/server market penetration highlighted by the appearance of the Internet/WWW, wireless technologies, and networked e-commerce applications.

commons, a sharing environment, these exotic precedents suddenly seem not so exotic. [Ivan] Illich argued that electronic devices (from the microphone to the computer) are a form of 'enclosure,'. . . In its general impact the march of information technology, personal computers combined with global telecommunications, seems to me to be taking us away from the idea of enclosure. My hunch is that the fusion of computers and communications will further empower the many. . . [emphasis added][1]

Cleveland extended this discussion in his 1990 book *The Global Commons*, and his "top-down" viewpoint clearly prefigured prevailing ideas about what we are here calling the virtual commons within its cultural context. However, he did not explore the complex problems inherent in helping individuals and institutions gain entry to its domain and make effective use of its resources. But *The Global Commons* did include a guest essay by Shirley Hufstedler, who at least acknowledged the vital practical question of how access to, and utilization of, this nebulous IC entity might be structured and managed:

> Technology is rapidly moving us toward a global information network that may transform itself into a global **information commons**. Nevertheless, we have only begun to think about the means of managing that commons and to develop structures that will enhance rather than diminish the incentives for creativity. [emphasis added][2]

The same questions were taken up, albeit briefly, by Robert W. Lucky, Executive Director of Research at Bell Laboratories, in his 1991 book *Silicon Dreams*. Lucky seems to have been among the first to articulate a full understanding that internetworking of computers would lead to new types of virtual communities, and thereby new levels of information gathering and dissemination that shared some features of libraries while also transcending traditional library models. Of course, Lucky was writing some five years after Harlan Cleveland's *The Knowledge Executive*, at a time when the icon of the stand-alone PC was already beginning to be superseded by basic forms of internetworking.

> Computer networks are much more than just highways for corporate data; they also put people together in a new and intelligent manner. These networks now link a number of closed, but worldwide,

communities, causing a new electronic informational proximity to emerge. Yet these networks are as yet only embryonic... Today there is little connectivity between local computer networks, and no national directory for data users. We have growing pains, but they will pass. Inevitably, the world will be encompassed by interconnected computer networks. Who really knows what capability will emerge from the computer-mediated networking of people and their information through data networks?... The **information commons** is a virtual place. It lies in the interstices of the electronic networks. It knows no political boundaries, and it will be accessible to everyone.... [I]t [provides] the kind of information that is very difficult to find in a library... [emphasis added][3]

Both Cleveland and Lucky seem to have assumed that the access and utilization issues raised by Hufstedler would be readily resolved, as in Lucky's sweeping assertion that the commons "...will be accessible to everyone." But the question remained: *how and where?* Would students and faculty sit in individual offices and dormitory rooms, physically isolated by the paradigm of the desktop, or in cubicles with what were usually referred to as "scholars' workstations?" How would they share or aggregate their learning experiences or apply their mastery of knowledge across an exclusively virtual domain? How would they then transition to new corporate workplaces in a knowledge economy typified by project teams cooperating laterally across old hierarchical divisions, in what Peter Drucker calls "reconfigurable organizations?"[4] And beyond the academy and the corporation, on the other side of the "digital divide," where would underclass and third-world citizens find access, how would they acquire hardware and software, and who would coach them in necessary skills?

Because these early theorists seem to have viewed the IC as only a virtual place, these authors never explored the underlying parallel between the centuries-old socially designated role of *libraries* as gathering agencies and access points to a common corpus of recorded knowledge, and the potential role of *libraries* as tangible anchors for the ephemeral cloud of the virtual IC they envisioned. Perhaps the closest any nonlibrary author came to confronting the issue of the end-user and his social environment was Al Mingioni, in a brief article for the *Journal of Systems Management* (1990), who described a "computer-based information commons" (CBIC) which he visualized as a civic network that embodied some aspects of what librarians would recognize as public library information and referral (I&R) services. Mingioni at least acknowledged the need for "public access terminals" in his CBIC model.[5] Nevertheless, a vital link between the theoretical and practical, the abstract and the concrete, still was missing from these early formulations of the IC concept. Also missing was a coherent discussion of the implications for higher education and scholarly communication of this gathering-place of knowledge communities and what Robert Lucky called the "new electronic informational proximity." Discussion of the cultural commons per se, however, has continued on its own discreet path since the 1990s, largely divorced from considerations of the physical commons, with important contributions by the aforementioned David Bollier and Nancy Kranich, among others.[6] (Chapters 8 and 10 specifically touch on the concerns of Bollier and the ALA IC Working Group, offering a new proposal to turn a linked group of academic library ICs into an experimental "Copyright-Free Zone (CFZ)," similar in certain respects to a "Free Trade Zone." This proposal could, in effect, offer the potential to further blend the cultural, virtual, and physical commons into a contiguous environment that would exemplify, and concretize, the long-standing but increasingly threatened tradition of academic fair use and open access to knowledge.)

IC Envisioning from the Bottom Up: Jackson Community College

Perhaps the first known formal proposal to bridge the gap and create a physical IC in an actual academic library took shape at Jackson Community College (JCC) in Jackson, Michigan, in the mid-1980s, and reached formal proposal status in 1987–1988. Ironically, the proposed facility was initially referred to as a *Learning Commons*. I was then Director of the Lee County Public Library System and coauthored a grant proposal on behalf of the JCC Learning Resource Center (LRC) that explicitly recognized the problem cited by Harlan Cleveland (in quoting Ivan Illich) arising from the fact that stand-alone electronic devices and media formats had become new information enclosures, and even local area networks had become isolated islands of functionality. The LC was proposed as a way for student learning activities to surmount the barriers between those enclosures and bridge these islands. I proposed the creation of a hypermedia shell that would provide a continuum of access to online and CD-ROM databases within a common graphical user environment, integrated with a suite of productivity software and multimedia learning tools, to be networked through a new computer lab within the community college LRC. The Learning Commons was envisioned as a way to move student usage of networked microcomputers from a pattern of narrowly defined productivity tasks to broadly integrative learning activities. The hypermedia shell would have shared certain characteristics with what we today call a course management system (CMS); although its integrative features might make it more accurately described as a *learning management system*, or virtual learning environment (VLE), with embedded information literacy, data retrieval, and multimedia components. The proposal described this commons as an initial step toward a more visionary model that would later incorporate "machine-based learning conversations" and "hypermedia knowledge exploration throughout the curriculum." Some of these ideas were also explored in correspondence and conversations with Jay David Bolter, then with the University of North Carolina at Chapel Hill and now with Georgia Institute of Technology (author of *Writing Space: The Computer, Hypertext, and the History of Writing*).[7] The community college Learning Resource Center LRC seemed an especially appropriate venue for this type of innovation for, as Russell Bailey has pointed out:

> ... community colleges (or junior colleges, as they were earlier known) have long provided multiple, integrated services in their libraries (Learning Resource Centers) out of practical necessity... Small liberal arts college libraries have done something similar, although there the integration had more to do with the concepts of "interrelatedness" and "interdisciplinarity" at the core of the liberal arts traditions. However, in neither of these two cases was the integration of services conceptually based on learner needs in a high technology environment."[8]

Although academic computer labs were already well-established in the late 1980s, it is important to distinguish between these early utilitarian labs and this early vision of a Learning Commons. This distinction reflected the functional gulf that then yawned between the two major personal computer operating systems (OS). The prevalent OS of the day, MS-DOS, featured what was known as a *command-line interface*, where the user interacted with the PC using textual commands that were arbitrary, cryptic, and program-specific. Because these programs did not always feature compatible data formats and utilized cumbersome import/export utilities, they tended to create and perpetuate isolated silos of digital information. (These silos are pictured as the ovals within the computer lab island schematic of Figure 2.2.) Students who used MS-DOS software applications in typical college computer labs tended to use them for narrowly-defined productivity tasks, not for broadly integrative learning activities.

Although online database searching was also quite common at the time, it utilized command-line interfaces roughly equivalent to MS-DOS, and was not always available in the early self-service computer labs. Instead, online search-and-retrieval from proprietary databases was often a mediated activity done in back-office consultation with librarians, and thus effected another sort of island or enclosure. So the functional barriers between individual applications was matched by the institutional and commercial boundaries between those productivity labs on the one hand and the gated communities of online database information on the other. While ideas about students, faculty, and librarians working as "learning communities" within a common "information environment" had already been advanced in theory, these ideas bore little relation to the daily practical experiences of students using typical computer labs or doing routine database searching. In fact, such theories were probably more relevant at the time to the use of print collections in traditional library settings!

This situation repeated itself in the lack of integrated media formats and presentation technologies. A typical reference (or information access) technology of the twentieth century, the microfiche reader, and a typical Media Services technology, the 16mm projector, did not "speak" to each other, and it would have been unusual for anyone to attempt to move content from one format to the other. Importantly, this division also defined a pervasive boundary between the technology of research and the technology of classroom instruction. The schematic in Figure 2.2 depicts the islands and enclosures resulting from the lack of integrated technology platforms in the 1980s: (1) computer labs, (2) online searching workstations, and (3) classroom media presentation devices. The significance of this early state of affairs should be stressed because it was crucial to the conceptualization of the IC as a physical access, learning, and service delivery continuum, and to the subsequent explosion of interconnectivity represented by the Internet and the World Wide Web.

Beyond MS-DOS, the newly developed OS for Apple's Macintosh family of computers was proposed for the JCC Learning Commons because it followed a very different paradigm (the first widely accepted version of Microsoft Windows, version 3.0, would not be released for another three years, on May, 22 1990). The Mac's graphical user interface (GUI) utilized the first commercially viable bit-mapped screen display and a hand-operated mouse. These features enabled the Mac OS to offer a menu bar with drop-down command options, a vital first step toward the creation of a common operational shell that could transcend the arcane and segregated command structure of individual DOS applications. The Mac also enforced new Edit menu utilities called "cut/paste" and "copy/paste" that eased the partitioning of data silos. And lastly, the convention of icons and windows as navigational elements on a

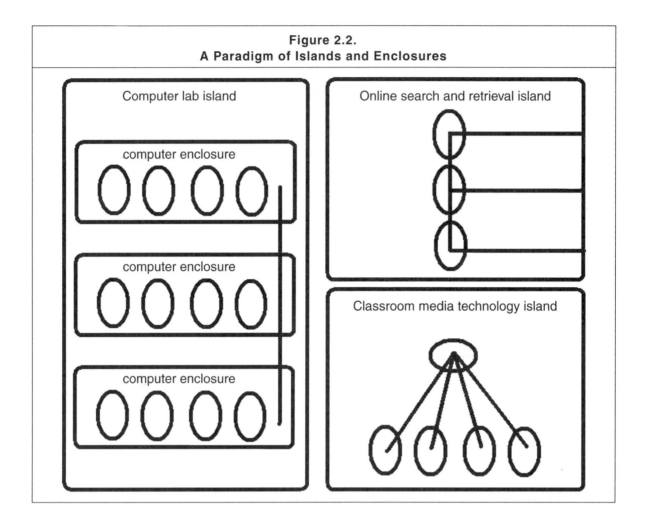

Figure 2.2.
A Paradigm of Islands and Enclosures

Computer lab island

computer enclosure

computer enclosure

computer enclosure

Online search and retrieval island

Classroom media technology island

desktop offered the future promise of user manipulation of complex data structures, knowledge environments, interactive media sources, and self-actuated search engines. Microsoft eventually enabled many similar features in successive versions of its own Windows OS. These innovations in turn became crucial to the implementation of multiple applications working within a unified *software suite*. Microsoft Office became a hugely successful example of multiple applications enabling the user to work across a *continuum of shared resources*, and thence, one forerunner of a virtual commons. However, this still did not directly address the boundary between the islands of productivity applications on the one hand and online database searching on the other.

The other innovation with great long-term potential bundled with the Mac OS was a deceptively low-profile application called Hypercard with an integrated scripting language called Hypertalk. Mac users quickly became engrossed with its adaptability for hypertext and hypermedia experimentation, and the flexibility of its recursive navigational structure based on the concept of the "Home Card." Hypercard demonstrated that GUI elements previously used for navigation could also be used for cross-platform communication, data search, retrieval, and manipulation. The JCC Learning Commons proposal was designed to explore Hypercard's potential for bridging the islands of learning media, but unfortunately, this LC grant proposal was not approved, and the coauthors each soon moved on to other positions. Thus, the first known attempt to create an academic IC never moved from planning to implementation, but it planted seeds that later came to fruition in other institutions.

While the initial proposal did not receive funding, I continued to explore the idea of a common hypermedia shell to bridge the islands of online searching, information manipulation, and integrative learning activities. In a March 1990 article for *Wilson Library Bulletin*, reprinted in the June 1990 issue of *OCLC Microcomputing*, I noted that

> ...a Mac-like interface for online searching would exploit some of the machine's more advanced hypertext capabilities. The great potential of the Macintosh operating system (as opposed to primitive command-line systems like MS-DOS) rests in its ability to create custom shells that can be used in a variety of information environments...by helping the user format search keys, and after the session by organizing search results. It could also offer a standard utility for importing and exporting text files to share search data with other applications...It would be entirely possible to devise a single Hypercard shell that could usher the user into online database gateways with built-in custom protocols for each.[9]

I later recycled portions of the original JCC Learning Commons proposal for a 1995 Apple Library of Tomorrow (ALOT) grant called the *Charleston Multimedia Project*, which prefigured later urban exploration virtual learning environments (VLEs) such as *City of Troy* and *Ancient Spaces*. This project, its implementation and implications, will be discussed in more detail in Chapter 3.

Hypercard, the Web, and the Growth of the Virtual Commons

Many early academic Mac users began using Hypercard as a communications front end for various data-intensive online resources, including Cray supercomputers. But Apple corporate leadership failed to grasp the product's potential and allowed an extraordinary strategic opportunity to slip away. At first, the Internet's early command-line utilities (Archie, WAIS, gopher, etc.) looked nothing like Hypercard. But when Tim Berners-Lee originated the World Wide Web and HTML, the similarity to Hypertalk became apparent.[10] (In fact, the original Berners-Lee proposal for a Web project at CERN was briefly in competition with a simultaneous proposal by another CERN computer engineer, Robert Cailliau, to create an Internet-extensible Hypercard network.[11]) Soon thereafter, early graphical Web browsers like Mosaic and Netscape Navigator popularized navigational and operational elements long familiar to Hypercard users, such as the now ubiquitous "home page." The similarity of Hypercard to the subsequent Web environment is now recognized in the mainstream IT literature, as described in the following CNET news story about the original development of the Web:

> The closest thing at the time to what was to become HTTP and HTML (Hypertext Markup Language) was Apple's Hypercard program—what former Apple CEO John Sculley recently said was one of Apple's biggest missed opportunities. "We weren't insightful enough to recognize what we had inside of Hypercard."[12]

However, even had Apple fully seized its strategic opportunity in the late 1980s, it seems likely in retrospect that the shadow of their potential proprietary claim to what eventually became Web-space might have slowed the Web's ultimate growth and adoption. The stunning growth of the Web into a digital environment touching all segments of the information society was facilitated by the fact that HTTP and HTML were born within the quasi-academic research milieu at CERN under the tradition of open access and fair use. In other words, *the World Wide Web was born within the tradition of the cultural information commons*. This in turn helped facilitate the rapid utilization of the Web by the higher education and library communities that then formed the seedbed for virtual and physical ICs.[13]

While this review of Hypercard, the Web, and early academic technologies may seem a digression, it presents critical lessons that we will revisit in a later discussion about the future implications of new end-user learning and entertainment technologies, such as iPod, from Apple and other vendors. These "fugitive" technologies are even now emerging in a semi-underground cultural and generational milieu that shares many characteristics with the earliest emergence of Hypercard. Our second reason for discussing the JCC proposal is that contemporary CMS/VLE and IC-enabled learning environments are only now catching up to its original vision of hypermedia knowledge exploration throughout the curriculum, with embedded cross-disciplinary information literacy, data retrieval, and multimedia components for serendipitous learning.

IC Planning from the Top Down: Maricopa Community College District

While the JCC proposal foreshadowed the ICs role in front-end service delivery and in reshaping the user's information environment from the bottom up, it did not address the equally urgent top-down issues of IT planning and integration within those rapidly changing educational institutions and government agencies that hosted and funded libraries. Perhaps the most cogent early discussion of the top-down aspect of IC developmental history came shortly afterward, in the Spring 1990 issue of *Library Administration and Management*, where Philip Tompkins discussed new organizational structures for teaching libraries. "A large group of workstations ([with] ... efficient consultation staff nearby) will be available in a computer commons, with access to computer courseware and information software ... this facility will also provide state-of-the-art equipment with software too sophisticated for most student computers."[14] In July 1990, Maricopa Community College District Chancellor Paul E. Elsner gave a presentation describing Maricopa's planning process for "... the integration of information technology on campus."[15] This important presentation was later expanded in a 1992 report from Tompkins, then Director of Library Information Services at Maricopa's Estrella Mountain Community Center, in which he critiqued the prevailing norm where "... libraries, learning centers, media centers, computer laboratories tied to separate media, functioned without a truly integrating instructional and informational technologies planning process."[16] The Elsner and Tompkins documents, issued together in EDUCOM's Executive Strategies Reports series, provided an overview of the planning concepts that led to the first successful implementation of a physical Information Commons within the Maricopa district. Tompkins' report never specifically mentions an IC or LC, but the concept is implicit in what he broadly described as:

...an era of reconceptualization and boundary spanning collaboration....This collaboration has implications for telecommunications, microcomputers, the redesign of the classroom and the need for new, sponsored learning environments (spaces) departing radically in design from the theater of the classroom or the traditional library or learning resource center.

Tompkins also foresaw that these new library environments would be developed synchronously with new approaches to teaching and learning: "...Collaborative and cooperative teaching, and independent, self-paced learning call for new spaces accommodating the massing of newer instructional and information technologies, remote from the theater style classroom. Multimedia accessibility can usher in changing roles for the instructors who learn to moderate the historic obsession with 'telling' to incorporate skillful coaching and facilitating upon call ('from sage on the stage to guide on the side')."

Early University ICs: Iowa and Southern California

Tompkins' paper was written at a time when parallel planning efforts were already underway at the University of Iowa, which opened its Information Arcade in September 1992, and the University of Southern California's Leavey Library, which opened its first constituent Information Commons in 1994.[17] Three key observations emerged about these groundbreaking IC projects at Iowa and Southern California. First, although the two institutions are very different, and located in disparate regions of the United States surrounded by diverse campus cultures, the guiding rationale behind their IC initiatives was quite similar. Second, though each used the term "information" in institutional nomenclature, neither viewed online information retrieval as the primary justification for an IC. Both initiatives were clearly aimed from the start at offering innovative arenas and venues for student *learning*. And third, both ICs were clearly viewed from the outset by their respective library management teams as opportunities for projecting the library's identity across campus as an agent for *collaboration*.

Figure 2.3 Key Lessons from Iowa and Southern California
ICs begun at divergent institutions exhibit converging patterns of service delivery, within the scope of local variability
ICs facilitate information search and retrieval, but typically address deeper and broader facilitation of learning
ICs can be initiated by library management as part of a strategy to project the identity of the library as a change agent for collaboration

These key points were implicit in the language contained in announcements from library managers as justification for their IC initiatives. Anita K. Lowry, Head of the University of Iowa's Information Arcade, stated: "A collaborative effort of the University Libraries, the Office of Information Technology, and the academic faculty, the Information Arcade is an ambitious facility designed to support the use of electronic resources in research, teaching, and independent learning."[18] Lowry further quoted University Librarian Sheila Creth: "The goal of the center is to bring new information technologies into the teaching and research process of the University of Iowa campus, using the library as the primary focus in order to link traditional print materials to the electronic information sources." Anne Lynch of the University of Southern California described USC's Leavey Library as "...a student-focused academic center for learning and intellectual discovery and exploration outside the classroom with information resources in all formats, services and spaces conducive to learning, and an active information literacy instruction program."[19] And elsewhere she added: "Chief among its primary roles is that of an intellectual center for undergraduates, whereby full access to the wealth of the Internet and a rich collection of monographs and periodicals are combined with individual and group study space, hands-on learning rooms, and expert research consultation and instruction programs."[20]

While this book makes the case for a phased evolution from Information Commons to Learning Commons, it recognizes that the entire notion of learning support was prefigured in these earliest ICs, just as it had been in the JCC and Maricopa proposals. Each early instance of the physical IC offered unique features, but all were characterized by what might best be called an underlying "continuum of service" that extended across three (or more) formerly independent core service "islands" or departments. These were typically the units shown in Figure 2.4, where information could be (1) identified and retrieved (reference core), (2) processed and manipulated (research data services core), and (3) repackaged for presentation (media services core).

The IC "emerges" at the technological intersection of these (and other) former islands, as shown in Figure 2.5. This intersection also marks the initial focal point of those physical,

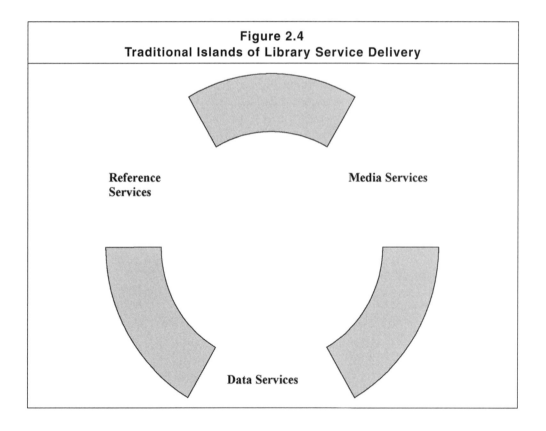

Figure 2.4
Traditional Islands of Library Service Delivery

Reference
Services

Media Services

Data Services

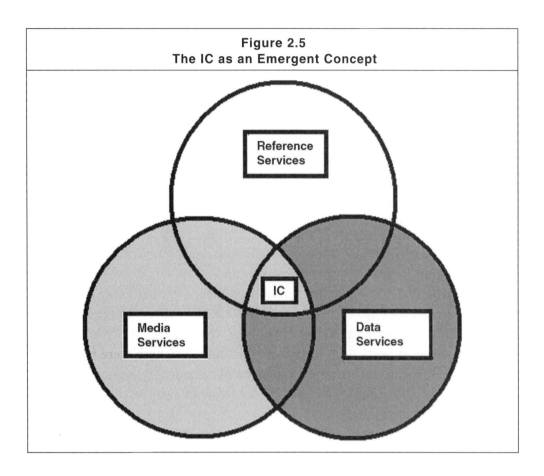

**Figure 2.5
The IC as an Emergent Concept**

Reference
Services

IC

Media
Services

Data
Services

digital, and human resources organized in support of learning that were included in the IC definition.

The social resources, as related to study teams, group-process learning, communities of interest, and communities of scholarship, would be integrated more gradually as part of the IC's evolutionary development toward a Learning Commons. That evolutionary development was perhaps best foreshadowed by the success and growth of the UWired project at the University of Washington. Beginning in 1994 as a pilot collaboration between the Office of Undergraduate Education, Computing & Communications, and UW Libraries, the UWired has grown from an initial Laptop Plug and Play Collaboratory in 1994 to a full array of Commons facilities, technology partnership programs, and campus-wide summits on information and technology literacy.[21]

Traditional Library Concerns

Such innovative IC facilities stood in sharp contrast to those traditional libraries that in the mid-to-late 1990s still maintained pronounced boundaries (and sometimes barriers) between reference, data processing, media services, and related activities, often in ways that subtly reinforced (and were an inadvertent legacy of) the old "islands and enclosures" paradigm. But for those traditional libraries, signs of uncertain waters ahead were beginning to appear. ICs emerged against a backdrop of reported long-term declines in reference transactions and other traditional library use levels. The Executive Summary of ACRL's SPEC Kit 268 *Reference Service Statistics & Assessment* put it: "...in recent years...many academic libraries have experienced a sharp reduction in the number of transactions recorded," and more specifically, "...77% of responding libraries reported that the number of reference transactions has decreased in the past three years."[22] That was written in 2002; it is not coincidental that Scott Carlson's famous "Deserted Library" article in the *Chronicle of Higher Education* had appeared only months earlier, in November 2001, anecdotally describing overall declines in academic library use levels.[23] And it is presumably not coincidental that the decline in traditional library statistics accompanied the public's mass migration toward online subject directories like Yahoo and search engines like Google. Such indicators of slackening demand were accompanied by a steady drumbeat of journal articles questioning the future viability of printed books and journals, academic publishing houses, and the general traditions of print scholarship and bibliography. In the same period, one new institution of the California State University system, Monterey Bay (CSUMB), made news by opening its campus without what some would consider an adequate physical library, amid reported internal debate about the future viability of the *library as place*. One side of the debate seems to have been influenced by the assumption that the end of the Age of Print was at hand, an assumption that has proven uncomfortably similar to earlier predictions of the paperless office. As of this writing CSUMB has begun construction of a new physical library and Learning Commons. The current Web page for the projected "Tanimura & Antle Family Memorial Library" expresses the need for an adequate physical facility, as follows:

> ...Even in the age of vast...digital resources, the library provides *place* in terms of facility and of people...[it] serves as the initial venue for exploration, research, and discovery; is a major source of information resources in all formats; and facilitates peer, faculty, staff, and technical support for learning." [emphasis added][24]

Recent Developments

As this book was being written, the University of Texas at Austin was making news by moving books out of its undergraduate library for the establishment of a dedicated IC facility in the former undergraduate library. As the *Chronicle of Higher Education* commented:

> Nearly all of the 90,000 volumes contained in the undergraduate library are being carted off this summer to other libraries on the campus to make room for an "information commons"—a growing trend at colleges and universities around the country.[25]

However, the Austin campus will still host the larger Perry-Castañeda Library, where the undergraduate collection is being relocated and consolidated. Thus the UT-Austin campus is not an experiment in library-in-absentia. While the Texas IC project generally reaped initial praise from students, one student quoted by the *Chronicle* expressed an interesting concern: "When I do research, I like to go to a section of the library where I might stumble on another book that's useful," she says. "It's different from plugging a keyword into the computer and having a fixed idea of what you're looking for." This concern about serendipitous discovery seems both valid and vital, and there are clear opportunities for the development of digital resources to meet this need, to be discussed later.

In contrast to softening use levels in traditional (and sometimes deserted) libraries, many libraries with newly developed ICs saw significant jumps in usage statistics; the physical commons appeared to offer a new paradigm of place not undermined or diminished by the virtual identities of Yahoo and Google. Preliminary usage data seems to indicate that a well-configured physical commons can not only comfortably coexist with, but actually leverage and synchronize with, increased usage of the virtual commons. For example, the University of Montana reported an annual total of pre-IC library building visits of 552,368 in 1999–2000, rising to an IC-enhanced total of 679,951 in 2001–2002. Concurrently, annual Web "visits" increased from 147,410 to 262,222 for those respective periods.[26] In measures of subsidiary services, the University of Calgary saw "Library Reference Queries" jump from a pre-IC total of 48,043 in 1998–1999 to an IC-enhanced total of 59,742 the following year, and, interestingly, a concurrent jump in print materials circulation from 477,360 to 640,645.[27] Figure 2.6 presents a somewhat broader "case study" of the measurable impact of the IC at Coates Library at Trinity University in Texas.

Figure 2.6
Impact of the IC at Coates Library, Trinity University[28]

From "Report on the Impact of the Information Commons"
(Prepared July 2004 by Diane Graves, University Librarian)

Comparing academic year (September–May) 2002–2003 (pre-Info Commons) to 2003–2004 (after it was complete), we found a number of increases in common measures of library success.

Circulation of library materials overall increased 2%. While this is modest, any increase in the use of library collections is significant, especially when circulation had been declining approximately 8% annually for the past five years or so.

Use of the building went up 14.56%, from a door count of 361,152 in '02–03 to 413,741 in '03–04. This increase reflects the number of people who came to the library during the course of the academic year. It's a good indicator of how the library is perceived as a place of study.

Searches in electronic resources jumped from 167,577 to 261,776, an increase of 56.21%. Librarians at Trinity agree that this is one of the most significant measures of the Commons' success. One of our challenges has been to lead students away from Google as a sole source of research information. This remarkable jump in electronic resource use reflects a much higher awareness of the vast array of high-quality resources available to our users.

Instruction increased almost 39%. The number of library instruction sessions offered (almost all of them in the Technology Training Room—room 310—in the Info Commons) went up 38.36%, from 73 in '02–03 to 101 in '03–04. Faculty have appreciated having a dedicated space for hands-on instruction in the use of technology and library research. Faculty members who have brought one class for an instruction session tend to be repeaters. They see the impact of the commons and the instruction session on their students' work.

The number of students taught in those classes increased 58.04%, from 1,263 to 1,996. This was one of the goals we stated in the grant proposal—we wanted to make the library a center of research instruction again, and it appears we're well on our way. Most first-year students (we estimate over 85%) have exposure to the information commons and the library through these class sessions, and that will pay off as they choose a major and focus more deeply on subject-specific resources and research techniques.

Reference questions rose 5.81%—an increase for the first time in years. The new design and intent of the Information Commons Help Desk made the library's reference service more obvious and approachable than it has been in a long, long time. That feature, along with the increase in library exposure through instruction sessions, has made students more at ease with the library faculty, which in turn made them feel comfortable seeking additional one-on-one assistance.

Viewing the topic from a slightly different angle, Mount Holyoke reported outcomes that compared student use of IC space with their use of other library spaces, as shown in Figure 2.7.[29] The Mount Holyoke figures dramatize how rapidly and enthusiastically students have migrated to the physical commons. But the continued use levels of the library's traditional spaces at Mount Holyoke also hints at why proposed experiments in a library-in-absentia campus might prove unsuccessful.

Robert E. Renaud similarly described the impact of a new IC at Dickinson College: "In 2002 the first phase of the Information Commons was completed, creating a facility with two classrooms, space for faculty and student collaboration, and housing 54 computers for student use...the gate count increased 13%, circulation 36%, and reference activity 52%, whereas the size of the student body increased 8%."[30]

No systematic statistical studies have been compiled as of this date comparing pre-IC and post-IC library usage levels across the board on a national scale. One complication to such a study would lie in the fact that many ICs have been initiated as components of new library building construction or renovation projects. Presumably, new library construction per se accounts for some undetermined percentage of increased initial usage. In fact, subsequent figures from Montana and Calgary indicate a modest (though temporary) decline in physical IC facility usage after its first year of operation, then maintaining an ongoing plateau or gradual increase thereafter, well above pre-IC library use levels. We suspect this second-year dip signals a "new building factor" hidden in the first year usage spike that washes out of subsequent year statistics.

Notwithstanding an unsustainable first year novelty effect, reports of continuing strong demand in both physical and virtual usage from early IC adopters prompted many additional institutions to initiate IC projects from the mid-1990s onward, both within existing buildings and as centerpieces of new library construction projects, with the work of the author at the University of North Carolina-Charlotte being just one representative example. And in many cases, the early thematic focus on *learning* from Iowa and Southern California was carried forward, as Susan Beatty and Peggy White of the University of Calgary describe:

Figure 2.7
Measurable Outcomes from the Mount Holyoke IC

- Of the 94% of respondents who conduct research in the Library, 55% of respondents to the Library Space survey indicated that they conduct research in the Information Commons.
- Of the 53% of respondents who get computer help in the Library, 83% get it in the Information Commons.
- Of the 79% of respondents who write papers in the Library, 47% write them in the Information Commons.
- Of the 65% of respondents who conduct group work in the Library, 71% conduct it in the Information Commons.
- Of the 71% of respondents who socialize in the Library, 57% in the Information commons.
- Increase in reference transactions while many peer institutions saw a drop in numbers.
- 8,484 circulations of wireless laptop computers in 2003/04
- 2,656 circulations of media equipment in 2003/04.
- The Fall semester of 2004 saw a 500% increase over the same period in 2003 in the number of items on Electronic Reserves.
- By September 2004, Media Services had mediated 68% of all scheduled classrooms.
- 50% of Information Fluency sessions delivered using the wireless classrooms.

...administrators identified an enhanced role for the library, one that would ultimately align it more closely with the primary goal of the academy: learning. The Information Commons seemed to offer this opening... [and] early evidence indicated that the Commons could be instrumental in reviving the life of the library;... by offering assistance and instruction with digital products and software...the new library would re-situate itself as a learning facility. It would accentuate and highlight these opportunities. The individual learner would be able to take advantage of the re-source-rich environment of the library as it is supported by technology.... Libraries emerged as a natural site for this facility due not only to their long association with technology as an enabler for learning and access to information, but as well to their service orientation and organizational cul-ture.... This culture of collaboration and teamwork and integrated learning prompted libraries to work with partners such as Information Technology in...the provision of an innovative service in a new physical environment.[31]

By 1998–1999, recognition was growing that the IC model also offered libraries the op-portunity to realign their services with a number of emerging trends in higher education, in-cluding new IT applications in distance learning, group process learning, and faculty development.[32] From 2001 to 2004, David Murray of Brookdale Community College mon-itored the early growth and development of the IC phenomenon and posted relevant links, descriptions, and documents on his sabbatical Web site.[33] In July 2004, the Association of Research Libraries (ARL) surveyed its 123 member libraries. Of the 74 libraries responding, 22 (30 percent) reported having established an Information Commons in their library.[34] In 2004, Susan Beatty and Peggy White conducted an environmental scan using various lists, bibliographies, and Web sites, including an array of sites extending well beyond those sur-veyed by ARL. They identified an initial group of 100 ICs, primarily in North America, of which 36 had more than 100 workstations and served university communities. They found that these 36 tended to fall into three categories, which Beatty and White classed as computer laboratories within libraries, integrated facilities within libraries, and IC buildings. These three categories were differentiated both by their scope of service delivery and by their range of collaborative partners. The computer laboratory type tended to focus on IT support and Web access, while the integrated facility and stand-alone building types featured the broader continuum of service, including reference and media services, that more closely characterizes the definition of ICs used in this book.[35] Also in 2004, David Vose of Binghamtom Univer-sity, in collaboration with the author, initiated the INFOCOMMONS-L listserv.[36]

During this period, OCLC commissioned an international study on information-seeking habits and preferences, with results published in *Perceptions of Libraries and Information Resources* (2005). When broken down by age groups, the results validated the library's role in hosting the physical commons and providing expert help for college students in accessing and interpreting online resources. "While 62 percent of U.S. respondents 65 and over never have used the library for computer/Internet access...only 14 percent of U.S. youth age 14–17 never have used a library for this purpose."[37] College student respondents were also signifi-cantly more likely to have asked for help in using the library's electronic resources or doing online searching than were total respondents, by 46 percent to 36 percent. And when asked to compare libraries with search engines, libraries were given the nod for accuracy and credi-bility, while search engines received higher marks for speed, convenience, and availability. A substantial majority of college student respondents agreed with the statement that librarians add value to the information search process. (Further aspects of this study will be considered in our discussion of IC branding in Chapter 8.)

While the OCLC study was being completed, Joanne Henning, Head of Reference Services at the University of Victoria, British Columbia, undertook a traveling sabbatical to visit IC installations on 25 campuses across Canada and the US. Her study found further evidence of ongoing service integration and collaborative learning-support activities with many variations, and we will recount some of her observations in the course of this book.[38] Collectively, the documentation of Murray, Beatty and White, and Henning provides evidence that the Information Commons is not a passing fad, but is rapidly becoming a normative fixture of the twenty-first-century academy. In recognition of this trend, it is also clear that many colleges and universities are only now preparing to enter the IC arena, and many early adopters are only now entering a second wave of LC enhancement.

Endnotes

[1] Cleveland, Harlan. 1985. *The Knowledge Executive: Leadership in an Information Society*. New York: E. P. Dutton. 101–102.

[2] Hufstedler, Shirley. 1990. "Private Property in the Information Commons." In *The Global Commons: Policy for the Planet*, edited by Harlan Cleveland. (Aspen, Colorado: Aspen Institute & University Press of America. 85.

[3] Lucky, Robert W. 1991. *Silicon Dreams: Information, Man, and Machine*. New York: St. Martin's Press. 11–12.

[4] Drucker, Peter. 1997. "Introduction: Toward the New Organization." In *The Organization of the Future* edited by F. Hesselbein, M. Goldsmith, and R. Bechkard, San Francisco: Jossey-Bass. 1–5.

[5] Mingione, Al. 1990. "Computer-based Information Commons." *Journal of Systems Management*. 41 no. 10 (October) 7.

[6] Kranich, Nancy. 2004. *The Information Commons: A Public Policy Report*. New York: Brennan Center for Justice, New York University. Available: http://www.fepproject.org/policyreports/InformationCommons.pdf

[7] Bolter, Jay David. 1991. *Writing Space: The Computer, Hypertext, and the History of Writing*. Hillsdale, NJ: L. Erlbaum. See also: Jay David Bolter, Letter to Donald Beagle. (March 31, 1991).

[8] Bailey, Russell. 2005. "Information Commons Services for Learners and Researchers: Evolution in Patron Needs, Digital Resources and Scholarly Publishing." INFORUM 2005. Available: http://www.inforum.cz/inforum2005/english/prispevek.php-prispevek=32.htm

[9] Beagle, Donald. 1990. "Online with a Macintosh." *OCLC Microcomputing*, OCLC. 6 no. 2 (April). 13–15, 25–26.

[10] The similarities between Hypercard and the Web owed a great deal to the long prior development of hypertext theory and practice, from Vannevar Bush to Ted Nelson. Unfortunately, this important backstory is too extensive for inclusion here.

[11] Gillies, James, and Robert Cailliau. 2000. *How the Web was Born*. London: Oxford University Press. 198.

[12] Loney, Matt. 2003. "Web creator Berners-Lee knighted." *CNET News.com* (December 31, 2003). Available: http://news.com.com/2100-1032-5134229.html

[13] See also: Branwyn, Gareth, and Peter Sugarman. 1990. "Computer Networks as an 'Information Commons.'" *The Futurist*. (July–August). 46.

[14] Tompkins, Philip. 1990. "New Structures for Teaching Libraries." *Library Administration and Management*, 4 (Spring). 79.

[15] Elsner, Paul E. 1990. "What Presidents Need to Know about the Integration of Information Technology on Campus." EDUCOM. Available: http://www.educause.edu/ir/library/text/HEI1040.TXT

[16] Tompkins, Philip. 1992. "Information Technology Planning and Community Colleges: A Variance in a Transitional Era," EDUCOM. Available: http://www.educause.edu/ir/library/text/HEI1040.TXT

[17] Creth, Sheila D. 1994. "The Information Arcade: Playground for the Mind." *Journal of Academic Librarianship*, 20 no. 1 (March).

[18] Lowrey, Anita. 1994. "The Information Arcade at the University of Iowa." *CAUSE/EFFECT* 17 no. 3, (Fall). Available: http://www.educause.edu/ir/library/text/CEM9438.txt

[19] Lynch, Anne. 2004. "Leavey Library Overview." Presentation for: *The Information Commons: A Learning Space Beyond the Classroom.* University of Southern California (September 16, 2004). Available: http://www. usc.edu/isd/libraries/locations/leavey/news/conference/presentations/presentations_9-16/USC_Lynch.ppt#1

[20] Beagle, Donald. 2004. "Learning Beyond the Classroom: Envisioning the Information Commons' Future," *Library Hi Tech News.* 21 no. 10. 4.

[21] "About UWired," 2001. Seattle: University of Washington. Available: http://www.washington.edu/uwired/about/index.shtml

[22] Novotny, Eric. 2002. "Executive Summary," *ARL SPEC Kit 268: Reference Service Statistics & Assessment.* Association of Research Libraries. Available: http://www.arl.org/spec/268sum.html

[23] Carlson, Scott. 2001. "The Deserted Library: As Students Work Online, Reading Rooms Empty Out—Leading some Campuses to Add Starbucks." *Chronicle of Higher Education.* (November 16).

[24] "Tanimure & Antle Library: Purpose." Monterey, CA: California State University. (2005) Available: http://csumb.edu/site/x5762.xml

[25] Mangan, Katherine S. 2005. "Packing Up the Books." *Chronicle of Higher Education: Information Technology.* 51 no. 43. A27.

[26] Samson, Sue, and Erling Oelz. 2005. "The Academic Library as a Full-Service Information Center, *Journal of Academic Librarianship.* 31 no. 4 (July). 350. Note: After 2002, physical visits declined somewhat, though still remained well above pre-IC levels, while annual Web visits continued to rise dramatically, reaching 389,688 in 2002–2003

[27] Beatty, Susan. E-mail to Donald Beagle. (October 6, 2005).

[28] Graves, Diane. 2004. "Report on the Impact of the Information Commons." Trinity University. (July). Available: http://lib.trinity.edu/libinfo/infocommons/index.shtml

[29] *Application from the Winner of the 2005 ACRL Excellence in Academic Libraries Award,* Mount Holyoke College. (2005). Available: http://www.ala.org/ala/acrlbucket/excellenceaward/holyokeap.htm

[30] Renaud, Robert E. 1997. "Space and Purpose: Repositioning the Liberal Arts College Library." *Transformations: Liberal Arts in the Digital Age.* Available: http://apps.nitle.org/transformations/?q=node/97

[31] Beatty, Susan, and Peggy White. 2005. "Information Commons: Models for eLiteracy and the Integration of Learning." *Journal of eLiteracy,* 2. 2. Available: http://www.jelit.org/archive/00000052/

[32] Beagle, Donald. 1999. "Conceptualizing an Information Commons." *Journal of Academic Librarianship.* 25 (March). 82–89.

[33] Murray, David. 2004–2005. "Information Commons: A Directory of Innovative Services and Resources in Academic Libraries." Brookdale Community College. Available: http://www.brookdale.cc.nj.us/library/infocommons/ic_home.html

[34] Haas, Leslie, and Jan Robertson. 2004. *SPEC Kit 281: The Information Commons.* Washington, D.C.: Association of Research Libraries. 11.

[35] Beatty, Susan, and Peggy White. 2004. "Information Commons: Models for E-Lit and the Integration of Learning."Presentation for *ELit 2004: E-Literacy for Learning and Life.* New York. Available: http://www.elit-conf.org/elit2004/docs/ppt/sess2rma2.ppt#1

[36] "Archives of INFOCOMMONS-L@LISTSERV.BINGHAMTON.EDU," Information Commons Interest Group (May 2004–current). Available http://listserv.binghamton.edu/cgi-bin/wa.exe?AO=infocommons-/

[37] "Part 2: Using the Library—In Person and Online." 2005. *Perceptions of Libraries and Information Resources* OCLC. Available: http://www.oclc.org/reports/pdfs/Percept_pt2.pdf

[38] Henning, Joanne. 2005. "Information Commons Study Leave: October 2, 2004–March 31, 2005." University of British Columbia. Available: http://jhenning.law.uvic.ca/

3

Information Commons, Information Literacy, and the Learning Commons

Overview of ICs and Information Literacy

As the first library-based ICs were beginning to appear, the IT revolution was also generating a new focus on what had already become known as "information literacy." Though it initially appeared to be only tangentially related to ICs, the conceptual space between the two movements steadily narrowed until today both seem destined to follow inevitably conjoined paths. Melanie Remy of the University of Southern California's Leavey Library has provided an excellent overview of this area of convergence from the librarian's perspective:

> In the learner-centered environment of Leavey's Information Commons, information literacy is part of our service mission. Here, there is a focus on the reference interaction as a learner-centered teaching opportunity. Librarians who teach in this context are ideally suited to help classroom faculty understand how students really think and work in the current information environment. We consult with classroom faculty to design curricula and assignments that integrate information-gathering in a discipline-based intellectual context. Through our partnership with the University Writing Program, we provide freshmen with a shared experience of the research process in the context of their "researched writing" assignments. . . . Librarians in the Information Commons see up close how students interact with digital resources and apply this knowledge to system design, whether it's the library's web pages, online instruction, course management systems, or complex information retrieval systems such as the Scholars' Portal. The virtual aspects of the Commons are equally if not more important than the physical, and as a group, librarians have many more significant contributions to make in this area. Well-designed, user-centered information resources allow librarians teaching information literacy to focus more on the intellectual work this entails and less on its practical elements. Ultimately, by combining well-designed physical and virtual library space, the Information Commons can achieve the purpose of reducing the efforts students devote to gathering information and save their time and focus for the scholarly application of that information.[1]

The point of intersection between the IC and information literacy is marked by a broadened definition of what the Educational Testing Service (ETS) now refers to as "information and communications technology" (ICT) literacy, a definition that roughly parallels what we refer to as the IC's "continuum of service." As ETS describes it: "ICT literacy is using digital technology, communications tools, and/or networks to access, manage, integrate, evaluate and create information in order to function in a knowledge society."[2] Figure 3.1 summarizes these five components of ICT literacy.

Figure 3.1 **Components of ICT Literacy as Defined by ETS**
Access—knowing about and knowing how to collect and/or retrieve information.
Manage—applying an existing organizational or classification scheme.
Integrate—interpreting and representing information, which involves summarizing, comparing, and contrasting.
Evaluate—making judgments about the quality, relevance, usefulness, or efficiency of information.
Create—generating information by adapting, applying, designing, inventing, or authoring information.

But what does it really mean to say that the ICT literacy definition roughly parallels the IC's "continuum of service?" The traditional library reference department projects a service profile that tends to place overriding (and sometimes exclusive) focus on the first activity of "access." Workstations in such departments sometimes exclude even the most basic productivity software, such as Microsoft Office, crucial to managing and integrating information. By contrast, the "continuum of service" within the Information Commons can provide the breadth of resources and skilled staff support needed to facilitate all five interrelated ICT literacy activities, as suggested in Figure 3.2.

Figure 3.2 **The IC Service Model Related to ICT Literacy**	
Identification & retrieval	*Access:* knowing about and knowing how to collect and/or retrieve information
Processing & interpretation	*Manage:* applying an existing organizational or classification scheme. *Integrate:* interpreting and representing, comparing and contrasting. *Evaluate:* judgments about the quality, relevance, usefulness, of information
Packaging & presentation	Create: generating information by adapting, applying, designing, inventing or authoring

Of course, traditional libraries have always collected *books* on the topics of managing, integrating, evaluating, and creating information. But e-learning, instructional media, and productivity software now provide online tools and resources for actively performing all five ICT activities *using a single workstation or a cluster of network access points and peripherals within a single workspace*, along with traditional print resources. In this context, the library manager (or university administrator) may wish to approach this book with the fundamental question: "Is there a workspace in my library (or somewhere else on my campus) where students and faculty can *carry to completion* a project that entails all five definitional activities of ICT literacy?"

How does ICT literacy support relate to the larger question of learning? To answer this question, you must further explore how the concept of the three IC levels and the IC's continuum of service relate to student learning modalities and faculty pedagogical goals. Barb Mann, Coordinator of Information Literacy at the University of Southern Maine, participated in a Spring 2005 conference session (ACRL's New England Chapter) titled "Teaching in the Information Commons." The session report describes Mann as stating that

> ...having an Information Commons in the library serves to strengthen and highlight the library's position as the central learning place on campus. Project-based and collaborative learning in particular flourish in the Information Commons, where users have access to both skilled staff consultation and an array of technology in a single welcoming environment.[3]

But why is the IC a good "fit" for project-based learning? Houghton Mifflin's "Project-Based Learning Space" describes project-based learning as "...a comprehensive instructional approach to engage students in sustained, cooperative investigation."[4] Four features are highlighted:

1. A key issue or "driving question" that is based in a real-life problem and typically touches on multiple subject areas.
2. Opportunities for students to conduct active exploration that exposes them to key concepts, and allows them to gather and apply information, and then represent their knowledge in a variety of formats.
3. Collaboration among students, faculty and sometimes resource people beyond campus so that knowledge can be shared and distributed among participants in the "learning community."
4. The development and application of cognitive tools in learning environments that facilitate student efforts to represent their ideas: such as computer-assisted laboratories, virtual hypermedia, statistical/graphing programs, and Web site development.[5]

The methodology of project-based learning has been described as "Searching—Solving—Creating—Sharing." "**Searching** requires the identification and representation of a scientific problem.... **Solving** involves gathering information and generating a solution to the stated problem.... **Creating** refers to the creation of a product, such as a presentation to class members.... **Sharing** involves the actual communication of findings and may also result in the generation of future search questions."[6] The IC's continuum of service, from *identification & retrieval* to *processing & interpretation* to *packaging & presentation*, clearly offers an opportunistic parallel to the sequence of searching—solving—creating—sharing of project-based learning. And because many K-12 educators have adapted project-based learning models to their needs, the model holds special significance when interpreting the learning expectations and preferences of NetGen freshmen having their first contact with the college or university library.

According to the session report, ACRL/New England Session copresenter Mark Caprio, e-Scholarship Program Manager at Boston College, further described the Information Commons as

> ...something fundamentally new and links it to two recent and growing trends in education. These trends involve the increasing importance of both collaboration and multi-media production for service providers and users alike. Thus the Information Commons is based as much on collaboration and cooperation among reference staff, computing, IT, media services, and faculty as they teach and provide services to students, as it is on collaboration and cooperation among students working in groups to produce complex audio-visual texts. It is no longer enough, Caprio asserts, for students to acquire and demonstrate traditional text-based literacy; they must also develop competency or literacy in sound- and image-based media. The principal role of the Information Commons is to support the development of this new multi-media literacy by providing seamless access to all necessary services and resources.[7]

Such generalized testimonials of IC-based instruction invite more specific substantiation, and Susan Beatty of the University of Calgary provides a faculty quote that describes how collaborative library-faculty instruction can reorient itself around the continuum of service in an opportunistic way:

> ...The instruction coming from the Commons is able to meet a timed need—during lecture time—and facilitates what I do. The skills have improved for the students. Students know now what to ask—they know what they need to know exists...integrated instruction [would be] more difficult without the Commons.[8]

The IC's adaptability and suitability as a venue for learning undergirds the concept of a phased evolution from Information Commons to Learning Commons. To trace the further direction this trend is taking, you can begin with an analytical summation by Thomas C. Greene, Professor and Gaines Chair in Psychology at St. Lawrence University. Writing for Project Kaleidoscope (PKAL), Greene described its goal to incorporate current empirical findings about learning in the design of spaces that support Science Technology Engineering and Math (STEM) education:

> ...we recognize the centrality of...cognitive processes that support learning and memory.... Humans are also social animals who typically work, play, and learn in groups. The influence of social data on PKAL principles is apparent in discussions of community and informal learning.[9]

In the sections to follow, you may examine how the Learning Commons can be a forum where librarians and faculty select, assemble, and interpret a confluence of human, physical, digital, and social resources that will support both the cognitive and social processes intrinsic to learning.

Human Resources: The LC, Information Literacy, and Cognitive Skills

Just as the three broad areas of the IC service schema—*identification & retrieval, processing & interpretation, packaging & presentation*—roughly correspond to the constituent activities of ICT literacy, these activities in turn can be broken down and associated with underlying cognitive skills. For example, the first activity of "access" can be broken down into processes of *need identification, query articulation, search strategy formulation*, and *retrieval transactions*. Numerous attempts have been made to list and categorize the cognitive skills associated with such processes in broad educational or learning contexts, dating back to Bloom's Taxonomy. Bloom's well-known list includes: Knowledge/recall, Comprehension, Application, Analysis, Synthesis, and Evaluation. When applied in social contexts, these skill frameworks entail foundational elements of what has come to be known as constructivist learning theory. The potential applicability of constructivist theory to library learning situations has long been recognized; Elmborg's 1992 proposal to develop a "reference pedagogy" is one good example.[10]

These correspondences indicate how and why the IC's organizational framework and cluster of technologies can allow it to be an effective forum for ICT literacy *instruction*. To take this analogy further, for as Remy and Beatty emphasize, the IC's instructional role blends expeditiously into its role as a launching pad for *learning*. Whether it be serendipitous, independent, and self-paced learning, or a programmatic initiative that leverages the IC as a testbed for pedagogical innovation, this role brings you to Scott Bennett's description of a *Learning Commons*:

> A learning commons, as imagined here . . . would bring people together not around informally shared interests, as happens in traditional common rooms, but around shared learning tasks, sometimes formalized in class assignments. . . . A learning commons would be built around the social dimensions of learning and knowledge and would be managed by students themselves for learning purposes that vary greatly and change frequently.[11]

Bennett's distinction offers a useful way to present the idea of a phased evolution from IC to LC, which we see as emerging when the resources supporting the IC are *organized in collaboration with learning initiatives sponsored by other academic units*. Seen in this context, the mapping of the IC's schema of services and resources onto ICT literacy activities and underlying cognitive skills is much more than a semantic exercise or a marriage of convenience. For even as librarians have been experimenting with expanded IC services, learning theorists have been enlarging the boundaries and contexts of their own discussions about, and interpretations of, information literacy.

Jeremy J. Shapiro and Shelly K. Hughes, in their influential article "Information Literacy as a Liberal Art," make the case that

> Information and computer literacy, in the conventional sense, are functionally valuable technical skills. But information literacy should in fact be conceived more broadly as a new liberal art that extends from knowing how to use computers and access information to critical reflection on the nature of information itself, its technical infrastructure, and its social, cultural and even philosophical context and impact—as essential to the mental framework of the educated information-age citizen as the trivium of basic liberal arts (grammar, logic and rhetoric) was to the educated person in medieval society.[12]

Shapiro and Hughes describe eight dimensions of information literacy, as shown in Figure 3.3.

The Shapiro-Hughes schema can be viewed as a liberal arts core curriculum per se; it can also be viewed, we feel, as a way to extend information literacy throughout a disciplinary

Figure 3.3 Shapiro & Hughes' Eight Dimensions of Information Literacy	
Tool literacy	the ability to understand and use the practical and conceptual tools of current information technology, including software, hardware and multimedia.
Resource literacy	the ability to understand the form, format, location and access methods of information resources, especially daily expanding networked information resources.
Social-structural literacy	knowing that and how information is socially situated and produced . . . about the institutions and social networks . . . that create and organize information and knowledge; and the social processes through which it is generated.
Research literacy	the ability to understand and use the IT-based tools relevant to the work of today's researcher and scholar.
Publishing literacy	the ability to format and publish research and ideas electronically, in textual and multimedia forms (including via World Wide Web, electronic mail and distribution lists, and CD-ROMs), to introduce them into the electronic public realm and the electronic community of scholars.
Emerging technology literacy	the ability to ongoingly adapt to, understand, evaluate and make use of the continually emerging innovations in information technology so as not to be a prisoner of prior tools and resources, and to make intelligent decisions about the adoption of new ones.
Critical literacy	the ability to evaluate critically the intellectual, human and social strengths and weaknesses, potentials and limits, benefits and costs of information technologies.
On-line community literacy	the ability to understand the personal and interpersonal impact of behavior, action, and interaction on-line and to act in ways that takes account of both the intertwinement of social and technological factors in on-line environments and of their distinctive cultures, including managing one's digital identity.

curriculum. As Dean de la Motte, Vice President for Academic Affairs at Belmont Abbey College, describes it:

> The emerging core curriculum stresses information literacy in English composition and across the major disciplines. In such a context, information literacy reinforces the skills and knowledge simultaneously developed in the core curriculum and in the major field: analytical thinking; qualitative judgment; broad familiarity with different academic disciplines; understanding and effective use of a range of forms of communication, including effective written expression in the evaluation and marshaling of evidence.[13]

Could a traditional library adequately support all eight dimensions of the Shapiro-Hughes model, whether structured as a stand-alone schema or integrated into disciplinary curricula? Or would the model presented in "Information Literacy as a Liberal Art" and further developed by Shapiro and Hughes find more effective support through student and faculty utilization of an IC/LC-type of facility? The latter seems more viable based on the interrelated dimensions of literacy identified by Shapiro and Hughes and their interesting correlations with the IC's context of *physical, digital, human, and social resources organized in support of learning.* One can visualize mapping the first basic literacies directly onto the framework presented in the Preface. As shown in Figure 3.4, Tool literacy, Resource literacy, and Social-structural literacy appear to readily map onto use of the physical, virtual, and cultural commons respectively.

But the true promise of the Learning Commons model lies in its interweaving of *collaborative* social resources with enhanced physical spaces, digital toolsets, and expert human support. To repeat Warschauer's comment: "Access to ICT for the **promotion of social inclusion** cannot rest on the provision of devices or conduits alone." [emphasis added] The same interweaving of resources that supports the active, contextual, and social components of learning identified by Malcolm Brown, also exposes students to the "ground rules" for navigating the interdependent levels of physical, virtual, and cultural commons, and thereby their *social inclusion* in a college or university as members of a *community of learning*, as well their later social inclusion in learning organizations, both corporate and cultural. Figure 3.5 shows the result of a focus group discussion among students about the eight literacies, and their perceived relationship to the four categories of supporting resources. The students identify Tool Literacy as indicating cognizance of physical resources, Critical Literacy as cognizance of human resources, Resource Literacy as cognizance of digital resources, and Social-structural Literacy as cognizance of social resources. Figure 3.5 shows these literacies aligned to draw upon their most natural area of resource support. But beyond this, in the students' view, mastery of all eight dimensions of literacy would require the supporting

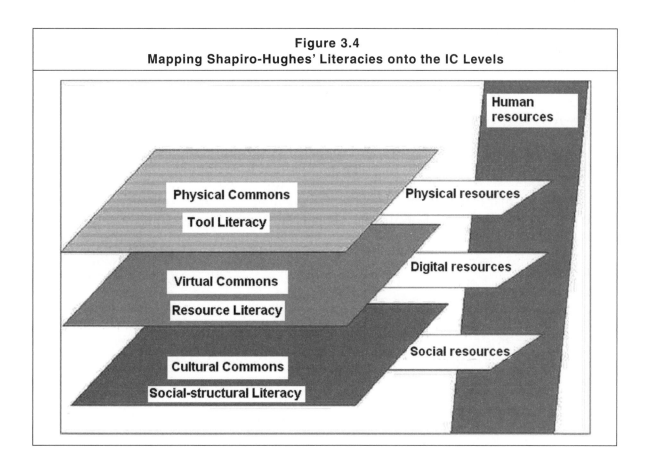

Figure 3.4
Mapping Shapiro-Hughes' Literacies onto the IC Levels

Human resources

Physical Commons
Tool Literacy

Physical resources

Virtual Commons
Resource Literacy

Digital resources

Cultural Commons
Social-structural Literacy

Social resources

Figure 3.5
LC Resources and the Eight Dimensions of Information Literacy

Tool Literacy

Critical Literacy

Emerging Technology Literacy

Research Literacy

Publishing Literacy

Online Community Literacy

Resource Literacy

Social-structural Literacy

---

interplay of all four resource categories, as reflected in their arrangement across the graph of supporting resources.

For IC managers and instructional staff, then, the challenge seems to be how to select, assemble, and interpret the four resource types to enable student assimilation of the eight dimensions of literacy. Student attempts to utilize these resources, as in online database searching, provides IC/LC staff with the opportunity to seize the "teachable moment" and apply the constructivist ideas discussed in Elmborg's reference pedagogy. In his NSSE-based study "Technology and Student Engagement," Thomas F. Nelson Laird reports: "...our results suggest that...there may be uses of IT (e.g., using the WWW to find academic resources) that are a completely separate form of effective educational practice."[14] Agreed, and in fact, you could argue that the ability to find, recognize, evaluate, synthesize, and utilize networked academic resources effectively involves *all eight* dimensions of literacy, and some new research which relates information-seeking behavior and learning styles will be discussed later.

Ultimately, the question of IC/LC use in effective educational practice will also need to be addressed within the framework of assessment, for recent years have seen a shift away from total reliance on output measures and toward more qualitative analysis of student learning outcomes. Chapter 8 discusses this more thoroughly, but it should be noted here in passing that the IC also offers libraries an avenue to become active and involved players in that emerging learning assessment arena. Stimulated by the Council of Regional Accreditation Commissions' (C-RAC) push to have student learning and achievement central to the accreditation process, the regional accreditation bodies have begun looking beyond traditional academic programs to ask: how do *student support services* contribute to student learning? Melanie Remy of the University of Southern California points out:

Today, the assessment movement in higher education is shifting the mission of the university from teaching to learning, and learning has become the new organizing principle for the academic library.... The Information Commons and its evolving cousins are uniquely qualified to foster the campus commitment to information literacy.... This is also how the Information Commons succeeds: by providing truly learner-centered service based on understanding how students actually behave and what they need to do outside of the classroom in order to learn.[15]

Physical Resources: LC Spaces and Technologies

Another aspect of the IC as learning space developed in the aftermath of Iowa and Southern California can be seen in the Miller Nichols Library Information Commons at the University of Missouri, Kansas City. Ted Sheldon, Director of UMKC University Libraries (1985–2004), emphasized his view of an information commons as a *space* that supports access, collaboration, and production for an optimum learning experience. And Associate Director of Libraries Helen H. Spalding emphasized the role this Information Commons *space* plays in *extending* the library's traditional missions.

The UMKC University Libraries have had a long-standing commitment to student-centered learning and to integrating information literacy skills into the curriculum, which have been evident in many of our services, including our collections in diverse formats, growing library instruction program, and the new Information Commons. Only in the library can students and faculty consult with library faculty, who facilitate inquiry, problem solving, and thinking critically in locating, evaluating, and applying appropriate information resources, whether they are available online, in print, on sound recordings, or in other formats.[16]

This vision of the IC's role as a *space* that *extends* the library's resources and services is somewhat different, of course, from the new model at UT-Austin, where the IC space has effectively *displaced* the undergraduate library. The UMKC Information Commons physically presents a warm and softened interior space that reflects and also extends the ambience of the traditional library, and differs rather strikingly from the austere or antiseptic look often associated with high-tech installations, without compromising its IT functionality. We see similar traditional library ambience in other ICs, such as the IC at Elon University in North Carolina, and these examples suggest that a phased evolution from library to IC to LC must be viewed not only as an extension of its continuum of service delivery, but also through its extensions of physical layout, furnishings, and IT infrastructure. However, Chapter 8 also presents the idea of marketing the IC in accord with the idea of *brand divergence*, and the complications and possible contradictions this may entail when presenting the IC as an *extension* of library spaces and services.

Traditionally, libraries allocated spaces and furnishings primarily to bring users in proximity to the dominant knowledge containers of the Age of Print: books and journals. They consequently tended to organize their furnishings repertoire around various configurations of tables, chairs, and carrels arranged in relationship to bookstacks and journal backfiles. This rather painfully limited traditional repertoire was expanded in early ICs with new types of aggregated pods, octagonals, cubicles, alcoves, and studios designed to bring users into more effective proximity to technology.

This development process also saw a new emphasis on small group study areas within discreet enclosures—normally soundproof, of course, but often visually transparent, to better convey to casual walk-in users the availability of spaces for group consultation. As Charlene Hurt wrote in 1997: "Teaching and learning are becoming more collaborative. Such library users need group-study rooms and tables, individual and group carrels, and a mix of seating comfortable for various styles of working together. They also need access to media and technology in shared environments."[17] Sometimes, due to budget constraints, group study rooms were not always infused with technology in the earliest ICs, an absence that was soon noticed by students themselves and quickly rectified. At the University of Southern California's Leavey Library, for example, user demand subsequent to the IC's opening led to the introduction of technology platforms in various group study areas. It is particularly noteworthy that *user demand* for broadened IT-based *learning activities* helped bring technology and group study spaces together. An evolution from IC to LC implies various schemas to bring learners into effective contact with their peers while in simultaneous proximity to their facilitative technologies, and to what one author has referred to as "knowledge media."[18] Just as every campus has innumerable spaces called "classrooms" originally designed around a "sage on the stage" paradigm of *instruction*, there is (as Tompkins predicted) a growing demand for spaces designed around emerging paradigms of *coaching*, sometimes referred to as "guide on the side," as well as group-process and self-directed *learning*, both faculty-initiated and spontaneous. The IC/LC seems uniquely well positioned to participate in this emerging agenda, and on many campuses, to play a formative, leadership role.

The attendant technology infrastructure also points to the LC's potential role as a campus-central anchor for high-end IT tools, especially those that might offer features useful for cross-disciplinary research and too expensive for duplication in multiple departmental workspaces. An excellent example of high-end collaborative technology extension can be found in a project recently initiated in the Collaboration Center of the Health Sciences Library (HSL) of the University of North Carolina-Chapel Hill (and also referenced in the Indiana University plan for a *Research Commons*). The HSL's Collaboration Center now features a RENCI DisplayWall (or VisWall), a 10×8 foot rear-projection display device with a native resolution of $4,096 \times 3,072$ pixels.[19] This digital video array can present a wall-size image from a computer display, whether it be satellite imagery of the earth's surface, a Renaissance fresco, electron microscope shots of molecular structure, or views from the Hubble Space Telescope. A number of critical features distinguish the RENCI DisplayWall from a simple aggregated set of high-definition LCD monitors; most important, its extraordinary 12.5 million pixel resolution is backed by robust processing power. This power of resolution allows researchers to probe imagery for small details while simultaneously viewing the full context of a surrounding visual environment. This bridging of micro and macro structure has application for projects in many disciplines, and consequently the DisplayWall is not only being made available for use in health sciences, but for research projects ranging from the engravings of William Blake to cloud patterns and climatology. Significantly, the Display Wall is not mounted in some vast arena for mass viewing by large audiences, for that would be a waste of its resolution power, but is positioned in a group-study space that can comfortably seat perhaps *thirty* students, researchers, or faculty. The scale of this large and powerful tool in such an intimate space at first might seem incongruous, but in fact, it is a superb application of the IC's important role in bringing powerful technology to the service of group-process learning and team-based research. And at the HSL Collaboration Center, the DisplayWall is being integrated with the AccessGrid, a collaborative teamwork infrastructure project that "... consists of large-format multimedia display, presentation, and interaction software environments; interfaces to grid middleware; and interfaces to remote visualization environments... [to] address the need for persistent electronic spaces... persistence is necessary to build true electronic communities, create lasting maps of the real world to distributed virtual environments..."[20] It represents a next-generation innovation in what once was simply known as "teleconferencing."

An objection can be raised to the LC as a central or neutral anchor for high-end IT tools which might be called the "put tools where the people are" viewpoint. Will specialized researchers actually trek across campus to use such a device, or might placement in a central facility actually reduce its utility to the point that instead of being used by many, it is used by few or none? The HSL Collaboration Center is already in a location designed for access by medical researchers, of course, so it may not be an ideal test case for supporting or refuting the central/neutral tool-access argument. Its DisplayWall has simply been made available for nonmedical research purposes as part of the Collaboration Center's role in supporting collaboration. But that in itself validates the concept of the inherent flexibility of an LC or a Collaboration Center, and the advantages of assembling key IT resources within its purview. It should be added that the DisplayWall clearly offers the potential to support those active, contextual, and social aspects of constructivist learning engagement stressed in earlier chapters. It also offers very interesting potentialities for extending these topics into future iterations of Internet technologies, such as Web 2.0 and the "semantic web." In Chapter 8, under the heading of "scanning the horizon," some implications of these technologies are presented, including RSS (really simple syndication), new and revised programming methods like AJAX and APIs, Web Services, instant messaging and virtual reference including co-browsing, Folksonomies, Tagging, and tag clouds, and social networking software. Display-Wall and AccessGrid installations also offer intriguing possibilities for future initiatives in metabrowsing and subject visualization, also discussed in Chapter 8. This leads to the reasonable proposition that high-end IT tools that do *not* lend themselves to active, contextual, or social learning utilization are probably *not* ideal candidates for central LC location.

Digital Resources: Hybrid Courses, Blended Learning, and Gaming

The use of digital resources in support of learning has been influenced by instructional models that can be generally categorized under the headings of *resource-based learning (RBL)* and *situated learning (SL)*. Formative elements of both RBL and SL can be found in the project-based learning schemas that began influencing K-12 educators in the early 1990s. Of course, cursory references to such ideas cannot adequately describe their subtleties and complexities. Nevertheless, many librarians have personally and collectively seen cases where faculty, motivated by their own interpretations of these models and anxious to explore their applications, have begun using IC resources and facilities in innovative ways. In addition, RBL and SL viewpoints have influenced the ways in which digital and social learning resources become related and interdependent. Such cases call for at least brief glosses on those theoretical approaches.

Resource-based learning (or pedagogy) has been defined by Ryan et al. as: "...an integrated set of strategies to promote student-centered learning...through a combination of specifically designed learning resources and interactive media and technologies," in contrast to "...traditional approaches where the main resource is a human teacher who delivers lessons, lectures and seminars to groups of students..."[21] While Ryan and his colleagues discuss RBL primarily in reference to e-learning, they are careful to point out its contributory role in blended or hybrid courses, and describe the incorporation of interactive media resources in traditional courses as "embedding." In fact, Ryan et al. stress that while some new courses are exclusively developed for online delivery, a more common pattern of change is one of gradual transformation of existing courses.[22] The authors elaborate: "...what is happening and is likely to happen in traditional institutions, where the bulk of the teaching is on campus, face-to-face and aimed at undergraduates...is that in the course of the next five to ten years a majority of such institutions will develop a number of 'hybrid' approaches to learning and teaching."[23] Describing the support staff needed for course hybridization, they emphasize the need for "...staff who work with media and information, graphic designers, desktop publishing and other lens media production staff, who may have new roles as Webmaster, instructional designer, or learning technology support staff...[and] there is an increased demand for librarians with...related skills and educational technologists to carry out research and development."[24] And, you might add, the need for this type of mixed support staff is matched by the corollary need for a suitable physical workspace for them to aggregate their technological tools and apply their expertise in proximity to students and faculty. We submit that the physical IC/LC offers the most effective, centrally located model to meet that need.

The early predictions of Ryan et al. that a majority of institutions would develop "a number of hybrid approaches to learning," now more frequently called blended learning, can now be seen to have been, if anything, underestimated. For example, the *Technology Enabled Teaching* newsletter reported a recent case study for Ohio State University:

> In FY04, 1,643 instructors in 135 departments at the university offered 2,507 courses (3,487 sections) through WebCT. Forty-five thousand students—about 77% of the student body—had a WebCT account...Large first year courses in the departments of biology, statistics, chemistry, and theater depended on WebCT's course management functions...[25]

In many respects the full scope of RBL can be seen in the proliferation of "learning objects," and their aggregation in digital repositories like MIT's D-Space. But D-Space also dramatizes the distinction between moderate and purist RBL positions in pedagogical practice. The purist RBL position would hold that embedded resources, sufficiently well-designed, can replace personal instruction. The moderate RBL position would hold that embedded resources should remain a subsidiary tool in blended courses, with teaching remaining central. Responding to some surprise across the higher education community that MIT would make its online course resources available freely to all, Phil Long explained the moderate RBL position to Steve Gilbert of the TLT Group:

...there are three 'legs' to an MIT education: extraordinary students, world-class faculty, and excellent content...An MIT education is the interaction among the three, facilitated by resources....quality of education is not something easy to accomplish disintermediated by the web. Distributing digitized course materials is not teaching.[26]

A full description of the conceptual underpinnings of situated learning (SL), like resource-based learning, is beyond the scope of this book, but William J. Clancy has provided a brief tutorial on some of the underlying tenets of situated learning theory:

> ...situated learning claims that every idea and human action is a generalization, adapted to the ongoing environment, because what people see and do [are]...adaptively recoordinated from previous ways of seeing, talking, and moving. Situated learning is the study of how human knowledge develops in the course of activity...[27]

In one respect, this notion that learning skills are adaptively recoordinated from experiences gained in the course of activity supports Phil Long's insistence on combining MIT's embedded resources with scholarly engagement and interaction. Some SL practitioners, however, come close to a purist RBL position in insisting that when multimedia resources are embedded within sufficiently interactive and immersive online environments (virtual reality), students can indeed learn without traditional instruction, on their own or in small self-directed groups. For example, the use of flight simulator software in aviation presents aspects of both RBL and SL. But a moderate RBL advocate would point out that most airline passengers would probably balk at boarding an aircraft piloted by someone with only flight simulator experience.

Regardless of your position on these viewpoints, there is no question about the relevance of situated learning models to libraries in general. Nor is the United States necessarily on the forefront of exploration in this area. Interesting initiatives in Scandanavia have begun charting the path of situated learning and libraries, as described by Erik Arnesen et al of Bergen University Library:

> The change now taking place is a move towards a *situated learning model* where the process of learning is contextualised. The development of information skills is linked to situations where the student directly experiences their value. Students acquire information literacy at the same time as they work with academic material...[28]

Arneson notes that the model requires closer cooperation between librarians and faculty, and the acquisition of new pedagogic skills by librarians. Similar research is under way in Australia, as described in the article "Information Literacy and the Library as a Learning Resource Centre":

> **Situated learning**...stresses informal learning...that takes place in communities...these environments of learning...require access to creative spaces such as studios and laboratories...to integrate physical and virtual modeling. This interplay between space, media technologies, learning and creativity will be studied as will the design of necessary collaborative learning environments.[29]

A very interesting study in Finland looked at the influence of personality factors on students' information-seeking behavior.[30] Author Jannica Heinstrom looked at core dimensions of personality, such as extraversion, openness, and conscientiousness, and studied their possible relationship to characteristic styles of information-seeking behavior, which she describes as "fast surfing, broad scanning, and deep diving." Perhaps not surprisingly, she found statistically significant correlations. What seems especially pertinent is that the same core dimensions of personality have also been related by other researchers to learning styles.[31] The implication is that there may be causative interdependencies between learning styles and information-seeking behaviors; i.e., the way we facilitate information-seeking may positively impact learning. If true, such research may become an additional argument for collaboration between faculty and librarians to embed information search and retrieval tools as carefully crafted resources within online learning environments.

Both RBL and SL predated the World Wide Web, but the Web's emergence has given faculty and librarians new ways to explore both approaches. RBL practitioners find the Web to be a suitable conveyance for embedded multimedia resources, while SL practitioners find in the Web a sort of "theater of the mind" for alternate SL virtual realities. Two other approaches to learning theory have been mentioned in the context of LC development: First, multiple intelligences, which posits sensory proclivities related to learning, as in visual learners or auditory learners, offers interesting connection to the rich multimedia resources of such modern LCs as Vassar's Media Cloisters. And second, a related approach to creative writing developed in the 1970s at the California Institute of the Arts by psycholinguist Josephine Harris, which is built around conceptual frames of *monologue, dialogue* and *discourse*.[32] The development of blogs and wikis offers new arenas of exploration for the monologue/dialogue/discourse learning model, and the LC labs offer a suitable facility for supportive innovation.

The significance of Web-enhanced RBL and SL learning tools for blended learning and mainstream library instruction was occluded for a time by the hype surrounding distance learning per se. Nevertheless, dedicated online library and information literacy instruction has undergone its own phased evolution and gradually gathered momentum. The first major article on the topic, by Nancy K. Getty, Barbara Burd, Sarah K. Burns, and Linda Piele, was entitled "Using Courseware to Deliver Library Instruction Via the Web: Four Examples." It demonstrated the use of course management systems to house and add functionality to library tutorials, to maintain source material for an already operational library course, to create BI modules for a faculty-taught literature and communications class, and to bring added online functionalities such as reading lists, quizzes, and threaded discussions to the BI (bibliographic instruction) arena.[33] More recent interest in active learning emerged in an article by Wenxian Zhang, which was notable for its emphasis on using CMS/VLE to develop an Information Fluency course that exposed students to the reasoning and critical thinking skills necessary for successful research, thus providing an example of cognitive style immersion within the framework of stand-alone library instruction.[34] Zhang states: "Interactivity in online education makes the difference between an information source and a learning experience. Active learning is active engagement by the students with the materials."[35] And according to the author, the key to developing a successful Web-assisted library instructional module "... is to link it directly with the pedagogical objectives of the course and to use technology effectively to enhance and enrich students' learning experiences."[36] This type of resource-based interactive or immersive learning also has roots in "The Learning Pyramid" diagram in Figure 3.6, sometimes attributed to research at the National Training Institute in Bethel, Maine.[37]

Figure 3.6
Learning Pyramid, Multimedia Resources, and Active Learning

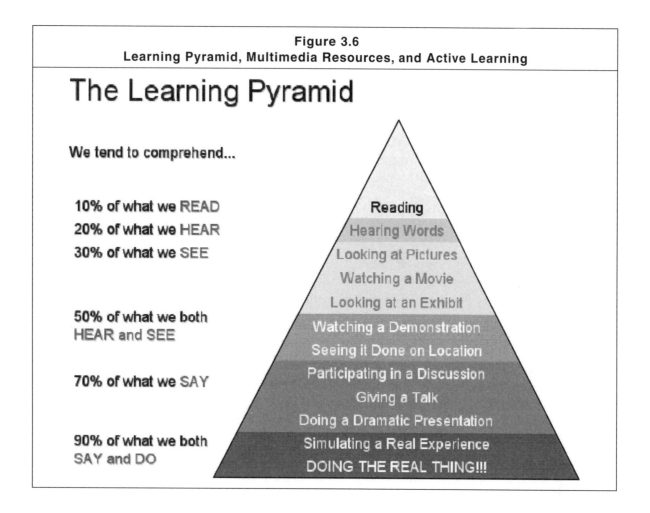

The multimedia-equipped group learning rooms of the LC offer faculty the opportunity to craft a custom learning environment where their students can look at pictures, watch a movie, view a demonstration, visit a Web-based exhibit, give a dramatic presentation, study the simulation of a real experience, rehearse a presentation, and also participate in a face-to-face discussion. This capability shows how and why social resources and digital resources can be blended to create active contextual learning experiences that immerse the students in the cognitive style of a discipline.

Computer Games as LC Digital Resources

By creating this type of arena, the Learning Commons also then positions itself as a potential testbed for the creative utilization of gaming and virtual reality simulation, often considered another element of RBL and SL. We want to stress that video and computer gaming per se has long been a topic of interest to learning theorists, dating back to its earliest development. For example, based on research in the 1980s, Patricia Marks Greenfield described key cognitive skills engaged in the early game *Pac-Man:* (1) inductive reasoning, because players must inductively ascertain the nature of obstacles in order to overcome them; and (2) parallel processing, which involves receiving information from multiple sources simultaneously. She added:

...Pac-Man embodies another cognitive complexity that was impossible in pre-computer games: the interaction of two elements yields results that could not be predicted from either one separately... Only by watching the monsters interacting with Pac-Man in different parts of the maze can you detect the dynamic qualities of the maze.[38]

Greenfield's early research is mentioned here because she uncovered two critical issues: inductive reasoning from the behavior of embedded resources, and parallel processing through visualization displays, that figure prominently in later formulations of RBL and SL. Pac-Man was also a good example of type of game prevalent during the time of "islands and enclosures," a game that young people tended to play individually (though sequential gaming among members of small peer groups was common in arcades). The cognitive skills described by Greenfield were typically engaged by solo players; social interactions were largely peripheral to the core challenges of the game's program. But with the arrival of the Web, of course, gaming has begun to engage cognitive and social skills in concert, most notably in the spread of Massive Multiplayer Online Games (MMOGs). And on the academic level, certain meta-theoretical aspects of game theory continue to become elevated in significance. For example, as this text was written, it was announced that the 2005 Nobel Prize in Economics was awarded to Thomas C. Schelling and Robert Aumann, who worked independently to apply game theory to social and political problems.

Traditional academic libraries, even those with strong IT infrastructures, are in most instances inadequate facilities for hosting student and faculty engagement with learning scenarios based on computer gaming and embedded virtual reality resources. By contrast, the IC/LC not only can become such a suitable facility, but on some campuses, *already is.* Crit Stuart of Georgia Institute of Technology has described how the Georgia Tech Information Commons has, since its inception, hosted a "gaming night" every semester.[39] In this context, gaming intersects the underlying concerns of both resource-based and situated learning. There are already cases in which components of games are embedded as multimedia learning objects in online courseware, and in some cases, these games present simulations of real-world scenarios that apply to situated learning. For example, a group in the Department of Classical, Near Eastern, and Religious Studies at the University of British Columbia has begun a virtual reality project called *Ancient Spaces*, which they describe as:

...interactive simulations of the environments of Mediterranean antiquity... We are developing an open-source, Internet-based format that can be freely employed by multiple institutions. Through collaboration, we aim to develop a compatible and comprehensive library of archaeological models, which will eventually be deployed in a more complete simulation of ancient Mediterranean society.[40]

This project recapitulates and builds upon the concept behind the revision of the original JCC/Learning Commons proposal, a 1995 Apple Library of Tomorrow grant entitled the *Charleston Multimedia Project.* That project, as described in Karen Commings' article "Libraries of the Future" in the journal *Computers In Libraries* (April 1996), was designed to use "...hypertext and hypermedia to explore collaborative history," and "allow someone to sit at a personal computer and take a tour of an historic building or travel down one of Charleston's streets simply by operating a mouse...The project began with Charleston's waterfront historic district, which includes about 4,000 structures in a 1,000-acre area first settled in 1690."[41] This project later developed resources touching on the city during its Walled City/Colonial, Revolutionary War, Antebellum, and Civil War periods. Although the *Charleston Multimedia Project* was developed using software tools primitive by today's standards, its decade-long tenure on the Web is now significantly longer than *City of Troy* or *Ancient Spaces*, and thus offers some longitudinal lessons. Interestingly, its uses now specifically include independent self-paced learning. John Van Dalen of the Charleston County Public Library reports that the *Charleston Multimedia Project* resource files (now largely incorporated within the Web site of the Charleston County Public Library) are sometimes used by persons preparing themselves to become officially licensed tour guides to the city's Historic District. Van Dalen has commented that learners find the online project files more richly associative than typical narrative study texts.[42] This coincides with the rationale of the *Ancient Spaces* home page, which describes this project as an "...immersive educational environment" and "...a large-scale simulation of the society and culture of antiquity." Presumably, students exploring the labyrinth of Knossos on *Ancient Spaces* will enable similar inductive reasoning and parallel processing skills discovered by Greenfield in the Pac-Man maze. And both skill sets have implications for the inclusion of subject visualization components in future online public access catalogs (OPACs), which we will briefly discuss in Chapter 8.

Social Resources: LCs, Group Learning, and Communities of Scholarship

The validating research on group process learning and its potential for higher education is, of course, far too vast to be dealt with here. Here is a brief representative quote from a "meta-analysis" that summarizes a range of studies, from a report coauthored by Leonard Springer of the National Institute for Science Education on research funded by the National Science Foundation on the "Effects of Small-Group Learning on Undergraduates in Science, Mathematics, Engineering, and Technology (SMET)." Springer, Stanne, and Donovan state their overall findings and conclusions:

> Students who learn in small groups...demonstrate greater academic achievement, express more favorable attitudes toward learning, and persist through SMET courses or programs to a greater extent than their traditionally taught counterparts...even minimal group work can have positive effects on student achievement...Small-group learning...holds considerable promise for improving undergraduate SMET education.[43]

In *Tools for Teaching*, Barbara Gross Davis identifies three characteristic types of student learning groups, and our experience suggests that her typology effectively describes groups we now see making use of shared technological environments within a physical commons:

> *Informal learning groups* are ad hoc temporary clusterings of students....*Formal learning groups* are teams established to complete a specific task such as write a report, [or] carry out a project....*Study teams* are long-term groups...to provide members with support, encouragement, and assistance in completing course requirements and assignments.[44]

These types of groups increasingly utilize learning technologies and IC spaces in ways that are distinct from the needs of solo learners and traditional library users. This utilization partly arises due to the development of related pedagogical models that call for student interactions with digital texts on levels not previously achievable with collections of printed books, and for interactions with peers in ways not well-supported by traditional classrooms or libraries. Such initiatives often flow from learning theories we have already referenced that support active, contextual, and social learning activities. As faculty put components of their courses on the Web to supplement traditional classroom instruction, and became more familiar with course management system (CMS/VLE) capabilities, there have been indications of further transformations in instructional strategy that invoke elements of both situated and resource-based learning. One example of a blended or hybrid strategy now being explored by faculty is sometimes termed the "classroom flip." A schema summarizing the classroom flip can be seen in Figure 3.7, and further information about the technique can be found in a paper by J. W. Baker.[45] Baker summarizes the process in four steps: (1) move lecture material out of the classroom through online delivery; (2) move homework into the classroom where faculty can serve as a guide; (3) use additional opened up class time for higher-level discussion, application, and practice; and (4) extend conversation out of class through threaded discussion.

The classroom flip presents instructional librarians with both risks and opportunities. Perhaps the greatest risk is that those librarians who restrict themselves to traditional classroom presentations in a guest lecture format may find their services less relevant to faculty who wish to move all lecture content online in order to devote class time to discipline-based discussion. But for those librarians who devise their own interactive course Web pages or CMS strategies, the classroom flip may offer the opportunity to collaborate with faculty to an unprecedented degree in the development of new online environments where modules for active learning and cognitive immersion are *embedded*. This further emphasizes the need for the mixed skills of the support staff identified by Ryan et al. in support of resource-based learning. From the perspective of both faculty and librarian, the IC/LC model provides a creative arena for these collaborative productions, and the toolset for embedding multimedia information literacy and learning components in the online portion of the blended course.

One aspect of the "classroom flip" deserves special attention, since it has never been adequately examined: the isolated and isolating nature of students' exposure to the online content

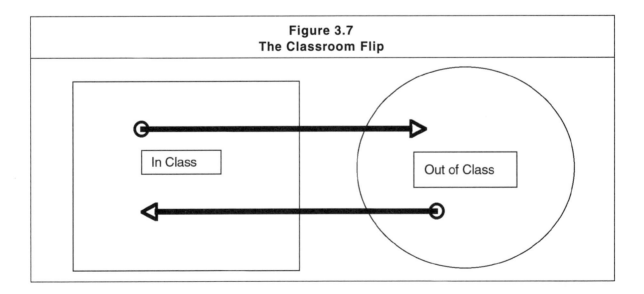

Figure 3.7
The Classroom Flip

In Class

Out of Class

of the hybrid course. The classroom flip implies that students will pursue the online portion of the hybrid model outside of class sessions; consequently, this learning activity would traditionally take place in the dorms or in other singular workstation settings, as shown in Figure 3.8.

But with research indicating the potential of socialized and group learning, faculty may wish to use the Learning Commons to create spaces where students may access and explore the online content of hybrid courses in group-process settings that allow further out-of-class discussion, exploration, and face-to-face interaction, as shown in Figure 3.9.

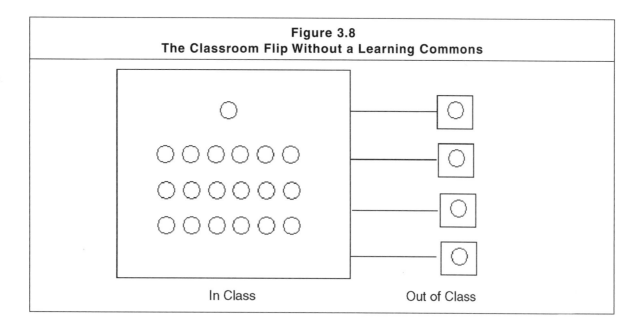

Figure 3.8
The Classroom Flip Without a Learning Commons

In Class   Out of Class

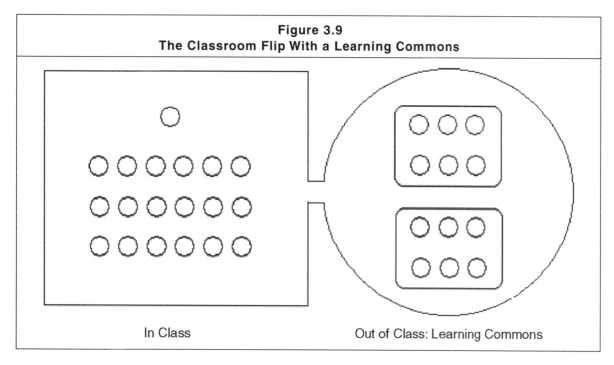

Figure 3.9
The Classroom Flip With a Learning Commons

In Class   Out of Class: Learning Commons

Such group-based access to online course material may be informally initiated by students themselves, but is often deliberately structured by faculty, as with Barbara Gross Davis's notion of study teams. The IT-enhanced group study areas of the IC clearly offer a plausible venue for either option, and we can foresee a time when the "classroom flip" might be elaborated as a pedagogical strategy to create a bi-modal instructional model balancing classroom-based instruction and IC-based out-of-class group learning activities. In one recent published study, 25 students were asked to rate their preference for level of course interactivity as compared to lecturing: (1) 100 percent lecturing; (2) 75 percent lecturing and 25 percent interactive; (3) 50 percent lecturing and 50 percent interactive; and (4) 100 percent interactive. Interestingly, all 25 chose number 3, 50 percent lecturing and 50 percent interactive."[46]

Given this increasing emphasis on out-of-classroom learning, both through multimedia-embedded online content and through small group engagement, Howard Strauss of Princeton University has recently questioned the investment of large sums in "smart classrooms," wondering whether more resources should be put instead into the creation of multimedia presentation studios and other extra-classroom facilities. He noted:

> The focus until now has been on classrooms...If learning is viewed as a continuous process... then our plan to improve learning must include the entire learning space...This will add to the richness of collaboration and interactivity...Given tools and training, the focus...will move from the classroom to the learning space environment...[47]

We are not advocating positioning the Learning Commons as a budgetary competitor to smart classrooms, but would simply note that if one were to mesh Strauss's vision of learning space multimedia studios with Springer's research on small-group learning, one would be led to the creation of a type of centrally located facility that offers (1) faculty the spaces and tools needed to craft the online environment, (2) librarians the spaces and tools needed to embed pertinent multimedia and data-retrieval resources in those environments, and (3) students the learning spaces and tools for group utilization of those environments; in other words, a space where situated learning meets resource-based learning. To summarize, *if the IC did not already exist, we would now be compelled to invent it.* Figure 3.10 offers this overview in a schematic.

Figure 3.10 The Learning Commons: Agents and Areas of Innovation	
For these agents:	**The Learning Commons offers:**
Faculty	Spaces, tools, and support helpful to craft the online learning environment for hybrid courses and the "classroom flip"
Librarians	Spaces, tools, and support needed to embed pertinent multimedia and data-retrieval resources in those environments; per "resource-based learning"
Students	Spaces, tools, and support for group/community utilization of those environments; per "situated learning"

The type of learning and social interactions that can thrive within the Learning Commons can also be of significant interest to the supporters of thematic learning communities. The phrase "learning communities" is being used in multiple and sometimes nebulous ways (much like Information Commons), but it also has very specific application to a particular approach to interdisciplinary ties across course and departmental boundaries that may depart from the traditional curriculum. The Evergreen Center at Washington State College has posted a Web page giving examples of types of student learning communities:[48]

Student Cohorts/Integrative Seminar: a small cohort of students enrolls in larger classes that faculty do not coordinate. In this instance, intellectual connections and community-building often take place in an additional integrative seminar.

For example, a cohort of eight students convenes around a special interest in T. S. Eliot's poem "The Waste Land." They may physically meet in a Learning Commons group study space, and they may further interact through "Webinar" space hosted on an LC server. At these venues, this thematic community meets with a faculty specialist on Eliot for integrative sessions that place total focus on that poem. On the advice of that specialist, and to learn more about the literary, historical, and cultural contexts of the poem, these eight students also enroll *as a group* in three larger classes: "Mythology of the Grail Legend," "Early Twentieth Century English and American Poetry," and "Modernism, Postmodernism, and Culture." Each of these courses is open to normal enrollment of perhaps 25–30 students, but each course also hosts the small "student learning community" of eight students whose group focus is on an appreciation of a poem by T. S. Eliot. Figure 3.11 illustrates the concept.

Related forms of learning communities described by the Evergreen Center's page include the "Linked Courses/Course Clusters" model which involves "...two or more classes linked thematically or by content which a cohort of students takes together. In this instance, the faculty do plan the program collaboratively." And in "Coordinated Study, learning communities

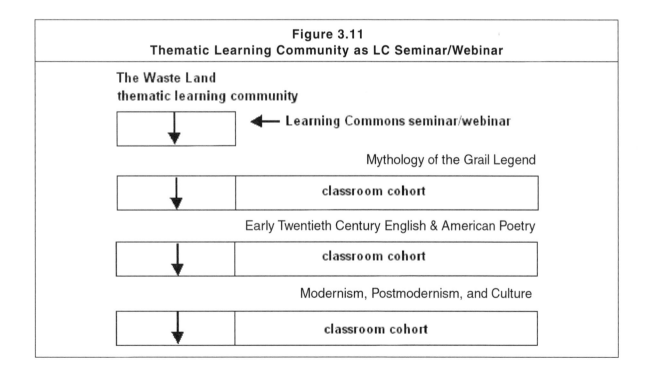

Figure 3.11
Thematic Learning Community as LC Seminar/Webinar

The Waste Land
thematic learning community

← Learning Commons seminar/webinar

Mythology of the Grail Legend

classroom cohort

Early Twentieth Century English & American Poetry

classroom cohort

Modernism, Postmodernism, and Culture

classroom cohort

may involve coursework that faculty members team teach. The course work is embedded in an integrated program of study."

The Learning Commons Summation: Collaborative Development of Human, Physical, Digital, and Social Resources

As Carole A. Barone of EDUCAUSE has noted, "Faculty have progressed from simply putting course content online to designing active learning and knowledge creating environments that immerse the student in the cognitive style of the discipline."[49] *Ancient Spaces* is a splendid example of a collection of embedded resources designed in support of cognitive immersive, resource-based, and situated learning. This type of associative, integrative learning environment, often conveyed through a course management system, stands in sharp contrast to older reductionist narratives that too often typified academic textbooks and lecture notes. The contrast in form and function is emphasized by John Seely Brown and Paul Duguid:

> The delivery view of education assumes that knowledge comprises discrete preformed units, which learners ingest in smaller or greater amounts until graduation or indigestion takes over. But knowledge is not a static, preformed substance. It is constantly changing. Learning involves active engagement in the processes of that change.[50]

The traditional academic reference desk has always excelled at delivering discrete facts and chunks of information in response to specific requests. Reference staff were trained to hone down patron needs to such specifiable facts and chunks. Those skills are still crucial as elements of critical analysis and problem-solving, but in themselves, are too narrowly defined to encompass the broad arena of service delivery needed in future library learning centers. As new learner-centered approaches to education are explored on many campuses, the synergy between the user support skills of computer staff, the information skills of reference staff, and production skills of media staff, gives the IC the flexible workspace all staff need to apply their combined expertise adaptively to blended learning scenarios enabled by course management systems/virtual learning environments, and, more generally, to the rapidly changing needs of a highly demanding user community.

The American Council on Education (A.C.E.) has produced a primer for change that includes a typology, or matrix, of change initiatives.[51] This matrix plots graph lines representing the depth of change, in terms of fundamental impact on basic activities and assumptions, and pervasiveness of change, in terms of extent and distribution of its influence beyond the library's walls. This matrix, adapted in Figure 3.12, may be helpful in characterizing the idea of a phased evolution from Information Commons to Learning Commons, and can serve to summarize the diverse arena of now evident collaborative learning initiatives as well as setting the stage for our discussion of strategic planning for the Information Commons.

1. Adjustment: neither deep, in terms of the library's core operations, nor pervasive, in terms of impact across campus. Described as a computer lab on the first floor of the library with a suite of productivity software (Microsoft Office) combined with access to electronic resources. Focus broadens from print to integration and coordination of information and technology resources for students.

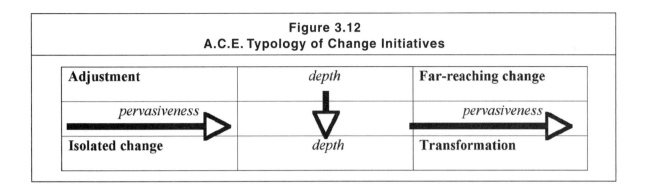

Figure 3.12
A.C.E. Typology of Change Initiatives

2. Isolated change: deep, in that the IC has substantially impacted library operations and services, but not pervasive, without broad impact across campus. Described as the same lab as (1) but with media authoring tools also included, and with coordinated in-library staff support designed to carry the user through a continuum of service from resource identification and retrieval on through data processing and format conversion to the desired end state of presentation, packaging, or publication. Here, the library has altered its pattern of service delivery to better align itself with changing campuswide priorities, and has done so by integrating functions formerly carried out by separate units within the library to project a new unified and comprehensive service profile. However, this level portrays an IC model that is still library-centric. While it better *aligns* the library with other campus priorities, it is still not intrinsically collaborative with other campus initiatives.

——*This marks the proposed threshold between IC and LC*——

3. Far-reaching change: the LC exerts a significant presence across campus, but that influence remains primarily associative, rather than truly collaborative. Described as (2) plus coordination with other unit(s) such as a faculty development center or center for teaching and learning, as well as the frequent inclusion of a campuswide course management system meaningfully linked to and integrated with library electronic resources and virtual reference services. Here, the library has further altered its pattern of service delivery to better align itself with changing campuswide priorities, and has done so by integrating those functions formerly carried out *within* the library with others formerly carried out *beyond* the library's purview. The service profile is no longer library-centric.

4. Transformation: both deep, in its impact on library services, and pervasive in terms of important campuswide collaborations. Described as (3) but carried out with reference to (or within a framework of) campuswide schema and/or faculty innovation such as core curriculum revision, information literacy across the curriculum, writing/authoring across the curriculum, cognitive immersion learning paradigms such as the "classroom flip," and/or learning object/IMS implementation, such as D-Space. At this level, functional integration continues across a horizontal plane, but vertical differentiation is beginning as the former service delivery profile projected toward students becomes enhanced with another (or multiple) service delivery profile(s) projected at the needs of faculty as course authors, knowledge creators, learning coaches, and scholarly communicators. This also involves an enriched suite of toolsets and services.

Endnotes

1 Remy, Melanie. 2004. "Information Literacy: The Information Commons Connection." University of Southern California, Teaching and Learning with Technology Conference. Available: http://www.usc.edu/isd/libraries/locations/leavey/news/conference/presentations/presentations_9-17/USC_Remy.pdf

2 ICT Literacy Panel, 2001. "Digital Transformation: A Report of the International ICT Literacy Panel," Educational Testing Service. Available: http://www.ets.org/research/ictliteracy/ictreport.pdf

3 Herrmann, Carol. 2005. "Teaching in the Information Commons." *Spring 2005 Conference: The Future of Academic Libraries*. Association of College & Research Libraries New England Chapter. Available: http://www.acrlnec.org/Springconf05/Infocommons.rtf

4 "Project-Based Learning Space: Background Knowledge and Theory." 2006. Houghton Mifflin. Available: http://college.hmco.com/education/pbl/background.html

5 Blumenfeld, P. C., E. Soloway, R. W. Marx, J. S. Krajcik, M. Guzdial, and A. Palincsar. 1991. "Motivating Project-based Learning: Sustaining the Doing, Supporting the Learning." *Educational Psychologist*, 26 no. 3/4. 369–398.

6 "Project-Based Learning Space: Background Knowledge and Theory." 2006. Houghton Mifflin. Available: http://college.hmco.com/education/pbl/background.html

7 Herrmann, Carol. 2005. "Teaching in the Information Commons." *Spring 2005 Conference: The Future of Academic Libraries*. Association of College & Research Libraries New England Chapter. Available: http://www.acrlnec.org/Springconf05/Infocommons.rtf

8 Beatty, Susan. 2003. "The Information Commons at the University of Calgary: Strategies for Integration." In *Information and IT Literacy: Enabling Learning in the 21st Century*, edited by Allan Martin and Hannelore Rader. London, Facet Publishing. 159. Available: http://www.facetpublishing.co.uk/458.pdf

9 Greene, Thomas C. 2005. "What Works, A PKAL Essay: Spaces for Learning Communities." Project Kaleidoscope. Available: http://www.pkal.org/documents/SpacesForLearningCommunities.cfm

10 Elmborg, James K. 2002. "Teaching at the Desk: Toward a Reference Pedagogy." *portal: Libraries and the Academy*, 2 no. 3 455–464.

11 Bennett , Scott. 2003. *Libraries Designed for Learning*. Washington, D.C.: CLIR. 38. Available: http://www.clir.org/pubs/reports/pub122/pub122web.pdf

12 Shapiro, Jeremy J., and Shelley K. Hughes, 2003. "Information Literacy as a Liberal Art." *EDUCAUSE Review*. Available: http://www.educause.edu/pub/er/review/reviewarticles/31231.html. See also: Shapiro, Jeremy J., and Shelley K. Hughes. 2002. "The Case of the Inflammatory E-mail: Building Culture and Community in OnLine Academic Environments." In *Handbook of Online Learning: Innovations in Higher Education and Corporate Training* edited by Kjell Rudestam and Judith Schoenholtz-Read. Thousand Oaks, Calif.: SAGE Publications. 91–124.

13 de la Motte, Dean. 2005. "Vision for Information Technology and Learning at Belmont Abbey College," Belmont Abbey College, Belmont NC. 5p.

14 Laird, Thomas F. Nelson. 2005. "Technology and Student Engagement: Lessons Learned from the National Survey of Student Engagement (NSSE)," National Survey of Student Engagement. Available: http://nsse.iub.edu/pdf/conference_presentations/2005/tech_and_stu_engagement.pdf

15 Remy, Melanie. 2004. "Information Literacy: The Information Commons Connection." University of Southern California, Teaching and Learning with Technology Conference. Available: http://www.usc.edu/isd/libraries/locations/leavey/news/conference/presentations/presentations_9-17/USC_Remy.pdf

16 "Miller Nichols Library Information Commons." 2001. Kansas City, MO: University of Missouri, Kansas City. Available: http://www.umkc.edu/lib/MNL/About/info-commons.htm

17 Hurt, Charlene. 1997. "Building Libraries in the Virtual Age." *College & Research Libraries News* (February). 75–76.

18 Daniel, Sir John S., "Why Universities Need Technology Strategies." *Change: the Magazine of Higher Learning*. 29, no. 4 (1997). 16.

19 "Introducing the RENCI HSL 12.5 Million Pixel DisplayWall." University of North Carolina Health Sciences Library. (December 2005). Available: http://www.hsl.unc.edu/Collaboration/ccdisplaywall.cfm

20 "AccessGrid: A Global Community." Available: http://www.accessgrid.org/

21 Ryan, Steve, Bernard Scott, Howard Freeman, and Daxa Patel. 2000. *The Virtual University: The Internet and Resource-Based Learning*. London: Kogan Page. 30–31.

22 Ryan, p. 164.

23 Ryan, p. 169.

24 Ryan, p. 163.

25 Dehoney, Joanne, and Rebecca Andre. "Case Study: CMS in Transition: Managing Change," *Technology-Enabled Teaching* October 6, 2005. Available: http://www.campus-technology.com/news_article.asp?id=11892& typeid=156

26 Long, Phil. E-mail to Steve Gilbert, as quoted in "TLT-SWG-19: Sharing MIT Course Content—Not Courses." (October 25, 2005, 9:30 am).

27 William J. Clancy, "A Tutorial on Situated Learning" *Proceedings of the International Conference on Computers and Education (Taiwan)*. Self, J. (ed.) Charlottesville, Va.: AACE. 49–70, 1995. Available at: http://cogprints. org/323/00/139.htm

28 Arnesen, Erik, et al., 2004. "New Pedagogic Challenges for the University Library." *Scandinavian Public Library Quarterly*. 37 no. 3. Available: http://www.splq.info/issues/vol37_3/05.htm

29 Lyons, Erik. "Information Literacy and the Library as a Learning Resource Centre." Available: http://web.bit.mah. se/konferens/ck2/cabinet/report/CreatingKnowledge2.pdf

30 Heinstrom, Jannica. 2005. "Fast Surfing, Broad Scanning, and Deep Diving: The Influence of Personality and Study Approach on Students' Information-Seeking Behavior." *Journal of Documentation*. 61 no. 2. 228–247.

31 Sadler-Smith, E. 1997. "'Learning Style:' Frameworks and Instruments," *Educational Psychology*. 17 no. 1/2. 51–63.

32 Harris, Josephine. Letter to Donald Beagle. May 5, 2003.

33 Getty, Nancy K., Barbara Burd, Sarah K. Burns, and Linda Piele. 2000. "Using Courseware to Deliver Library Instruction via the Web: Four Examples," *Reference Services Review*. 28 (Winter). 349.

34 Zhang, Wenxian. 2002. "Developing Web-Enhanced Learning for Information Fluency." *Reference & User Services Quarterly* 41. (Summer). 356–363.

35 Ibid., 360.

36 Ibid., 362.

37 Hagner, Paul R. "Mobile Learning Environments for the 21st Century." Presentation for 2006 NITLE-CIC: Technology and Learning Spaces. Available: http://www.pkal.org/documents/MobileLearningEnvironments For21stCentury.cfm

38 Greenfield, Patricia Marks. 1984. *Mind and Media: The Effects of Television, Video Games, and Computers*. Cambridge: Harvard University Press. 110–113.

39 Stuart, Crit. "Learning from the Commons: Experiments in Collaboration and Transformation," Chapel Hill, N.C.: Triangle Research Libraries Network 2005 Winter Conference. Available: http://www.unc.edu/~pmpittma/ InfoCommons/Stuart%20presentation.ppt

40 "Ancient Spaces: Antiquity Comes Alive." University of British Columbia, Department of Classical, Near Eastern, and Religious Studies. 2005. Available: http://www.cnrs.ubc.ca/ancientspaces/

41 Commings, Karen. 1996. "Libraries of the Future" *Computers in Libraries*. April. 22–23.

42 Beagle, Donald. 1996. "Charleston Multimedia Project (files)" Charleston County Public Library. Available: http://www.ccpl.org/content.asp?id=14676&catID=5405&action=detail&parentID=5402

43 Springer, Leonard, Mary Elizabeth Stanne, and Samuel Donovan. 1997. "Measuring the Success of Small-Group Learning in College-Level SMET Teaching: A Meta-Analysis." Wisconsin Center for Education Research, University of Wisconsin-Madison. Available: http://www.wcer.wisc.edu/archive/cl1/CL/resource/ scismet.htm

44 Davis, Barbara Gross. 1993. *Tools for Teaching*. San Francisco, Calif.: Jossey-Bass. Excerpt available: http://teaching.berkeley.edu/bgd/collaborative.html

45 Baker, J. W. 2000. "The 'Classroom Flip:' Using Web Course Management Tools to Become the Guide by the Side." In *Selected Papers from the 11th International Conference on College Teaching and Learning*. Edited by J. A. Chambers. Jacksonville, FL: Florida Community College at Jacksonville. 9–17.

46 Roberts, Gregory R. 2005. "Technology and Learning Expectations of the Net Generation." In *Educating the Net Generation*, edited by Diana G. Oblinger and James R. Oblinger. EDUCAUSE. Available: http://www.educause. edu/educatingthenetgen/

47 Strauss, Howard. 2005. "New Learning Spaces: Smart Learners, Not Smart Classrooms." *Campus Technology*. October 11. Available: http://www.campus-technology.com/article.asp?id=6702

48 "What are Learning Communities?" Evergreen Center, Washington State College. Available: http://www. evergreen.edu/washcenter/lcfaq.htm#21

49 Barone, Carole A. "Leadership & Technology: Infrastructure is Not the Issue." Presented at EDUCAUSE Southeastern Regional Conference, Charleston, S.C., (June 19, 2002). Available: http://www.educause.edu/ir/ library/powerpoint/SER0213.pps

[50] Brown, John Seely, and Paul Duguid. 1996. "Universities in the Digital Age." *Change: The Magazine of Higher Learning.* 28 (July/August). 17.

[51] Eckel, Peter, Madeleine Green, Barbara Hill, and Bill Mallon. 2000. *On Change III—Taking Charge of Change: A Primer for Colleges and Universities.* Creating the Context: American Council on Education Occasional Paper #3. Section I, p. 16. Available: http://www.acenet.edu/bookstore/pdf/on-change/section_I.pdf

II

Designing and Building the Physical Commons

In this section, Chapter 4 begins the discussion of planning an Information Commons, Learning Commons, or Collaboration Center. It introduces some key concepts of strategic planning critical for IC development, and introduces the self-discovery step of the planning process. Chapter 5 continues with two further steps in strategic planning: Scenario-Building and Projecting the Future Commons. Chapter 6 then completes the last two steps of the sequence, Managing the Conversation and Drafting the Project Documentation, thereby moving the process into and through tactical planning. In total, this planning template is intended as a flexible guide to either plan an IC or LC from its inception, or to plan for a phased enhancement of an existing Information Commons toward the more collaborative and integrative model of a Learning Commons.

4

Strategic Planning I: Discovering Needs through Surveys and Focus Groups

Paul Duguid, in his keynote speech to the Association of College and Research Libraries (ACRL) conference in Charlotte of April 2002, commented that during the previous 25 years of the information revolution, publishers had been thinking strategically while librarians had tended to think only tactically. Duguid characterized the strategic thinking within the publishing community as "how & why" thinking, with focus on the long-term. He described the tactical thinking within the library community as "what & when" thinking, aimed primarily at the near term. He went on to challenge librarians, both individually and as a profession, to begin thinking—and planning—strategically.

In one sense, Duguid's critique may seem unfair; even a cursory Web search on library plans and planning reveals a rich and ever-growing population of library strategic plans. He may be correct, however, in that private sector strategic planning began earlier and more vigorously than its academic counterpart. In IC consulting, the author has seen cases where IC plans fail to achieve funding or management support in part because planning documents labeled "strategic" are actually tactical in nature. The difference becomes critical as the planning process undergoes campus administrative review, and also because it shapes subsequent stages of implementation and development. This is not a textbook on strategic planning, of course, but the following material will take a fresh look at a few key aspects of strategic planning especially pertinent to IC development. Readers who consider themselves already well versed in strategic planning may wish to skip ahead to the section "The IC Planning Group."

IC Strategic Planning Overview

Some library strategic plans are stand-alone, while many others are developed within the rubric of larger institutional planning regimes. In either case, in planning the startup of an Information Commons or the enhancement of an IC into a Learning Commons, it is essential to meet Duguid's challenge. The physical IC phenomenon first took shape as a direct outgrowth of new strategic planning initiatives within a select group of institutions such as

Maricopa, Iowa, and Southern California. Its importance is magnified by the four-model typology of adjustment, isolated change, far-reaching change, or transformation, because through strategic planning library managers can make sound decisions about where on this matrix to target an IC initiative on a particular campus at a particular time. And if the commons is indeed proposed as part of a far-reaching or transformational change, then the strategic planning process becomes a framework for incorporating cross-campus and interdepartmental goals and objectives in collaborative LC program formulation. But none of this should be seen as diminishing the significance of subsequent tactical planning. Strategic planning in isolation will remain a mere academic exercise. It should ideally precede and then effectively flow into the vital and practical traditions of tactical planning. This book spends more time discussing strategic planning than tactical, largely because it recommends blending tactical planning into implementation using project management (PM) techniques, and preferably using standard software such as Microsoft Project. Therefore, some follow-up comments on tactical planning will be also presented as the first section on implementation in Chapter 8.

Duguid's statement forms the basis for a good distinction between strategic and tactical planning. In Figure 4.1, the left side of the table lists the pitfalls of *only* doing tactical planning, in contrast to the right side of the table which lists the practical benefits of including strategic planning as a precedent.

Figure 4.1 Characteristics of Tactical and Strategic Planning	
Tactical Planning in Isolation	**Strategic Planning as Precedent**
what and when	how and why
summative, focuses vision	formative, expands vision
library-centric	campus-wide view
concept-thin; typified by checklists & timetables	concept-rich; flows into narrative; tells a coherent story
implementation & assessment may be compartmentalized	incorporates or anticipates implementation & assessment

The five key aspects of strategic planning in the right column of Figure 4.1 are interdependent, and it can be difficult to separate them out even for purposes of illustration and discussion. Still, the distinction is useful because planning is truly the proverbial journey that begins with a single step, and the care with which the first few steps are taken can have lasting reverberations through the entire history of a project or program.

Strategic planning efforts must turn on an axis that extends between two key relationships: (1) the relationship between the library and its users (students AND faculty), and (2) the relationship between the library and its hosting or funding institution. In the simplest articulation, the library should align its resources and services with the priority goals of its hosting institution by meeting the needs of its users. However, significant complexity hides

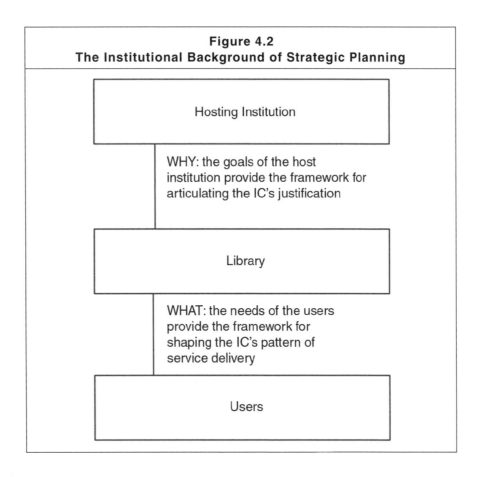

Figure 4.2
The Institutional Background of Strategic Planning

Hosting Institution

WHY: the goals of the host
institution provide the framework for
articulating the IC's justification

Library

WHAT: the needs of the users
provide the framework for
shaping the IC's pattern of
service delivery

Users

in the fact that goals of the host tend to be abstract and static generalizations, while the needs of the users tend to be changeable and specific.

The IT revolution brings users into the library with a broader, more fluid, and more unpredictable range of needs than can be effectively met by the traditional pattern of service delivery of old school academic libraries. When these needs are not adequately met, or collaborative opportunities are not pursued, the library risks falling out of alignment with the needs of its users and, eventually, with the goals of its hosting institution. If the library could meet these needs simply by plunking down a computer lab into the middle of a reference room, all talk about strategic planning might be superfluous. But as Young and Von Seggern's research showed, such a generic computer lab solution would lead only to student (and staff) frustration. Beyond that, the library management team that contents itself with hosting a mere computer lab would miss vital strategic opportunities to reposition itself for even greater challenges and opportunities in the future.

As noted in the historical overview, development of ICs has frequently been incorporated into either expansion of existing buildings or the design and construction of new buildings. In the scaffold of supporting resources, the building becomes the single most important physical resource, the arena within which all other physical, digital, human, and social resources are assembled. This book does not offer a specific chapter on building expansion or construction; rather, the IC planning template introduced in this chapter is structured to inform a "Project Sequence" described by Stephens, Kirby, Kamal, and Ellis in their Project

Kaleidoscope (PKAL) essay on institutional building planning.[1] These authors present a three-stage sequence for planning buildings that includes a conceptual stage, a design stage, and an implementation stage. The IC strategic planning section here is structured to inform their conceptual stage, and the IC tactical planning section is structured to inform their design stage. "Inform" means that the initial steps of organizational planning for the IC will normally precede building planning and design, with the two processes thereafter following converging paths. And sometimes, as you will note later, there comes a tipping-point or turn-about where the building design and construction timetable begins to drive subsequent tactical stages of organizational planning.

The IC Planning Group

The starting point is the creation of a planning committee, here called the IC Planning Group. The initial IC Planning Group may draw entirely upon library staff at one extreme, or pull key stakeholders from across campus (or even beyond campus) at the other extreme. In some cases, an internal group may later transition into a campuswide task force. These extremes relate, of course, to the presumptive target for the project on the A.C.E. matrix: adjustment, isolated change, far-reaching change, or transformation. A planning group based on internal library staff, aiming initially at adjustment or isolated change, may be built around an ongoing preexisting group such as a regular "public services committee" or "technology services committee," newly charged to take a look at IC options. Or, it may be a newly formed internal group drawn from various parts of the library organization chart and charged specifically with the task of IC strategic planning. Either type of internally staffed group may later grow to include key stakeholders from other academic departments if and when IC planning reaches beyond initial expectations of scope.

At the other extreme, institutional leaders may initially convene a powerful, widely-based IC Planning Group to target far-reaching or transformational change across campus from the "starting gate." An outstanding example of such a group was described by Scott Walter of the University of Kansas as a "Collaborative Learning Spaces Working Group."[2] Walter's presentation is recommended as a model for highly ambitious planning group formulation. That group's membership is shown in Figure 4.3.

Figure 4.3
University of Kansas Collaborative Learning Spaces Group

- Assistant Dean of Libraries for Facilities & Public Services
- Assistant Dean, School of Architecture
- Director, Center for Teaching Excellence (CTE)
- Director, Instructional Development & Support (IDS)
- Student Technology Coordinator
- Associate Director, Thematic Learning Communities (TLC)
- Campus Architect
- Librarians, Classroom Faculty, Students

It should be stressed that the Kansas group included both the Campus Architect and the Assistant Dean of the School of Architecture. But what about an IC Planning Group on a campus that will contract with an outside architect in the event that IC planning will lead to a new or expanded building? At what point should an architect or firm representative be brought into the IC strategic planning process? One could do so as soon as the likelihood of construction or renovation emerges as a viable option. But the reality on many campuses is that initial phases of strategic planning are often seen as synonymous with needs assessment. Stephens et al. describe in their essay a conceptual stage of building planning that begins with recognition of a perceived need, and moves through envisioning and goal-setting to a feasibility study.[3] The reality is that IC organizational planning may need to gain momentum and reach a certain state of clarity, critical mass, and consensus before one can or should bring an architect into the process. As an alternative to enlisting an architect at such an early point, campus leadership could designate a key faculty member as a "project shepherd." As Stephens et al. describe in their essay, the project shepherd is given the authority to represent the educational mission of the new building, to liaison with other faculty, and to articulate their ideas within the leadership team that will eventually work closely with architects and design engineers.[4]

Joanne Henning notes in the "Gleanings" from her sabbatical visits that IC partnerships should be planned before spaces are planned. Both management and service functions can be enhanced by co-location of office space, for example. This is another reason we advocate an IC Planning Group that draws together potential partnership representatives prior to the inclusion of an outside architect.[5]

Another key decision is whether to convene the IC Planning Group itself before or after deciding on the planning framework or methodology to be used. Should the framework be presented in advance, or should the group simply be given a general charge, and invited to formulate a planning approach that suits them? Once again, this relates to the perceived scope of the project, from adjustment to transformation. A "power" committee, such as the Kansas group, may expect more autonomy and exhibit more self-direction, appropriate to a more ambitious vision, and a general charge may suffice. The University of Kansas group's charge was very simply premised: "To evaluate the needs of faculty and students for learning spaces that bring together print and electronic resources with learning tools that assist in collaborative learning." Such a group may still want to directly involve itself in one or more steps of the planning template, such as *Scenario-Building*, and leave other steps delegated to subordinate or satellite groups. However, even a high-level group might benefit from a prior conversation with library management in which the full template of planning options are discussed.

The IC Planning Template

From many IC planning variations in evidence, this book presents a generic five-step *planning template* meant to accommodate a range of local needs. There is little point in reinventing wheels, so this template is meant to be sufficiently flexible that various specific planning methodologies, including some marketed by corporate consultants, can be effectively harbored within its framework. In fact, along the way a few possible models from the planning literature and marketplace are mentioned as examples of how a campus-approved or mandated planning regime might be accommodated and customized to support an IC initiative. As noted earlier, the template is meant to inform the conceptual building planning stages described in the PKAL essay, and to incorporate a specific building-design sequence at whatever point that becomes possible.

The planning template, shown in Figure 4.4, consists of five steps: *(1) self-discovery, (2) scenario-building, (3) projecting the future commons, (4) managing the campus conversation,* and *(5) drafting the project documentation.* The first step described in this chapter, *self-discovery,* includes techniques of referral analysis, surveys, and focus groups. Chapters 5 and 6 discuss the rest of the planning template. From a practical standpoint, this sequence should not be set in stone. Not all steps will need to be separated out in every case. Library managers may emphasize one or two steps and subordinate others. Steps may be combined, or the order of steps may be changed. The farther one moves from theory to practice, the more important it becomes for the local library manager to adapt and customize the template examples for individual needs. The right column of Figure 4.4 presents the equivalent building-planning steps identified in the Project Kaleidoscope (PKAL) essay by Stephens et al. that may optionally be linked to, or run in parallel with, this organizational planning template. If a new or expanded building is even a possibility, it would be advisable for the college or university leadership to begin the project shepherd's orientation during the first two steps of the planning template. In fact, that orientation can include review of the *self-discovery* results and observation of the *scenario-building* process. By the time the planning template reaches the step of *projecting the future commons,* the project shepherd should be better prepared to advise university

Figure 4.4 The IC Planning Template			
Step	**Activity**	**Players**	**PKAL Building Planning equiv.**
Self-discovery	Staff feedback on unmonitored referrals; Conversations with users; surveys, focus groups	Library; Institutional Research	Preliminary: Project shepherd selection
Scenario- building	Envisioning likely or possible futures, local and/or global	Library staff plus selected key stakeholders	Preliminary: Project shepherd orientation
Projecting the future commons among the scenarios	Place real and potential library resources and services among those scenarios.	Library staff plus selected stakeholders, perhaps Task Force; Project shepherd; architect(?)	Conceptual stage: Perceived need Visions Goals
Managing the campus conversation	Summarize and extend the results of the first three steps in a campuswide forum.	Task Force plus more selected stakeholders; Project shepherd; architect(?)	Conceptual stage: Feasibility study
Drafting and disseminating the project or program documentation	Assemble discovery data, scenario summaries, Potential future cases, Proposed solution(s)	Library + Key stakeholders + Task Force; Project shepherd; architect(?)	Conceptual stage: Define Scope, Goals and Budget

leaders on the direction of the planning endeavor, and if that leadership views the prospect favorably, help initiate a parallel building planning track that begins to articulate the perceived need, visions, and goals for a new facility. Again, the organizational planning precedes building planning because we agree with Joanne Henning's "Gleanings:" the space should not be planned until the partners resolve how they intend to offer integrated services.

Some readers may find that the entire template seems overly complicated or elaborate. Such a perception might arise due to this method of assembling real-world examples. By magnifying the self-discovery methods of library A, the scenario-building phase of library B, and the projection diagrams of library C, each step is here artificially highlighted. The challenge for the local manager is to pick and choose those elements he/she sees as most useful for an integrated, organic local process. However, as noted at the outset, a library IC/LC project can be somewhat equivalent to a corporation that restructures or reinvents some or all of its operations. Private-sector corporate restructurings are a good deal more complex and intimidating than anything presented in this book.

It may be helpful to think of the template as a process where you should begin by making *discoveries* and you should end by making *decisions*. While you may strongly favor this transition from discovery to decision, sometimes "the writing is on the wall" and the end-state of the projected IC may be imposed from above, constrained by conditions, or simply self-evident. If an end-state of adjustment or isolated change is handed down, strategic planning becomes tactical planning quite quickly, the discovery phase may transition into decision-making at a relatively early point, scenario-building may be kept very circumscribed, and campus conversations largely informative rather than collaborative. Nonetheless, these efforts can still be valuable as preliminary steps toward later expansion or elaboration of the IC toward an LC as time brings further opportunities and challenges.

When the IC's end-state is not self-evident, and when various initiatives and innovations across campus seem to invite library involvement or collaboration, then the discovery process becomes lengthened, scenario-building more ambitious, campus conversations more collaborative, key stakeholder involvement more crucial (and at an earlier stage), and strategic planning transitions to tactical planning only toward the very end of the template. The discovery process identifies the types of physical, digital, and human resources needed; the decision process involves selection of those specific resources and articulates how they will be organized and interpreted for users. Social resources play a role in the IC, but enter the picture most prominently when the plan envisions a Learning Commons or Collaboration Center (such as the University of Kansas example noted earlier) that is intended to project far-reaching or transformational change.

Planning Template Step: Self-discovery, Including Referral Analysis, Surveys and Focus Groups

At the earliest stage of the planning template, a *discovery step* frames what and why discussions for all subsequent how and when phases of the planning enterprise. At the most practical level, from the starting point of existing library services, one can think of the self-discovery step as a fact-finding effort to answer the initial questions posed in Figure 4.5.

Figure 4.5
Key Initial Questions for the Self-Discovery Step

What IT and media tools and are students currently using in the library, and why?

What are key areas and examples of dissatisfaction with library IT, and why?

What needs are being unmet and causing these areas of dissatisfaction, and why?

What resources can be identified to meet these needs?
- Physical resources: spaces, furnishings, peripherals, supplies, hardware
- Digital resources: software, databases, utilities, media
- Human resources: IT support, application training, coaches, help desk
- Social resources: teaching and learning initiatives, writing center outreach, communities of interest or practice; student study teams

---

The techniques discussed here include referral-analysis, surveys, and focus groups. Another powerful tool (or set of tools) can be found within the methodologies of ethnographic research. Chapter 10 introduces ethnographic research in the context of guiding the development of an Information Commons into a Learning Commons.

Referral Analysis

Insights can be gained from staff feedback about reference interviews, and may especially cluster around what Catherine Sheldrick Ross calls "unmonitored referrals."[6] Ross defines this as any referral to another part of the library or beyond the library where there is no traditional follow-up. You may find that you emphasize unmonitored referrals that revolve around the scope of the patron's need, especially as it relates to information manipulation, technology access, or multimedia. Figure 4.6 presents one very basic example of how a

---

Figure 4.6
Example of an Unmonitored Referral and IC Resources Needed

Bob, a business student, was given the task of taking twelve product fact sheets for a new sports drink, including graphics and text, and developing a marketing campaign around them. One sheet gives general nutritional information, three others compare the drink to specific competitor products, another gives testimonials from test market consumers, and so forth. Bob's assignment is to present his campaign with a PowerPoint presentation that incorporates content from these fact sheets. The library workstations do have PowerPoint, but Bob needs a scanner to input the content. The library has no public access scanners, but the librarian that night bends the rules and lets Bob use a scanner in a staff workroom. However, Bob also soon realizes that he needs to manipulate the text, not just paste it in as an image. He does not have time to type in all the text. The librarian recognizes that Bob needs optical character recognition (OCR) software, which the library does not have. The librarian is pretty sure the Media Services office has some scanners available to students, but isn't sure if they have OCR software available. Bob is sent to Media Services and no one knows how his assignment turned out. *Bob's reference query has become an unmonitored referral.*

Physical resources: large-size carrel or worktable suitable for workstation plus scanner

Digital resources: scanning utility; OCR software, PowerPoint

Human resources: IT support, application training, coaches, help desk

reference desk query becomes an unmonitored referral, and how it points to potential IC tools and resources that can meet an easily identifiable need.

Take the simple practical step of asking library staff to flag all user queries that turn into unmonitored referrals, for whatever reason. The IC Planning Group will review and analyze these at a later point in the process. A small number of unmonitored referrals may mask a larger need or range of needs, because word-of-mouth from one nonserved or under-served user can dissuade dozens of potential users whose needs are then never to be registered or measured.

Surveys

Further answers can flow from surveys and focus groups. Both can be useful tools for the entire IC discovery process, but surveys seem to be especially suited to discovering current use of (and needs for) physical and digital resources, while focus groups seem especially well-suited to learning more about usage of (and need for) human and social resources. Survey questionnaires and focus group interview scripts should not be limited to yes/no, fill-in-the-blank, or multiple choice Q&A, but should always include open-ended space and encouragement for "other" thoughts, anecdotal comments, testimonials, and narrative digressions. Through this sort of unrehearsed feedback one escapes the danger that the most vital parts of the conversation never emerge because the script or questionnaire has been too rigidly structured around library jargon or limited by the manager's preconceptions.

Any number of academic libraries have posted user surveys on the Web that are readily accessible, and many contain the types of questions that can be adapted to elicit areas of need and dissatisfaction important to IC planning. You can't copy actual questions (unless specific permission to do so is sought and obtained), but can seek out examples for adaptation and updating. To construct a survey for IC strategic planning, you can review, modify, and recombine sections of various Web-access surveys from other institutions. Start with three questions adapted from the Rochester Institute of Technology's "RIT Library Users Survey,"[7] in Figure 4.7.

Figure 4.7
RIT Survey: User Feedback on Services/Resources

Check any and all of the following resources that you use when you conduct research for a topic:

Reference Desk	Web surfing
Library Research databases	Subject specialist/librarian
Library's catalog (subject/keyword searching)	Online Reference
Browsing the shelves	

If you discover that the library lacks the materials you need, what further steps do you take?

Request an Interlibrary Loan	Use the Web
Try other libraries	Other:

The Library has recently introduced a number of new services; check all that you are aware of:

Wireless laptops	Flatbed scanners/digital cameras
Online Reference	[other examples]
Microsoft Office on student-access workstations	

The first question is designed to ascertain student use of current library services and resources *in the context of their typical research habits*. The second queries their choice of alternative services or resources when the library fails to meet their needs. The third is meant to gauge student awareness of any resources and services recently added. In the above example, we included the question "When you find that the library lacks the materials you need, what do you do?" This question could be modified with specific reference to technology and media services, as follows: "Do you ever find that the library lacks the hardware, software, media resources, or technical assistance you need, and if so, what do you do? Please give examples of such needs." The Planning Group may especially want to compare student answers to this question with the flagged unmonitored referrals.

The RIT survey then makes especially good use of open-ended questions related to physical resources, further adapted in Figure 4.8.

Figure 4.8
RIT Survey: Open-Ended User Feedback

How could the library improve group study rooms and their equipment?

Tables would be better if...
Chairs would be improved by...
Equipment, such as...
Wall displays or decor, such as...
Other ideas:

How could the building be improved in general?

What new services should the library offer, or how else might the library better meet student research needs?

These adapted RIT survey questions form a good opening framework for both student and faculty IC planning surveys because the information gained should help library managers position new IC resources in the context of prevailing research tactics and habits, as a solution to current problems, and as a platform to promote awareness and use of new resources. In addition to the open-format questions about physical resources in Figure 4.8, you may want to add one or more specific questions with reference to size and configuration of group study areas.

A section of the survey can be set up to probe more deeply into student and faculty use of digital resources, especially workstation-based activities and productivity software. These results will help drive decisions about ubiquity of software. Should all software be available on every machine, or will there be thematic or functional application clusters on groups of specialized machines? The University of Washington has posted survey questionnaires for undergraduate students, graduate students, students in professional programs, and faculty. The undergraduate survey[8] includes well-designed questions about library hardware and software use, and two are adapted in Figures 4.9 and 4.10.

As good as they are, both the RIT and University of Washington surveys tend to be less detailed on multimedia services and IT support than you might wish for IC planning. To include these features, turn to other examples that can be found in media center and IT center user surveys, also available on the Web. A 2002 survey instrument for Indiana University/Purdue

Figure 4.9 **University of Washington Undergraduate Survey: Software Use**	
How critical to your academic work is it to have the following software programs available on computers in the Library?	[scale of perceived importance 1–10]
Word processing Spreadsheets Presentation software (e.g. PowerPoint) Database software (e.g., Access) Publishing software (e.g., Acrobat) Graphics software (e.g., Photoshop) Scanners and OCR software for images and texts Bibliographic citation software (e.g., EndNote) Web-based collaboration tools **Comments: (wiki, blog)**	

Figure 4.10 **University of Washington Undergraduate Survey: Workstation Use**	
How frequently do you do the following when you use a Library workstation?	[scale of need or frequency 1–10]
Read or send e-mail Search the Library catalog Search an index to journal articles Look for full-text electronic journals Look for e-books Do course assignments/readings on the Web Use Google or another general Web search engine Look at a specific Web site without using a search engine Request assistance from library staff Work on your own Web page Use application software (e.g., word processing, spreadsheets) Listen to music Play games	

University at Indianapolis (IUPUI) has pertinent sections in its faculty survey, and is an example how a number of specific digital media tools and services have been grouped under three broad headings.[9] Such broadly grouped areas may also be used for the student survey, as shown in Figure 4.11.

Another pertinent section in the IUPUI student survey groups existing facilities, tools, and human support services. While survey forms may prove the best tool for probing digital and physical support services, it is still a good idea to include questions about human resources/support services at some point in the survey; Figure 4.12, excerpted from the Indiana survey on Student Technology Centers, offers one approach. You may want to include a section to gauge use of and satisfaction with any existing campus units that may fill a niche somewhat similar to the proposed IC.

Figure 4.11 **2003 IUPUI User Survey: Multimedia Production**	
Media Acquisition (Digital Audio Production, Digital Video Production, Slide/Photograph Scanning, Digital Photography, Media Conversion)	[scale of need or satisfaction +/–]
Production (Macromedia Flash Animation, Interactive DVD Production, PowerPoint Presentations, 3D Animation, Digital Video Editing, Web Site Production and Redesign)	[scale of need or satisfaction +/–]
Distribution and Technical Support (Streaming Audio and Video, Tape, CD and DVD Duplication System Administration)	[scale of need or satisfaction +/–]

Figure 4.12 **2003 UITS IUPUI User Survey: Student Technology Centers**	
Student Technology Centers hardware (computers, scanners, etc.)	[scale of need or satisfaction +/–]
Student Technology Centers software	[scale of need or satisfaction +/–]
Student Technology Centers consulting overall	[scale of need or satisfaction +/–]
Knowledge/ability of Student Technology Centers consultants	[scale of need or satisfaction +/–]
Courtesy/ helpfulness of Student Technology Centers consultants	[scale of need or satisfaction +/–]
Student Technology Centers overall	[scale of need or satisfaction +/–]
Network storage space	[scale of need or satisfaction +/–]
Central instructional and general purpose computers	[scale of need or satisfaction +/–]
Audio-based learning (tape duplication, streaming audio)	[scale of need or satisfaction +/–]

In some cases, planners may want the media-related questions in Figure 4.11 to be broken out to a level of greater detail, and the questions related to facilities and support services in Figure 4.11 also broken out into discrete subsections. It may also be useful for the survey to capture faculty or student use of pertinent tools and resources elsewhere on campus *beyond* the current library or IC offerings, to ascertain those necessary or optimal for enhancement of IC services and resources. An example of a survey tool that does both has been posted by Northwestern University's Digital Media Services unit.[10] It has been aimed at faculty, but we believe portions can easily be adapted to student surveys as well.

The first sample question, shown in Figure 4.13, queries faculty about media tools and resources available within departments.

The survey then queries faculty about software and media use for classes; see Figure 4.14.

Another survey, shown in Figure 4.15, queries faculty about current and potential future use of the central digital media services (DMS) center.

Figure 4.13
Northwestern DMS Survey: Dept. Equipment for Faculty

What equipment does your department own?
    Camera
    Digital camera
    Scanner
    Camcorder
    VCR
    Video editing station
    Other

Figure 4.14
Northwestern DMS Survey: Faculty Software/Media for Classes

What software do you frequently use for classes/research?
    Powerpoint
    PDF
    Web editing
    Video editing
    Photoshop
    Other

What media do you frequently use for classes?
    Video
    Streaming video
    Audio
    Streaming audio
    Images from slides
    Other

Figure 4.15
Northwestern DMS Survey: Faculty Use of DMS Equipment

If you use the DMS Drop-in Service, what equipment do you use?
Scanner
Streaming
Video editing
Making DVDs
Text scanner
Film recorder

What services or equipment would be helpful and are not currently available?
Scanning
Video capture/editing
CD/batch duplication
Image editing
Video editing
Other equipment or software

A summary and review of proposed student and faculty IC planning surveys is presented in Figures 4.16 and 4.17. These replace the earlier sample questions with descriptive annotations to encourage planners to develop original and up-to-date questions suitable for a given situation:

Figure 4.16 Summary Student IC Survey Sections and Examples	
Student use of current library services and resources *in the context of their current research.*	**Figure 4.7:** RIT examples
Student feedback about situations where the library failed to meet their needs and their choice of alternative services or resources when that happens.	**Figure 4.7:** RIT example; question #11
Student awareness of any innovative library resources and services recently added.	**Figure 4.7:** RIT example
Student open-format feedback about needed improvements to physical facilities.	**Figure 4.8:** RIT examples
Student use of/need for productivity software, applications and utilities.	**Figure 4.9:** University of Washington example
Student patterns and frequencies of workstation use.	**Figure 4.10:** University of Washington example
Student use of/need for multimedia production resources and tools.	**Figure 4.11:** IUPUI example, or **Figure 4.15:** Northwestern example
Student use of/need for central "student technology center" facility.	**Figure 4.12:** IUPUI example, or **Figure 4.15:** Northwestern example

Figure 4.17 Summary Faculty Survey Sections and Examples	
Faculty use of current library services and resources *in the context of their current research.*	**Figure 4.7:** RIT examples
Faculty feedback about situations where the library failed to meet their needs and their choice of alternative services or resources when that happens.	**Figure 4.7:** RIT example; question #11
Faculty awareness of any innovative library resources and services recently added.	**Figure 4.7:** RIT example
Faculty open-format feedback about needed improvements to physical facilities.	**Figure 4.8:** RIT examples
Faculty use of departmental media resources & tools.	**Figure 4.13:** Northwestern example
Faculty use of software applications, utilities, and multimedia resources for classes.	**Figure 4.14:** Northwestern example
Faculty current use of media production equipment in any current centralized digital media services unit.	**Figure 4.15:** Northwestern example, or **Figure 4.11:** IUPUI example
Faculty perceived future needs for media production equipment in a centralized digital media services facility.	**Figure 4.15:** Northwestern example, or **Figure 4.11:** IUPUI example

What about situations in which an existing IC facility is targeted for expansion and enhancement? A logical approach here is to fashion ongoing assessment surveys in such a way as to provide needed data for second-stage strategic planning. A tested example of an IC-based survey for students was conducted by Shahla Bahavar of USC's Leavey Library. Bahavar's survey included 18 multiple choice and 3 open-ended questions. Although Bahavar was surveying students using an existing IC, her premise included data-gathering for future IC enhancements. It was through the survey instrument's open-ended questions that Bahavar uncovered the need for scanning and audio-video editing capabilities and for a presentation room facility, features subsequently added to the Leavey Library IC.[11] This text of this survey is included in Chapter 9.

Focus Group Self-study

Consider the use of focus groups in your planning template, but in addition to, not instead of, surveys. It should be kept in mind that focus groups are not necessarily synonymous with scenario-building. Scenario-building, which is discussed in Chapter 5, is a specific technique often carried out by focus groups. But this section on focus group self-study looks first at how the focus group can gather information on current usage patterns that tends to slip through the cracks of survey results. As indicated earlier, anecdotal comments suggest that focus groups can be especially well-suited to discoveries about the use of and need for human and social resources. As Young and Von Seggern state:

> Focus group interviews are recommended when you are looking for a range of ideas or feelings, when you are trying to understand differences in perspectives between groups of people, when you want ideas to emerge from the group...this qualitative method can provide descriptive data derived from open-ended discussion.[12]

But the use of focus groups can be fairly demanding and time-consuming, and for IC planning, especially careful attention must be given to four elements, listed in Figure 4.18.

Figure 4.18
Four Key Focus Group Process Components

- Composing the script(s) or outline(s)
- Selecting the group(s) participants
- Staging and facilitating the session(s)
- Recording, summarizing, and interpreting the results

As noted previously, the steps of the strategic planning template may be combined or conjoined, and the focus group is one example where *self-discovery* may overlap or blend into *scenario-building* and/or *projecting the future commons*. This can be a good development; some preliminary scenario-building during focus group conversations may spark ideas that will benefit a later, more highly structured scenario-building phase. Whether this happens depends upon the script, the selection of participants, and how the sessions are facilitated. The planners must take care to keep the process coherent. Don't draft a very pragmatic, narrowly premised script and then select a group of dreamers and visionaries as participants. Don't convene a group of hard-headed "lets-get-this-done" pragmatists and then try to facilitate a visionary or improvisatory session. It is no crime to explore multiple style-options in parallel; a pragmatic script presented to a brass-tacks group in a narrowly defined facilitation can unfold in one session, while an open-ended script presented to visionaries in a conceptual way can unfold in another, and both may yield benefits to IC planning.

Composing the Script(s) or Outline(s)

If you have surveys preceding the focus group initiative (and you probably will) planners should first review assembled survey instruments and results for potential questions to use in focus group scripts. This is not "cheating"; any redundancy of results may be outweighed by the depth and context provided in focus group conversations. The key lies in "mining" survey results for critical points that need further exploration, extended discussion, pro-con debate, etc., and to draft focus group scripts accordingly.

The example in Figure 4.19 is a very pragmatic and tightly drawn script written for Pennsylvania public school teachers in evaluating school media centers, and includes the types of questions that might well also be found on survey instruments:[13]

Figure 4.19
Pennsylvania School Librarians' Association Focus Group Scripts

What library media services do you use in your teaching?
When (or how often) do you use them?
What do you think about these services?
How beneficial are these services to students?
How do you think improvements could be made in delivering these services to you?

The use of such directive, survey-type questions in a focus group places greater demand upon participant selection and group facilitation to ensure that quality conversation emerges. It is a possible lead-in phase to questions that will stimulate more broadly and deeply probing conversation. Figure 4.20 is a good example of a script that can do this and also entail some preliminary scenario-building; it is adapted from a Rutgers University focus group script.[14]

Figure 4.20
Rutgers University Faculty Focus Group Script (Adapted)

Part 1: The Library as provider of information and assistance.
  1.1 Where and how do you gather information for activities such as research, grants or teaching?
  1.2 How do you stay current with new tools and resources, and how do you master their use in your discipline?
  1.3 Describe an ideal model for a library that provides the information resources, learning tools, and support services you need for your professional work.

Part 2: The Library as a physical space.
  2.1 How do you typically access the library now: virtually, physically, both?
  2.2 Describe your ideal library as a building or facility. Would it include more rooms for collaborative coursework; expanded media labs; conference and program spaces, cafes, presentation support services? Other?

Part 3: Library involvement in Instruction
  3.1 How do your students acquire information needed for your course(s)? Do you use a course Web site; assemble a course pack; other; and do you seek collaboration with librarians or enlist library instruction?
  3.2 What other kinds of library support would enhance student learning?

Young and Von Seggern authored an interesting focus group script for students and reported on its use in a 2001 article, "General Information Seeking in Changing Times."[15] Although conducted in a library that did not then feature what we would define as an Information Commons, their script remains highly pertinent as a model to be adapted and extended for particular IC planning situations, because it avoids jargon and resource-specific (or even library-specific) queries, and reaches instead for the larger context of the students' entire information-seeking experience.

Figure 4.21
Young & Von Seggern Focus Group Script

Introduction of Topic

Let's begin with each of you sharing your name, your major [or department, if faculty], your hometown [or number of years at UI, if faculty].

1. Can you tell me about the sources you use to gather information for any purpose, such as classes [academic], projects you're working on outside of school, buying an item or product, etc.?
2. Thinking back over the last three to five years, can you describe how sources for gathering information have changed?
3. Can you describe what was the biggest obstacle to getting information you needed in the past?
4. As you think about gathering information now, what is the biggest obstacle?
5. I would like each of you to take a few minutes to write a list of what is important to you when you're looking for information. [Take a few minutes to allow them to write a brief list, then ask them to share in turn. Collect lists.]
6. When are you satisfied with the results of a search for information, and when do you decide that the information just doesn't exist or that the answer can't be found?
7. Now I would like each of you to imagine a perfect information source, one that suits your personal needs. Please describe what this information source would be like. Use your imagination; do not be limited by current technology or reality. Describe your dream source.

Summary by Moderator

I would like to summarize what's been said during this focus group session. [Give summary}. Is this an accurate summary? Do any of you have anything else you would like to add?

[If time permits and people are willing to stay and talk, introduce additional topics such as use of Help features, preferences for learning how to use sources versus getting the answer, the future role of libraries and how to improve library services.]

Focus group scripts can also "focus" more specifically on IC or LC examples. After a session discussion based on the "ideal physical library" or learning space of the Rutgers script, for example, focus group participants might then be taken on one or more site visits to IC facilities, and then reconvened to share their specific impressions of how that facility seemed to compare to their earlier idealized vision, and how such a facility might be fashioned and configured for their own campus.

SELECTING THE GROUP(S') PARTICIPANTS

If the institution's leadership has already designated a project shepherd, it may be valuable to consult with him/her regarding focus group participation and even process. The project shepherd may wish sit in, observe, or even participate in the focus group process to some degree. Regarding faculty participants, to repeat an earlier dictum, don't draft a very pragmatic, narrowly premised script and then select a group of dreamers and visionaries as participants. But the more a project is aimed at far-reaching change or transformation, the more important it becomes to select some faculty participants who are known to be IT early-adopters, creative thinkers, and pedagogical innovators. Look back to Chapter 3 on LCs and information literacy, and look for faculty and administrators who are known to be interested in ideas related to resource-based learning, situated learning, virtual reality, computer gaming, and group-process learning. Include a good number of staunch library supporters, but be willing to live dangerously and invite at least a few faculty and/or students who have been known to be critical of library services and resources in the past. As Joan Henning notes in her "Gleanings," the purpose is to identify who the Commons will serve. On some campuses, the focus is on undergraduates, while others devote significant Commons resources to the needs of faculty. One goal of focus groups will be to find a way to learn from potential users what they would like to see the Commons become. This effort should start in this discovery phase and extend through *scenario-building* and *projecting the future commons*.

The points outlined in Figure 4.22 are taken from the University of Texas QuickTips guide for focus group participant selection.[16]

STAGING AND FACILITATING THE SESSION(S)

Staging and facilitation of focus groups is covered effectively in many guidebooks on focus group practice, and only one aspect seems crucial for IC planning: all focus group facilitators must themselves be familiar with IC and LC concepts and examples, and reasonably familiar with the literature. The facilitator will need to place these sessions in a meaningful context for participants, and be able to answer questions about IC/LC concepts and examples that may arise. Beyond this, repeating our earlier dictum, don't convene a group of hard-headed "lets-get-this-done" achievers and then facilitate in a dreamy, improvisatory manner. It is also strongly advisable that all facilitators familiarize themselves with survey results before convening groups.

RECORDING, SUMMARIZING, AND INTERPRETING RESULTS

Some books on focus groups place great attention on the creation of scripts and the facilitation of the groups, but give little attention to the follow-up process of assembling, summarizing, and interpreting results. In this planning template, the "final product" phase is crucial because it may form the basis for the following steps of scenario-building and projecting the future commons. In fact, managers should at least consider keeping the groups intact and reconvening them to begin scenario-building. In any case, it is vital to record, aggregate, summarize, and interpret the results of initial focus group conversations, though this need not be an extremely complex or elaborate undertaking. The LC planning process at Queens University (Canada) provides some especially interesting examples of a variety of focus group summaries.[17] Figure 4.23 is an example of a simple brief summary of "emerging themes."

From here, the Queens University report moves on to offer a range of comments from various representative stakeholders (undergraduates, graduate students, faculty, etc.). It is fine

---

Figure 4.22
University of Texas QuickTips Guide

How to Select Focus Group Participants: Most commonly, contact people by phone or e-mail, explaining the purpose of the study and asking a few screening questions to determine if they qualify.

Explain the Study: Tell the purpose of the study, who is sponsoring it, and how the results will be used.

Explain the Focus Group: Include details about the date, time, location, and incentives.

Ask Screening Questions: To determine the eligibility of the prospective participant, based on the characteristics you want, you may include questions about major, demographics, habits, or other topics.

Example:

Hello, my name is _____ and I am calling to see if you would be willing to participate in a small group discussion hosted by the Division of Instructional Innovation and Assessment regarding the Webcasting of UT Austin's courses.

The discussion would take about 1–2 hours, and you will receive a complimentary lunch. _____Yes _____No

What is your classification? ____freshman ____sophomore ____junior ____senior

What is your major? _____

Do you live on campus? _____Yes _____No

If you live off of campus, how far is your commute to school?_____

Of the following times, which sessions would you be able to attend?
_____ Monday, March 17, 2005 @ 10:00 a.m.
_____ Tuesday, March 18, 2005 @ 3:00 p.m.
_____ Wednesday, March 19, 2005 @6:00 p.m.

Could I get your e-mail address so I can send you directions to the location?

E-mail: _____

Make Attending the Group Easy: Send each person a confirmation e-mail with clear directions to the focus group location, including a contact phone number for questions or problems. Emphasize that, because the focus group is very small, their participation is important and that you are counting on them. Transportation problems are sometimes a barrier to attending focus groups. If transportation is an issue for participants, consider ways to help them, such as offering bus tokens or including information about public transportation.

Provide Incentive for Participation: Although most marketing firms offer substantial monetary incentives for participation, this is not always possible in educational settings. Some alternative incentives are food or gift certificates.

Follow-up e-mail: A day or two prior to the session send e-mails thanking persons for agreeing to take part in the discussion, describing the purpose of the focus group, and identifying the date, time, and place of the focus group. Remind participants of the incentive for taking part and ask them to contact you if they are unable to attend.

Some Recruits Will Not Show: Because some individuals may forget, run into a scheduling conflict, or just decide not to take part, it is recommended that you select one or two more participants than needed to take part in the discussion session. If all participants do show up, you can still conduct the focus group.

Figure 4.23
Queens University Focus Group Summary of Emerging Themes

- A convenient, central location that supports learning
- A comfortable facility that provides a variety of spaces for learning
- A safe space that is secure but also welcoming—a place where students can feel they can ask any question.
- A social space that allows coffee and snacks
- A place where partners work together to provide services and spaces to support learning

to include superficially conflicting viewpoints, such as "too quiet" and "too noisy," because they may help delineate the need for varied functional spaces within a commons. Figure 4.24 gives a sampling.

Figure 4.24
Queens University Focus Group Narrative Comment Examples

"I want all information to be available electronically. We go right to the Internet and right now our expectations are not being met." **Undergraduate student**

"We use food as a break-out from work. It is the social part of studying and an important one at that." **Undergraduate student**

"A lot of people assume that the circulation desk is the place to ask for help, they wait in line, only to find they can't help us—very frustrating." **Undergraduate student**

"It would be great if the library would use the Web more for how to find information on a particular topic." **Undergraduate student**

"If students can't easily get between buildings, they will not go." **Graduate student**

"Software needs to be driven by the learning task—they learn the mechanics on their own." **Graduate student**

"The library has a real role to play in supporting student learning." **Graduate student**

"Students are becoming more and more sophisticated and need technology and productivity tools to complete their work." **Graduate student**

"Students right out of high school have no ability to discern what is useful or accurate. This facility will be important to showing them how to use research in their course work." **Faculty member**

"Think carefully about the layout of the classroom, traditional approaches may not be the best for this use." **Faculty member**

"Students really need resources for audio-visual equipment and the ability to view a DVD or video." **Faculty member**

"If you are going to create a facility where there is noise, you must also provide areas that are quiet." **Faculty member**

The Queens report then goes on to sort and summarize key discussion points in a set of structured tables such as the summary in Figure 4.25 of a focus group discussion about information sources, spaces, skills, and LC services. This is also a good example of how a results summary can include some preliminary results *analysis*, as the comments under **Spaces**, **Skills**, and **Services** indicate.

The Queens LC Planning Report also presents some results summaries and analysis in quantitative form. Focus groups are not normally associated with the sort of quantitative analysis attached to survey results but the example in Figure 4.26 shows how it can be effectively carried out and reported:

The Queens focus group process also included staff conversations, distinct from students and faculty. As you might expect, summary reports for these groups tended to bring out very specific issues and concerns, as in the summary in Figure 4.27 of an ITS (Information Technology Systems) staff focus group:

Once again, as with the summaries for student and faculty groups, the staff report moves from the short list of key emerging issues to a more expansive range of narrative comments, shown in Figure 4.28.

Figure 4.25 Queens University Information/Spaces Summary Matrix			
Information	**Spaces**	**Skills**	**Services**
-Students get their information from the Internet, the Web, from professors and reserve reading lists, textbooks and finally the library.	-Classroom is important for both faculty and graduate students but not so important for undergraduate students.	-Students are becoming much more sophisticated in their assignments and are using different formats. Learning facilities must reflect this.	-Single point or in close proximity to each other—IT and Library information should be close and easily identifiable.
-Students (undergraduate) want more electronic sources. - Faculty and students also want more multimedia formats. -Graduate students wanted greater access to the full range of information in a number of formats—print and electronic.	-Preview rooms were very important to students. -Professors are using materials in different formats for their course work and there is no place to view the materials.	-Students identified essay and study support as important. They felt that a central location would allow them to access the services when they needed it. It was too difficult for them to predict when they would use or need the service.	-Laptop support is becoming increasingly important as more students use them and more faculties are providing them. Network configuration is the main issue although diagnostic services are also important.
-Students want full productivity on all computers whether in the Learning Commons proper or library floors.	-Group study areas are one of the most important components of the new Learning Commons.	-Students confirmed their need for research support with their assignments. Students and faculty indicated that on-going research support (drop-in) would be important to offer instead of just at the beginning of the year.	-Students want longer hours—24/5 (Sunday through Friday)—all students have different study habits. Some study late in the evening and others in the early morning. Learning facilities on campus should reflect this.
	-Access to computers is important but should not be the focus of the Commons. It is important to support learning activities of students. Computers are part of that support.	-Faculty and students wanted a greater connection between the librarians and staff at the library. They felt that the library could really help to support student learning in a central facility.	-Web pages and library guides need to improve. They are confusing and should use the language that students understand. Libraries use too much "lingo."
	-The library is too noisy. There is a need for quiet and not so quiet areas.	-Statistical support was identified as required on campus—it made sense that this service should be provided with Data, GIS and Maps area. -Productivity training (e.g., excel) is important but should be offered on a one-on-one basis or drop-in basis. -Bibliographic and reference tools support is always needed.	-Interlibrary loans service needs to improve. As collections become more focused on electronic, turnaround times for ILL services will need to be quicker and more reliable. -Staff felt that ILL should be combined with Document Delivery and Access services to be more convenient for those using the library.
	-Storage areas are important to creating a welcoming facility	-Skills development should focus on more complex software	-Make the desk more visible and provide signs to let people know where to go for help—e.g., IT, Circulation or Reference.

\multicolumn{3}{c}{**Figure 4.26** **Queens University Focus Group Human Resource Criteria**}	
Faculty			
Rank	**Criteria**		**Relative Importance**
1	**Reliability**	The ability of the library to perform the promised service dependably and accurately.	32.5
2	**Responsiveness**	The willingness of the library to help clients and provide prompt service.	18.3
3	**Assurances**	The knowledge and courtesy of the library's employees and their ability to convey trust and confidence.	15.0
4	**Empathy**	The caring, individualized attention the library provides its clients.	15.0
5	**Tangibles**	The appearance of the library's physical facilities, equipment, personnel and communication materials.	14.2

Figure 4.27
Queens University ITS Staff Focus Group Emerging Themes

Services that should be offered in the Learning Commons:
- Connectivity (support)
- Printing and scanning (support)
- Statistical help (consulting)
- Workstation configuration (support)
- Workstation hardware (support)
- Ad hoc training (at point of need)
- Formal training (course driven)
- Roving (from the desk)
- Introductory IT courses

General Comments and Questions
- Hardware support (network, servers, etc.) could be elsewhere in the building
- Virtual and physical
- What are the real opportunities to integrate?
- What can be co-located?
- What services do we provide to students? Training (formal) or Just in Time or both.
- What about statistical help and data together?

And once again, the report then summarizes and analyzes IT staff focus group discussions in a more formalized matrix, as in this example presented in Figure 4.29: "Three issues were identified that participants agree will need to be resolved over the next few months and will form the basis of the partnership [between ITS and library]—Governance, Identity, Operations."

The concerns with governance, identity, and operations expressed within the Queens University ITS Staff Focus Group are well founded, and point to the fact that the whole question of the IT-Library relationship looms as the "elephant in the parlor" during the course of all IC initiatives. Questions about future collaboration, and potential convergence between the units need to be raised, explored, and resolved throughout the planning process, and the

---

Figure 4.28
Queens University ITS Staff Focus Group Narrative Comments

Is the focus for students? The primary focus is student-oriented. In a perfect world, it is faculty and students, but starting with students. If there is no physical link, there needs to be a virtual or pedagogical link. It's a communication piece.

What's the draw for faculty? Faculty could book spaces and do small group work with students. It's a way of supporting the needs of students to develop specific skills around a specific task. (i.e., Photoshop)—something that is integrated in their coursework. It's impossible to accommodate the needs of large classes. We're looking for a different model to meet their individual needs / shared needs in large classes.

Where is the commons? It should probably be the entire first floor. Have the expertise in one area. Have the opportunity to put current periodicals next to electronic journals—where one format supports another. Offices for staff—access to staff for consultation. The lines get blurred because there are no distinct boundaries. Areas / things can be connected in various ways and areas delineated subtly. Some activities complement one another. There are relationships between our units depending upon the questions we get.

What are they? Everything from hours to registrar. 75–80% get handled by front line. Others are referred. Not unlike what library does and the reference desk. For the store—how to use Photoshop? Library? And immediately begin asking questions. Some of the same issues arise at both service points. If this is the single point of contact, some people will want library-only info, or IT-only info or some blend of library and IT help.

Figure 4.29
Queens University ITS Staff Focus Group Summary Matrix

Governance "Focus on the User"	Identity	Operations
▪ Services offered ▪ Quality provision ▪ Team Functioning ▪ Leadership	▪ Of units and departments ▪ Confusion for users ▪ Roles for IT and Library IT ▪ Identity of the Whole—branding the learning commons	▪ Service hours at the desk ▪ Levels of training ▪ Budgets—ongoing ▪ Expectations of users/reality ▪ Spaces (what are the priorities)

focus group component of the self-discovery step can be a good starting point. If the previous relationship has been a turbulent one, then the initial focus group process can help planners locate and chart potential land mines that lie in wait, and help them begin to formulate strategies to avoid or surmount them. This issue is further discussed in Chapter 6, which presents a template for a *Memorandum of Understanding* to formalize cooperative IC relationship arrangements between IT and library management teams.

Endnotes

[1] Stephens, Cahal, Charles Kirby, Leila Kamal, and Kip Ellis. 2004. "The Politics and Process of Change: Institutional Building—Planning Teams." AL Volume IV. Project Kaleidoscope. Available: http://www.pkal.org/documents/Vol4PoliticsAndProcessOfChange.cfm

[2] Scott Walter "Collaborative Planning for Collaborative Learning: Designing and Promoting New Learning Spaces on Campus." Presented at the Ninth Annual October Conference at Dartmouth College, October 7, 2005. Available: https://kuscholarworks.ku.edu/dspace/bitstream/1808/612/1/OC_05.ppt

[3] Stephens, Kirby, Kamal, Ellis. http://www.pkal.org/documents/Vol4PoliticsAndProcessOfChange.cfm

[4] Ibid.

[5] Henning, Joanne. 2005. "Information Commons Study Leave: October 2, 2004–March 31, 2005." University of British Columbia. Available: http://jhenning.law.uvic.ca

[6] Kluegel, Kathleen, Catherine Sheldrick Ross, et al., 2003. "The Reference Interview: Connecting in Person and in Cyberspace." *Reference & User Services Quarterly*. 43 no. 1 (Fall). 40.

[7] Rochester Institute of Technology, "RIT Library Users Survey," Available: http://wally.rit.edu/general/user survey.html

[8] "2004 Undergraduate Library and Information Use Survey." University of Washington. Available: http://www. lib.washington.edu/assessment/surveys/survey2004/UNDERGRADUATE_LIBRARY_USE_SURVEY_SPRING_200 4.mht

[9] "2003 UITS IUPUI User Survey Summary." Indiana University/Purdue University at Indianapolis. (2003). Available: http://www.indiana.edu/~uitssur/2003/iupui/iupui_summary03.doc

[10] "Digital Media Services." Northwestern University. (2004). Available: http://2east.northwestern.edu/2004_ spring/_article_4.html

[11] Bahavar, Shahla. "Information Commons User Assessment: Perspectives from the USC Leavey Library." Presentation for: The Information Commons: A Learning Space Beyond the Classroom. University of Southern California (September 16, 2004). Available: http://www.usc.edu/isd/libraries/locations/leavey/news/conference/ presentations/presentations_9-16/Assessment/USC_Bahavar.ppt#1

[12] Young, Nancy J., and Marilyn Von Seggern. 2001. "General Information Seeking in Changing Times: A Focus Group Study," Reference & User Services Quarterly. 41 no. 2 (Winter). 159–169.

[13] "Sample Instruments for Data Collection." Pennsylvania School Librarians' Association. (2002) Available: http:// www.psla.org/pslaworkshops/fall2002_files/act2samp.doc

[14] "DLI-II Faculty and Student Focus Group Report." Rutgers University. (July 20, 2004). Available: http://www. libraries.rutgers.edu/rul/staff/groups/strategic_planning/reports/DLI-II_fac_student_focus_group_report.shtml

[15] Young, Nancy J., and Marilyn Von Seggern 2001. "General Information Seeking in Changing Times: A Focus Group Study," Reference & User Services Quarterly. 41 no. 2 (Winter). 159–169.

[16] "Data Gathering: Selecting Focus Group Participants." Division of Instructional Innovation and Assessment, University of Texas at Austin DIIA Instructional Assessment Resources Web Site. Available: http://www. utexas.edu/academic/diia/assessment/iar/resources/quicktips/quicktip_6-21.pdf

[17] "Queens Learning Commons Project: February 9–12, 2004." Queens University. Available: http://library.queensu. ca/webdoc/learningcommons/files/PlanningResultsSummary-1_20Feb04_rev1_pgs1-43.pdf

5

Strategic Planning II: Preparing Scenario-Building Techniques and Projecting the Future Commons

This book stresses the *formative* nature of the strategic planning process, and at first glance, this formative approach might seem to conflict with the measurable outcomes-based performance testing now prevalent in higher education, since it places clear emphasis on end results. But effective definition and measurement of agreed-upon outcomes requires prior articulation of shared purpose and vision. And this shared purpose and vision, in turn, does not materialize a priori, but grows best out of the formative process of strategic planning.

Planning Template Step: Scenario-Building

One technique that fits the formative discovery and decision process model is called *scenario-building*. To quote Joan Giesecke:

> In scenario driven planning, managers develop scenarios to design possible futures... then design strategies that will move the organization forward. Scenario driven planning helps managers identify their assumptions about the future and the organization, describe their own mental models of the future, and use that information to renew the organization.[1]

Some use the term scenario-building to describe group efforts to map out very specific elements of IC design, such as actual floor plans. For example, Robert E. Renaud of Dickinson College writes: "The analysis team surveyed users, gathered data, built cost models, and defined alternative planning scenarios... The use of alternative scenarios proved to be a particular aid in decision making... the need to sketch out actual floor plans helped task force members visualize the consequences of various actions."[2] In the planning template presented here, however, the process described by Renaud would come under the next step: *projecting the future commons*. This distinction is noted here to clarify the fact that the scenarios described in this section will relate to service delivery and learning outcomes, while more specific space-related and facility-based projections will follow. But the Dickinson College description also exemplifies how steps in this template might be associated or even conjoined. In the last chapter it was noted that some steps in the template might be combined or conjoined, and this is particularly true of scenario-building and projecting the future commons. They are separated here primarily for clarity of discussion, but also because the special challenges of planning new building construction may require sharper demarcation between the nebulous brainstorming that sometimes propels scenario-building and the more concrete and disciplined projection exercises.

Scenario-building can be a narrative process, a visual process, or both. We will offer examples of both scenario narratives and scenario diagrams. Scenario-building conversations can be hosted by the IC Planning Group, subordinate or satellite groups, or both. This step may also involve some level of participation by the project shepherd. However it may be structured, we recommend the same level of care taken for the four components of focus group process:

1. creation of a script or selection of "envisioning" methodology;
2. selection of participants;
3. facilitation of sessions; and
4. reporting/interpretation of results.

Scenarios of possible futures can be developed individually or by teams, and can focus on futures within the library, across campus, around the world, or all of the above in a relationship matrix. When focus is placed on the library, then the documented results of earlier focus group sessions and surveys can once again provide valuable starting points and raw material for scenario-building exercises. These considerations will obviously drive composition of the script, selection of participants, and facilitation of sessions. Once again, keeping these coherently related and moving in parallel becomes important.

The first example concerns a scenario-building group charged as follows: "Take a flagged unmonitored referral, or a problem example from survey or focus group results, and compose a narrative scenario where the same student brings the same question or need to the IC help desk. Describe how new IC/LC resources would be used to effectively meet that need and further our goals of supporting student learning, in contrast to the old library model that proved inadequate." Group participants should be given this charge and examples of unmonitored referrals or focus group problem examples well in advance.

A good example of the utility of this technique emerged in a scenario crafted around the unmonitored referral described in Figure 4.6, where business student Bob was given the task of taking product fact sheets for a new sports drink, including graphics and text, and developing a marketing campaign around them. A focus group was charged with framing a scenario to solve Bob's problem. The group's scenario not only described the obvious solution of scanning and OCR capabilities, but extrapolated the need for a presentation rehearsal studio for students preparing PowerPoint projects. And in fact, testimonials from multiple ICs across the country confirm that presentation rehearsal studios are becoming heavily used facilities within ICs. This small example helps validate the concept of a scenario-building approach that grows out of earlier self-discovery findings.

As an alternative to using problem examples, the facilitator may instead give participants other brief narrative scenarios to use as a guide, then charge the group with building scenarios of an exciting, innovative space for promoting learning.. The planning appendix for the IC at Case Western Reserve University presents three interesting examples of narrative scenarios that might be used as seedbed examples.[3] These are a good way to start because they are very specific, and address real-world "case studies" of how library users may come to utilize the range of resources in an Information Commons. The following quotes are used courtesy of the Kelvin Smith Library at Case Western Reserve University. The first scenario, in Figure 5.1, addresses learning outcomes based on a specific project assigned by an instructor in a regularly scheduled course.

But ICs have always been justified on the additional basis of independent learning, and the Case Western strategic planning document also anticipates improved learning outcomes for this role as well. The second scenario, in Figure 5.2, presents an example of student independent learning based on research in an academic context, but outside of any assigned project for a course:

Lastly, the Case Western plan offers the scenario in Figure 5.3, which is based on the IC's role of supporting group-process learning through IT tools and study rooms.

Examples such as these may also be especially useful for faculty asked to visualize special cases of future IC support in their respective disciplines, whether this might be nursing, engineering, business, physics, or music.

Figure 5.1
CWRU Scenario 1: Course Assignment

Literature—Discovery and a New Medium for New Learning

The Tuesday assignment for a sophomore seminar class: English Literature and Language Study for the Internet. Four students head to the Commons at KSL. The students want to save time, and that means no Web surfing. At the Reference/Research Consultation Desk, librarian Bob starts them on a database cluster search. They narrow it down to a theme, target classical and modern poems, find folklore and religion, and take Bob's suggestion to add a sound file for illustration. Bob has introduced them to Adam, who helps them embed a foreign language video clip in their document. A week later after a follow-up from Bob, the group takes it to another level and decides to build a Web page to showcase their summer solstice celebration poems—complete with text, sky charts (from the astronomy librarian), sound files in 3 languages, and reviews of the most famous poems. Their assignment has evolved into a practical project and will be used by a nearby junior high school where another KSL librarian does outreach. Research became fun to explore . . . and will entice new, younger scholars, as well.

Figure 5.2
CWRU Scenario 2: Independent Learning

History Comes to Life, with Art

A graduate art history student discovers Calvino's book Invisible Cities. She has worked before with Ericka, a Commons librarian, who now suggests that the student identify a modern city that interests her. She identifies Seattle, using historical newspapers and primary resources, and also refers back to thirteenth-century works for the Cities. She places the imaginary cities of the book against a backdrop of Seattle, re-creating them through digital photography and digital painting, using Photoshop available in the Commons, and with a referral to a staff member in the nearby Digital Library, Multimedia, Language Resource Center. Finally, she collaborates with David, a librarian-specialist in urban policy, as she creates a work about the fundamentals of the urban environment—throughout the centuries. After securing copyright permission for images and text from the original Italian and translated English, her work evolves into a book that has already received an inquiry from a publisher.

Figure 5.3
CWRU Scenario 3: Group Process Learning

Information Commons Group Rooms

Jenny, Jim, and Bill are working on a project for their graduate marketing course. Using relevant business databases at the suggestion of a business librarian, the group gathered market share and annual sales information and even downloaded data in an Excel format from the Census Web site. The use of census data sparked a thought in Jenny, who wondered if it was possible to match the demographics of those likely to purchase pizza with their location in and around Cleveland proper. With this in mind, the three again consulted a reference librarian who introduced them to the Center for Statistics and Geospatial Data. Using GIS software, Jim was able to show the neighborhoods and areas in and around Cleveland that likely purchase delivery pizza, including the prices of their homes, annual incomes, and ethnic makeup. Very excited by the power of mapping statistical data, Jim captured the images created by the GIS software and gave them to Bill, who used them to prepare detailed graphics for the PowerPoint presentation the three would have to give on their topic. In the Multimedia Center, Bill was able to not only import the images in to PowerPoint, but to incorporate video outtakes Jenny made of the neighborhoods she visited; in addition, Bill was able to add the Excel data to the PowerPoint slides and have that data appear as graphs and pie charts on the slides. With their presentation completely constructed, all that remained was to practice delivering it, so the presentation would not only look finished, but the three would be coordinated in their individual parts. Surprisingly, Jenny, Jim, and Bill found the perfect space in the same place where they did their research and built their presentation! The Information Commons provided group presentation rooms for just this purpose.

For LC planning initiatives aimed at far-reaching or transformational change, planning group members should review documentation of every other pertinent campus initiative that offers some potential relationship to LC services and resources. Take a close look at statements of justification, rationales for grant proposals, and especially *projected learning outcomes* for initiatives such as writing centers, course management systems/virtual learning environments, smart classrooms, wireless laptop initiatives, corporate learning partnerships, teaching and learning centers, pedagogical innovations, game/virtual reality environments, and even core curriculum revisions. Beyond reviewing documentation, you should hold conversations or interviews with key managers, initiators, or champions of such projects and programs.

By scanning documentation for projected learning outcomes, the facilitator will want to look for opportunities to refashion them as scenario-building Q&A scripts. The facilitator may draft *partial* scenarios based on these varied statements of projected learning outcomes and then use the scenario-building exercise to have the group extend those by projecting involvement of, or collaboration with, the LC. By embedding outcomes at this very early stage of the planning process, the IC Planning Group takes an important first step toward establishing what Amos Lakos calls a "culture of assessment" within the IC initiative.[4] A charge to student focus groups might be phrased as follows:

When students are using the [writing center/cms-vle/smart classrooms/wireless laptops/etc.] build scenarios showing how their demands on library might change, and how IC/LC might meet those demands. How might IC/LC collaborate with initiatives [writing center/cms-vle/smart classrooms/ wireless laptops/etc.] to proactively prepare for these new demands?

Similarly, faculty focus group(s) might be given the following charge:

When faculty are utilizing the [teaching center/pedagogical model/game simulations/cms-vle/core curriculum] how might their needs for library support change? How might IC/LC collaborate with initiatives [teaching center/pedagogical model/game simulations/cms-vle/core curriculum etc.] to proactively prepare for these new demands?

Following are more specific examples. The Writing Center at Middle Tennessee State University authored a "2000–05 Institutional Effectiveness Plan" which included a new "Writing Center Outreach Initiative."[5] Figure 5.4 presents the goal, outcome, and projected measurable result of that initiative:

Figure 5.4
MTSU "Writing Center Outreach Initiative"

Goal: Improve Writing Center outreach to academic disciplines other than English

Measurable outcome: Increased number of student contacts outside English

Results: Tutors visited 51 class sessions in departments other than English

---

In Figure 5.5, we offer (A) a case where a hypothetical Learning Commons Planning Group has discovered a problem with a writing center (WC) outreach initiative, and (B) offers a scenario whereby the problem is viewed as an opportunity for LC/WC collaboration.

Figure 5.5
Scenario for Writing Center/Learning Commons Collaboration

Problem: The writing center outreach results have not fully translated into effective learning outcomes. After visiting those class sessions, several tutors report having difficulty finding suitable space within those department computer labs for their writing tutorials. Writing Center workstations themselves are so heavily booked for composition class sessions that the influx of new students from the outreach program overtaxes the Writing Center itself. Tutors discover that many students in their outreach departments were/are using library workstations because of needed access to databases. This would be a logical place for Writing Center outreach tutors to schedule appointments with students from these other departments, but library workstation carrels currently are single-user models, not suitable for side-by-side tutorials at a workstation. *[Note: we emphasize that this problem statement does not apply to the actual Middle Tennessee State University initiative, but is a hypothetical problem statement adapted from a generic writing center/Learning Commons scenario-building exercise.]*

Scenario: The new Learning Commons will offer many side-by-side workstation access points where coaching and tutorials can be conducted in proximity to all necessary writing center software, course management system resources for the student's disciplinary class, and library database resources, as well as a richly stocked print collection of handbooks and guidebooks to effective writing techniques. The WC and LC also will share a booking calendar utility that allows tutors and students to book tutorial LC workstations when those resources are needed, or WC workstations when Writing Center meetings are needed.

The next example, in Figure 5.6, presents a sample learning outcomes statement for a business course adapted from a series posted at Texas Tech University.[6]

The group is presented with a problem: "While the business course sessions are held in a smart classroom, students working in out-of-class-session groups are having difficulty finding appropriate IT-equipped sites to fulfill all elements of the course outcomes statement." The group is then charged to build a scenario that presents key digital, physical, and human resources needed to support LC/Business Course collaboration, as shown in Figure 5.7.

Figure 5.6
Texas Tech Business Course Learning Outcomes Statement

Business Course

At the end of the course/program, students will be able to:

- Identify and describe current domestic and international business trends
- Explain how proper business management benefits consumers and employees
- Define the basic rules related to Human Resources management
- Compare and contrast the different types of business ownership
- Evaluate and classify various marketing strategies
- Summarize how technology can help a business manage information

---

Figure 5.7
Scenario for Business Course/Learning Commons Collaboration

Scenario: In its collaboration with the Business Department, the LC will offer

- Business online services with realtime domestic and international business trends
- Fulltext databases with content on business and human resource management
- LC staff will host "skill sessions" on utilizing those databases
- Small group spaces where local business owners can be invited for Q&A sessions
- Access to simulation software lab for visual evaluation of marketing strategies
- A model corporate intranet lab featuring key business technology tools
- Access to PowerPoint rehearsal studio for polishing business class presentations

---

The last example of building scenarios around collaboration based on learning outcomes involves faculty rather than students. IC Planning Group staff research the forthcoming projects of the Center for Teaching and Learning (CTL) and discover that the CTL Director has attended a workshop sponsored by the Knowledge Media Lab of the Carnegie Foundation for the Advancement of Teaching. The CTL Director feels that the Knowledge Media Lab's KEEP Toolkit offers some exciting potential for turning faculty teaching and research projects (currently in print form) into engaging multimedia Web sites. The IC Planning Group staff read the Carnegie Knowledge Media Lab's white paper "Using Multimedia to Advance the Scholarship of Teaching."[7] They note that the white paper assumes faculty will individually acquire and learn how to use all the multimedia support and Web site hosting hardware and software applicable to the KEEP Toolkit projects. In conversation with the CTL Director, they learn she feels that the burden of individual acquisition and mastery of software will be a significant disincentive to faculty involvement. She is looking for a collaborator unit that can help her make these hardware and software resources centrally available to interested faculty, and also host small faculty learning groups to share the experience of mastering the KEEP Toolkit. They invite the CTL Director to join an LC scenario-building planning group, and their scenario-building exercise is based on the four resources (Figure 5.8).

Even if one develops scenarios limited to campus-specific futures—such as a scenario related to Writing Across the Curriculum, or wireless laptops being made standard for all students, or a new graduate program in International Business being approved, or the psychology faculty deciding to apply situated learning via hybrid courses—such scenarios in themselves will be impacted by trends and forces beyond the campus and ultimately extending

---

Figure 5.8
LC/Center for Teaching Scenario to Support the KEEP Toolkit

Physical resources: workstations; single-user carrels for faculty who prefer working individually; **double-user carrels** for faculty who prefer working in teams, with student assistants, or with LC media skills coaches; **small group presentation rooms** for faculty groups to gather and review KEEP Toolkit resources and to present draft multimedia documentation examples. **Media equipment** for professional-level audio capture, video capture, large-screen display, etc. **Server** to host project's faculty multimedia Web sites.

Digital resources: the **KEEP Toolkit** itself; **media software** needed for all audio and video capture, transfer, reformatting, display, and archiving; **conversion utilities** for moving content to and from all pertinent campus-based CMS solutions; **databases** with pertinent ERIC and other educational technology articles. Selected **discipline-specific software** used by faculty who want to use the KEEP Toolkit project in support of teaching projects already utilizing packages such as GIS, system simulation, statistics, etc.

Human Resources: a Faculty KEEP Toolkit User Group to provide peer support; all or some meet regularly with LC management, review outcomes; LC **tech support staff** for IT, media, and specialized hardware; LC **instructional staff** for faculty skill sessions.

Social resources: collaborating planners brainstorm other campus partners to help organize a semi-annual **Faculty Showcase** to present project achievements to entire faculty and administration. An ideal partner appears in a new **Learning Communities Task Force** that happens to have a faculty member interested in the KEEP Toolkit.

---

to broader contexts. Similarly, global scenarios can be valuable as conceptual tools for continually repositioning the LC in an environment of increasing complexity. Some scenario-building groups take on an independent "life of their own," and leap ahead to global blue-sky brainstorming. The facilitator needs to be adept at determining how loosely or tightly to reign in such a group. If real enthusiasm and energy emerges, the facilitator may legitimately let the process play itself out, even when the results may seem to have little immediate or direct application. Sometimes later analysis will reveal unexpected linkages and surprisingly practical applications. In addition, Chapter 8 will present the idea of a type of current awareness programming within the Learning Commons called *horizon-scanning*. Some valuable groundwork for later horizon-scanning programs may be laid by allowing one or more scenario-building exercises to leap beyond the boundary of IC startup planning.

An interesting example of such far-reaching scenario-building can be found in the article "Four futures for scientific and medical publishing."[8] Authors Abbasi, Butterfield, et al. postulate four possible scenarios for scientific and medical publishing in the future, which they humorously name after the members of the television family "The Simpsons." Their scenarios are condensed and rephrased below:

Lisa scenario: a world of global conversations

Information moves not through publication but through electronic interchange. Constant voice and electronic conversations goes on between all involved in any given area of research. Publication of research loses importance because research is archived on university-sponsored and research center Web sites. Academic credit accrues from the "buzz" across the communities. Shared awareness develops of who is pursuing original lines of research and doing interesting work. Word of developments spreads very quickly across linked communities. The communities are self-sufficient; maintaining their own databases. Information is a side product of professional activities.

Homer scenario: a world of no significant change

Academics and research specialists continue to publish much as today. Consequently, no major changes emerge in the academic reward system. However, publication explosion continues to make it increasingly difficult to keep up. Need for recertification in disciplines builds aftermarket for distilled information and current awareness services. Some are free—supported by advertising, some by licensing fees, and some by professional societies or institutions (a hospital, in this example, which works through commercial and professional channels—to keep staff up to date). Publishers seek to add value to content—through sifting, condensing, and sorting—and have progressed to provide electronic access to much more material for just slightly more money.

Marge scenario: a world of academic innovation

New research results are posted on the Web for free access—on Web sites sponsored and administered by universities and research institutes, or academic-corporate partnerships. The researcher is electronically alerted to everything directly related to his research specialty. His tenure review status is based partly on the number of citation links and traffic his research draws on the Web, and whether his research leads to new discoveries or improves clinical practice...Decision support systems have emerged to help with clinical work. These run on handheld devices, and draw from constantly updated knowledge bases. Patients and the general public have access to the same information sources and decision support systems. Publishers no longer find it profitable to publish pure science. They produce magazines that deal with value-added issues (like IT applications in health care) and that are distributed to hospitals, health care providers, insurers, and regulatory offices.

Bart scenario: a world of corporate dominance

Nearly all scientific and medical information is funded and generated by large corporations and multinational conglomerates—as a side product of their in-house research labs or through grants to academics. Traditional independent scientific, technical, and medical (STM) publishers have disappeared. Editors now are on the payroll of the corporations, and their priority is to further the strategic plans of their employers. Most research is driven by the business plans of large organizations. Academics are typically employed by the companies, or in academic labs living on grants provided by the organizations. Academic achievement comes to be measured primarily by the ability to draw funding support from the organizations. Most universities are now teaching institutions, only superficially connected to research labs located at nearby quasi-academic campuses...The old notion of independence of information seems naive. The idea of research for the sake of research, or neutral unsponsored information, is viewed as old-fashioned. The market in ideas and the money markets are now closely connected, which ensures that good ideas are quickly exploited.

Although these scenario examples address the future of medical and scientific information, they have broader implications for scholarly communication at large, and corollary implications for future library IC/LC support services. At this juncture, these examples show how the scenario-building process can construct and articulate a range of possible global futures. The planner might charge a group with using these global scenarios as starting points and project localized scenarios for how IC services might be utilized on a particular campus were one specific global scenario to come to pass, as shown in Figure 5.9.

Visual diagrams can be a useful tool to help focus groups make sense of their alternative or complementary visions of the future. The template in Figure 5.10 is a possibly useful

Figure 5.9 Linking Global Scenarios to Local Scenarios	
Homer scenario	Current library service patterns remain relevant, but the IC staff directs increasing attention to helping students learn to cope with the continuation and acceleration of current data and information overload.
Lisa scenario	IC staff might devote much more time and energy to helping students learn to map and navigate the labyrinth of special interest communities and their interconnecting channels of online monologue, dialogue, and discourse.
Marge scenario	IC instructional staff helps students learn to utilize the information architecture and data structures undergirding decision support systems, and perhaps applying visualization software to conduct ongoing citation network analysis.
Bart scenario	IC staff called upon to collaborate with business faculty to help students track the hidden hand of investment-driven research, to sort out inherent problems of objectivity, bias, and ethics, and possibly use game theory simulations to identify and analyze the role of corporate research sponsors and their underlying profit agendas.

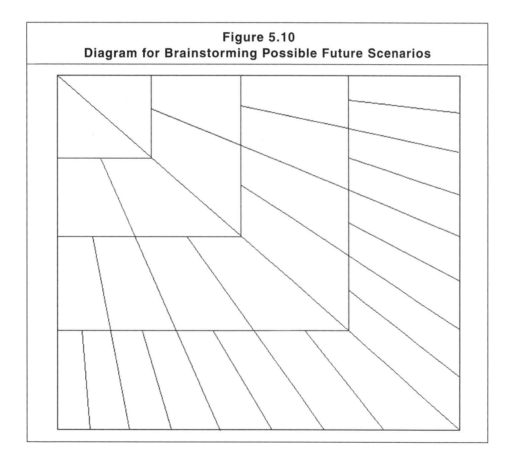

Figure 5.10
Diagram for Brainstorming Possible Future Scenarios

visual device to be posted by the facilitator at the beginning of a session. The diagram is a variant on a curved graph often referred to as a "Harman Fan," informally named after Willis Harman, who mentions it in his book *An Incomplete Guide to the Future*.[9] Harman did not originate the diagram—it had already entered generic use—but he applied it to the process of envisioning the future, or futures, of social and technological change. Harman used a model based on concentric quarter-circles, as if one took a photo of a pebble dropped in a pond with the rings of water widening out, and then turned the lower-right quarter of that image into a diagram. He then placed future developments as "stepping-stones" arrayed out among the concentric rings of the future, showing how future choices and developments could spread and multiply. Our diagram uses diagonally segmented rectangles instead of circles, and even-numbered stepping-stone divisions instead of odd.

In Harman's preferred usage the group would be asked to assemble a free-form list of possible future scenarios (technology innovations, social trends, economic factors, etc.). The facilitator labels each with a name and then takes the four scenarios most similar to the present and writes these on stick-up notes to the upper-left corner at positions a, b, c, and d. The most extreme or farthest-removed scenarios are labeled and applied to the far bottom and right subdivisions. The group is asked to place intermediate scenarios (or developments) as stepping-stones leading, in related ways, from the conservative a, b, c, d region to the scenarios on the farthest fringes. Or, one might try a modification of this approach, where the top-left regions are filled and the group is left to extrapolate eventualities out to the edges. Figure 5.11 labels regions a.1, a.2, b.1, b.1, etc., and also shows how sections around the fringes can be subdivided by diagonals to indicate either/or conditionalities or good/bad eventualities.

The diagram can be adapted to a great variety of group processes, and used in multiple ways. For example, a facilitator might label a, b, c, d with Homer, Marge, Lisa, and Bart

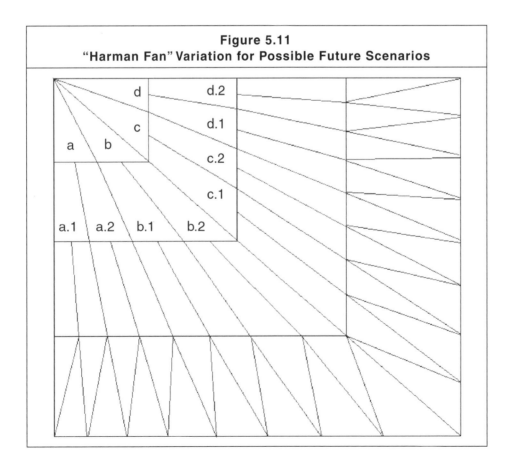

Figure 5.11
"Harman Fan" Variation for Possible Future Scenarios

scenarios from the article discussed earlier. Subsections a.1 and a.2 might then be labeled with two key implications or effects of the Homer scenario, with further subsequent implications or developments radiating out. Alternatively, each rectangle iteration from upper-left to far-bottom and far-right can be used as a cause-effect sequence, or a situation-implication relationship, or simply multiplying specific examples from a small number of initial general states or categories. Sometimes one scenario may overwhelm a neighbor; the group might consider the Homer scenario in section "a" to be a dead end, and want to move on to implications from the Marge scenario in "b." The facilitator can simply show the dead end with a marker in "a" and give sections "a.1" and "a.2" to further variant iterations of the Marge scenario. Be creative!

Planning Template Step: Projecting the Future Commons

As noted previously, the scenario-building step and the projecting the future commons step could be conjoined or combined. In general we recommend that a free-wheeling, brainstorming scenario-building step can be a good lead-in to a more disciplined projecting the future commons step that places much more emphasis on focal points of service delivery, the relationship between users and staff, and the optimal adjacencies among functions and activities. At this juncture, the IC Planning group will especially want to take stock of where the process has trended up to this point with regard to possible building construction, expansion, or renovation. If it is possible to foresee the need for design consultation or full-fledged architectural planning, then the projecting the future commons step becomes a plausible point where organizational and building planning processes could converge. In Figure 5.12, the projecting the future commons step is completed in time to inform what the PKAL essay by Stephens et al. call the "feasibility study" and its programming process, described as "an iterative one in which the users discuss the goals and purpose of the space with the design team. Out of this dialog emerges a coherent list of desired spaces with their key characteristic in terms of size, quality, location, and special facilities."[10] However, there are also successful cases where the projecting the future commons step or its equivalent was carried out entirely by campus (or even library) staff, and the results conveyed to design consultants and/or architects at a later date.

For exercises in projecting the future commons, use both narrative summaries and visual flowcharts. The narrative summaries should draw upon earlier focus group and scenario-building documentation, such as the Information/Spaces Summary Matrix shown in Figure 4.24. If earlier documentation does not include such matrices, draw some up as the first step in the exercise. The overall goal of projecting the future commons is captured in a phrase from Joanne Henning's "Gleanings: Identify how you understand your space. If it is just seen as learning space, then design it for that. If it is also seen as a social space, then different criteria need to be considered." Other key reference points from Henning's list include breaking up banks of computers into smaller clusters to help humanize the space, integrating sub-collections of books with the technology as space allows, and discrete spaces for quiet study and noisy collaborations. But probably the most important issue to confront at this stage is that of single or multiple service desks. As with other authors, Henning noted the alternatives she had seen in IC visits, ranging from single omnibus service desks that combine information, reference, and IT support, to multiple specialized service points that refer users across the IC floor space. Of various functionalities, media services was the one most often offered from a specialized location.

While "Harman fan" diagrams may be useful visual tools for scenario-building, more traditional flowchart methods are recommended for the visual component of projecting the future commons. Flowcharts can be used to project relationships across space, time, or both. The following examples show how Queens University LC planning groups drew up spatial flowcharts describing potential arrangements of user service points, work areas, and technologies. In Figure 5.12, the emphasis is placed on placement of help desks and consultation areas in association with offices, productivity workstations, and the reference collection.

In Figure 5.13, the main help desk is projected as a "triage" area that includes greeters and rovers. The LC entrance is presumably top-center. This triage desk is envisioned as adjacent to and mainly responsible for a coffee shop/lounge, quick-access workstations (e-mail checks, etc.), study skills and writing centers, a media center, and an e-classroom. More specialized help is set off in a separate area as ITS help levels 1 and 2, reference rovers, and what is

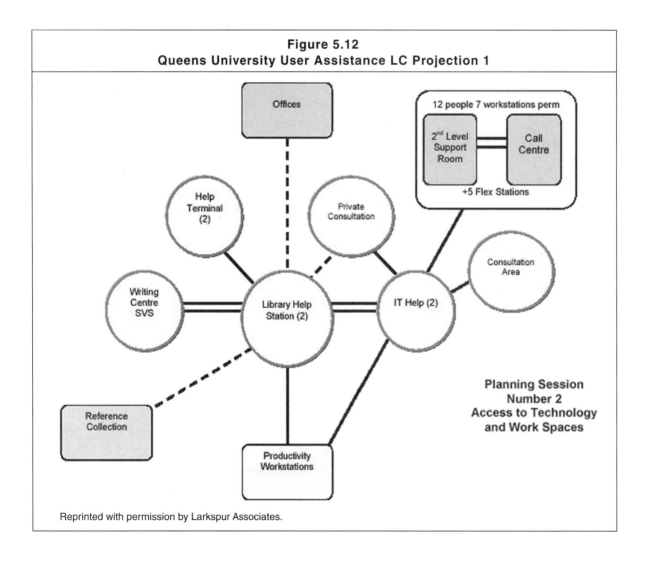

Figure 5.12
Queens University User Assistance LC Projection 1

Reprinted with permission by Larkspur Associates.

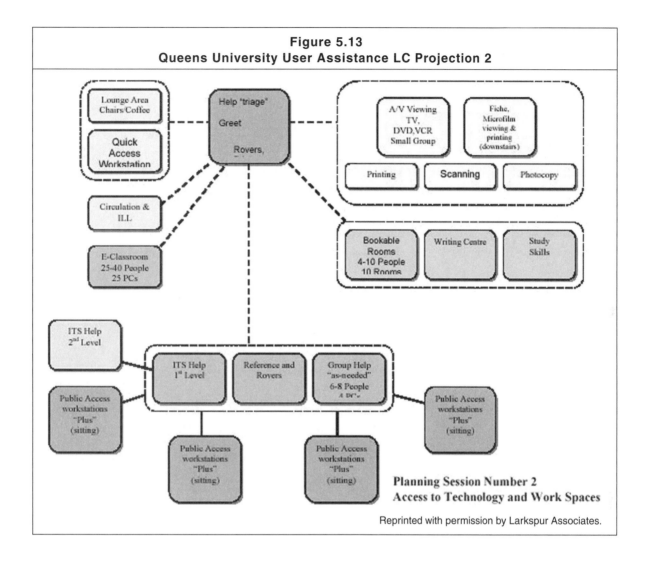

Figure 5.13
Queens University User Assistance LC Projection 2

Planning Session Number 2
Access to Technology and Work Spaces

Reprinted with permission by Larkspur Associates.

termed "group help." This locus is adjacent to and responsible for four areas of public access workstations.

In Figure 5.14, the LC entrance is specified at bottom-center of the diagram, and all varieties of help and user assistance are grouped in adjacency. The head desk area adjacent to the multimedia center actually becomes the central "star" of this system, around which all other spaces and services are arrayed as satellites.

In Figure 5.15, the LC entrance is not specified, but all user assistance is centralized, with satellite areas for adaptive technology, print and copy center, an area for more specialized labs such as GIS, data manipulation, multimedia, and preview studios, and another area for all social resource functionalities, including group study, group learning, and e-classroom.

The Queens process also included more detailed diagrams projecting the "transactional areas" for service points. One of these, Figure 5.16, is a particularly good illustration of how a variety of services at a multifunctional desk may be graphed or charted in a visual diagram. Many LCs have a single multifunctional desk simultaneously staffed by IT specialists, reference librarians, media support staff, and student assistants. In projecting such an inclusive service center, it may be particularly helpful to review the Queens example in Figure

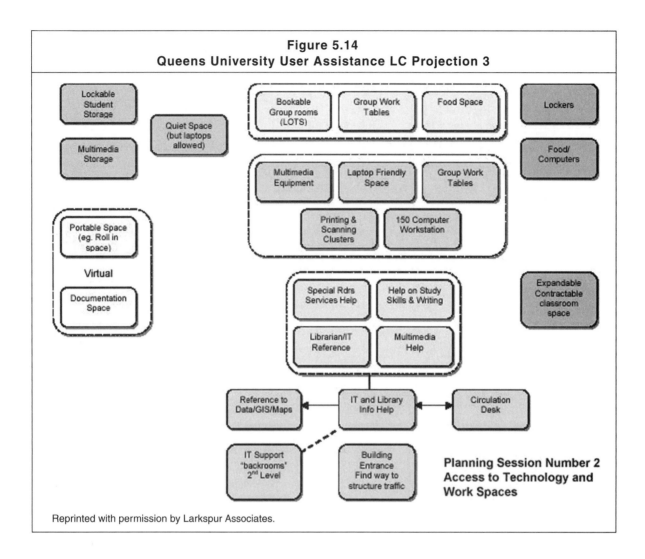

Figure 5.14
Queens University User Assistance LC Projection 3

Reprinted with permission by Larkspur Associates.

5.16; while the particular functions diagrammed here relate more to a business/circulation service point, they can be adapted and extrapolated for other situations.

Finally, we include one last example from Queens' fine planning report, showing how the same LC projection visualization process can be applied to the more traditional problem of physical materials collections. It would be a sad mistake to overlook the print and media collections that still form a vital component of the library-commons future. Even in current ICs such as UNC Charlotte, where much emphasis has been placed on technology access and the old reference collection has been drastically reduced, the IC users and staff still are adjacent to a core collection of some 30,000 items. Figure 5.17 offers a good example of how these physical resources can be mapped into the process of projecting the future commons.

In cases of building renovation or construction, the strategic planning step of projecting the future commons may include both flowcharts similar to the Queens examples and also "building-block diagrams." A building-block exercise could begin with a table that lists functional areas, as shown in Figure 5.18, before creating the diagram (Figure 5.19). This exercise is intended to capture the significant distinction between "swoopable" and "bookable" workstations noted by several IC initiators.

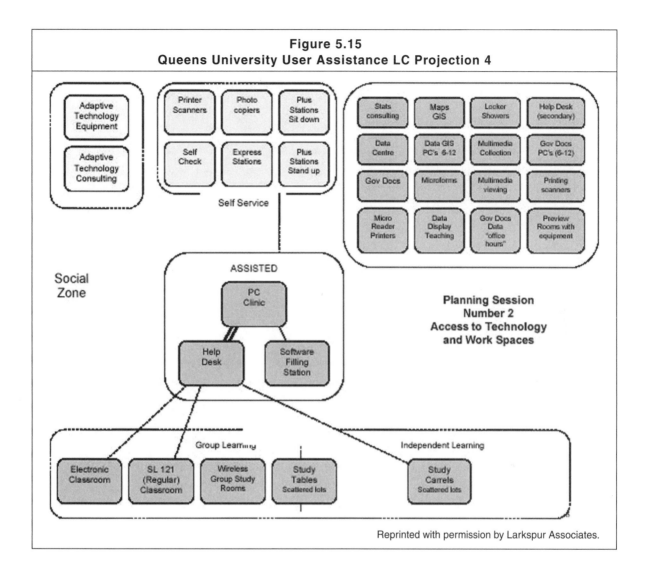

Figure 5.15
Queens University User Assistance LC Projection 4

Reprinted with permission by Larkspur Associates.

These elements can be recombined to work in a variety of custom or preexisting spaces. Figure 5.20 shows the same building blocks in a more enlongated, corridor configuration.

At the opposite extreme from these relatively simple, generic examples, Figure 5.21 gives the space statement headings from the plan for a Research Commons at Indiana University. The headings as a whole form a good exemplar for projecting a high-end, specialized facility aimed at meeting faculty research needs.

In addition to spaces, projection exercises can extend to brainstorming more detailed aspects of an IC installation, such as fixtures, furnishings, and equipment (F,F&E). The following examples present a schematic design developed through preliminary projection exercises during a Learning Commons planning process at Belmont Abbey College. The fixture is informally referred to as the "Commons Curve," and represents an attempt to attractively mix solo-access and dual-access workspaces without creating hard area divisions across a commons floor plan, such as those implied in the division of swoopable and bookable workstations in the preceding building-block diagrams. Figure 5.22 shows a single Commons Curve with five solo-access workstations around the convex side (these could be

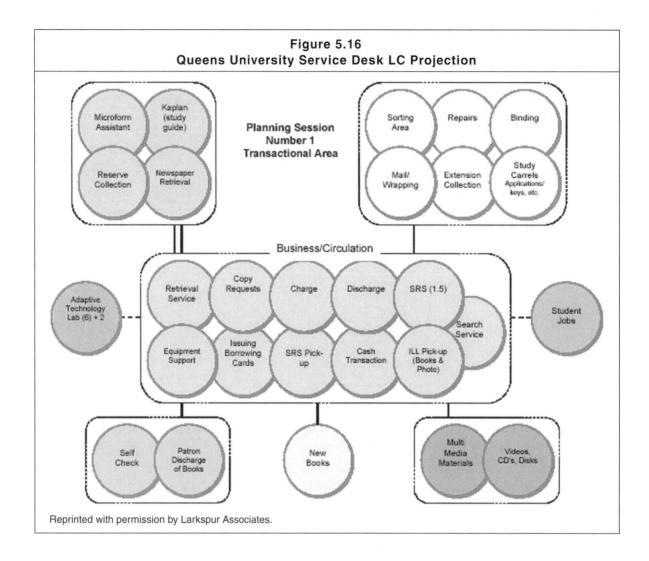

Figure 5.16
Queens University Service Desk LC Projection

Reprinted with permission by Larkspur Associates.

standing or sitting position) and a single large workspace (shaded) for coaching, teamwork, or tutorials on the concave side. A curved screen to inhibit sight and sound distraction is assumed to divide the concave and convex regions, with smaller dividers optionally placed between the convex-side access points. The concave region is meant to be large enough to handle a large-screen LCD monitor, scanner, and various other peripherals.

In a large open-space floor plan, multiple "Commons Curve" units are visualized as being conjoinable in pairs, or stretching in various extended combinations, as suggested by Figure 5.23.

And the units could even be coupled face-to-face to create freestanding small group work areas, as shown in Figure 5.24, with an optional work table placed between.

By the completion of the projecting the future commons step, the initial start-up phase of a building planning process may already be under way. Stephens et al. describe this as beginning with a conceptual stage, where the perceived need, visions, and goals for the new facility are drafted and articulated, followed by a design phase that will include a feasibility study and programming discussions and analysis. It would be useless here to try to spell out the sequencing of the building planning track in detail because so much depends

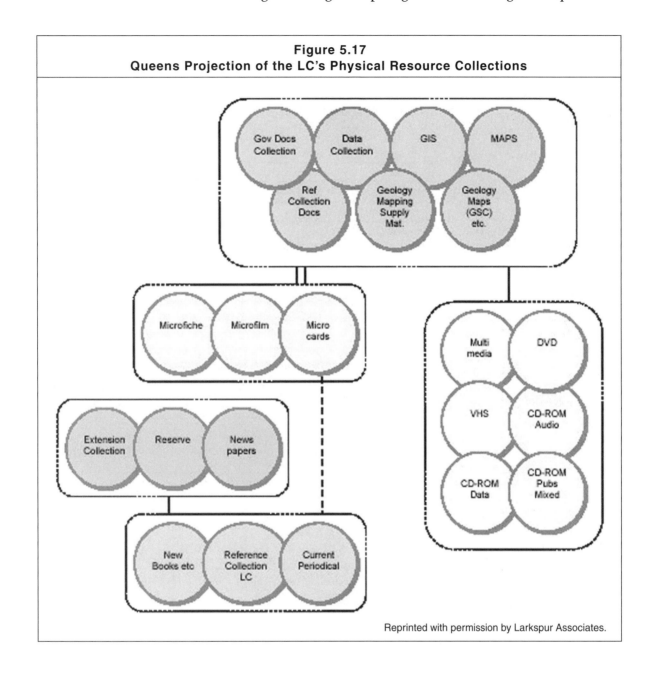

Figure 5.17
Queens Projection of the LC's Physical Resource Collections

Reprinted with permission by Larkspur Associates.

Figure 5.18
Sample Short List of Generic IC Functional Areas

Help desk
Quick-access workstation pods [swoopable]
Single-user workstation carrels [bookable]
Double-user workstation area(s) for tutorials & coaching
Group study area(s)
Smart classroom(s)
Coffee lounge
IT support w/ data manipulation center & faculty studio
Multimedia center & faculty studio

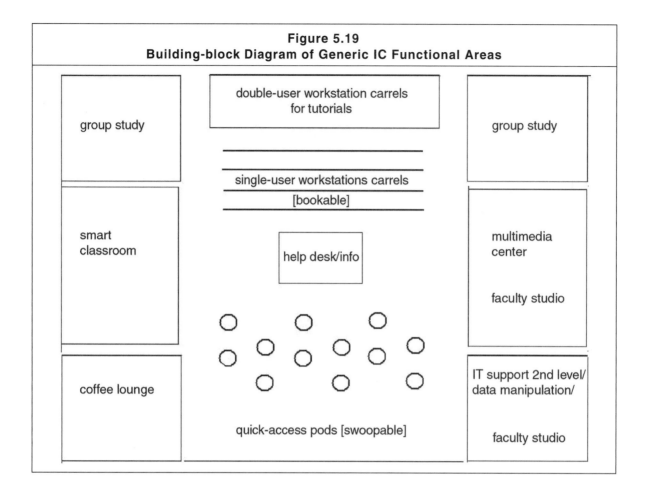

Figure 5.19
Building-block Diagram of Generic IC Functional Areas

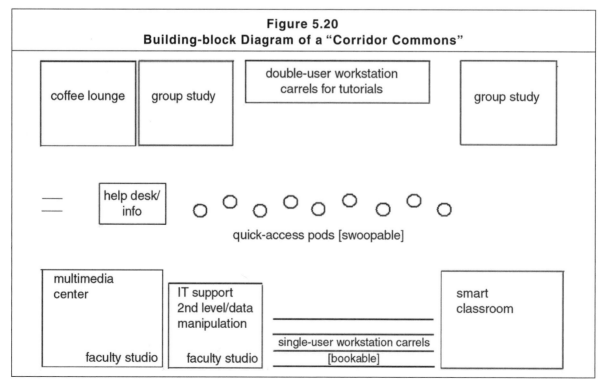

Figure 5.20
Building-block Diagram of a "Corridor Commons"

Figure 5.21
Space Designation Headings for IU's Research Commons

General Information Services—Point of Entry for the Research Commons

Reference and Research Collections

Digital Media Production, Delivery, Archiving, and Online Delivery of Text and Information

Research Compliance, Intellectual Property, and Technology Transfer

Data Analysis and Advanced Computation

Collaboration and Visualization

Software Support and Distribution and Support for Scholarly Writing

---

Figure 5.22
A Single "Commons Curve" Unit to Mix Solo and Dual-Access

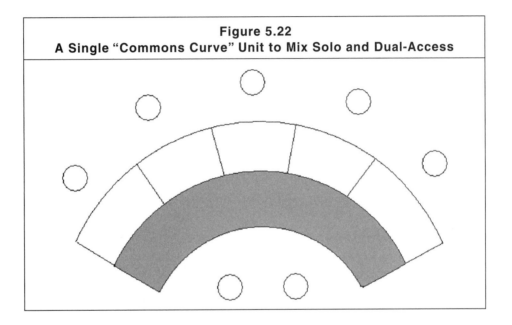

upon the individual methodological approach of the architect and design firm(s) chosen. In general, the purpose of the architectural programming process "...is to define and confirm the quantity and quality of the spaces that will make up the building...by gathering information in writing...about the specific needs of the people and departments that will use the building."[12] The project shepherd should infuse this start-up phase with insights gleaned from his/her overview of the first three steps of the IC planning template, and the flowcharts developed during projection exercises should become the basis for the iterative programming conversations between organizational and building planners. And if the project entails development of a Learning Commons that will involve substantial collaboration with, or perhaps even co-location of, other academic units from across campus within the new facility, the building planning processes of programming and design will likely be pushed back or "stepped down" to extend in parallel with the next steps of the planning template to be discussed in Chapter 6: *managing the campus conversation* and *drafting the project/program documentation*.

It may be useful to briefly summarize and review the group process strategic planning steps: *self-discovery*, *scenario-building*, and *projecting the future commons*. In the preceding

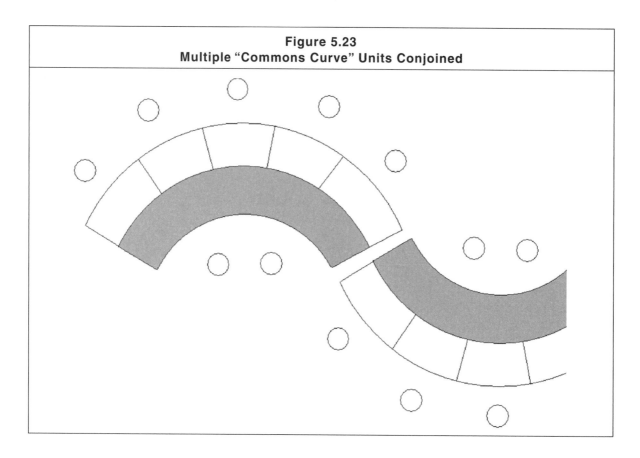

Figure 5.23
Multiple "Commons Curve" Units Conjoined

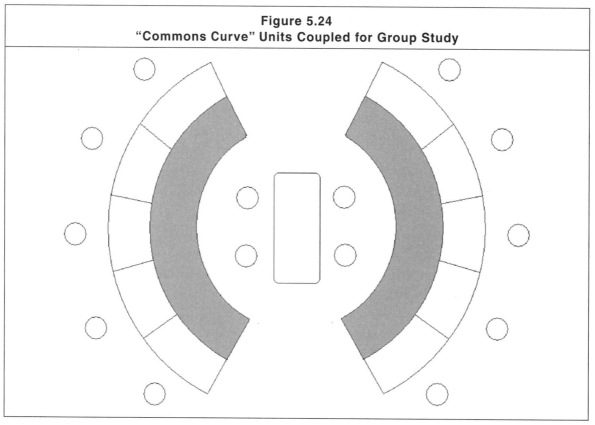

Figure 5.24
"Commons Curve" Units Coupled for Group Study

chapter, the first focus group section was part of the initial self-discovery phase, where the groups looked at basic ongoing service delivery issues and questions, using scripts similar to, or even drawn from, questions on user survey instruments. This can be very pragmatic, or it can be more visionary in a way that leads into scenario-building. In the scenario-building phase proper, the group(s) may be encouraged to grapple with the complex and difficult issue: "what the future might bring." A number of ways to approach such scenarios were presented, ranging from thumbnail narrative single-user case studies drawn from unmonitored referrals to projected campuswide collaborations based on learning outcomes and even to the horizons of the future of academic information and its potential impact on local services and resources. Lastly, with *projecting the future commons*, the group(s) were asked to identify all the LC service spaces and components from their focus group results and scenario-building results and start diagramming them out onto spatial maps of help desks, technology areas, group learning and study areas, and media centers. This concludes the discussion of the strategic planning phase of our IC planning template. The following chapter moves us into steps we present as a tactical planning phase. However, in large projects with multiple collaborators, these further steps will still involve significant strategic elements.

Endnotes

1 Giesecke, Joan. 1998. *Scenario Planning for Libraries*. Chicago: American Library Association. viii.

2 Renaud, Robert E. 1997. "Space and Purpose: Repositioning the Liberal Arts College Library," *Transformations: Liberal Arts in the Digital Age*. Available: http://apps.nitle.org/transformations/?q=node/97

3 "Whitepaper: Digital Media Services at the Kelvin Smith Library. Appendix B—KSL Information Commons Plan." Case Western Reserve University. (September 2004). Available: http://library.case.edu/ksl/freedmancenter/archive/AppB_InfoComm_purposepaper.pdf

4 Lakos, Amos A. "Implementing a 'Culture of Assessment' Within the Information Commons." USC Leavey Library 2004 Conference. Information Commons: Learning Space Beyond the Classroom, (September 16–17, 2004). Available: http://www.usc.edu/isd/libraries/locations/leavey/news/conference/presentations/

5 "2000–2005 Institutional Effectiveness Plan: Academic Units." Middle Tennessee State University. Available: http://www.mtsu.edu/~mtsacs/IEPlans/English.doc

6 "Sample Learning Outcome Statements: Introduction to Business." Texas Tech University. Available: http://dev.tltc.ttu.edu/Redesign/assessment/sample.asp

7 Pointer, Desiree, Thomas Hatch, and Toru Iiyoshi. "Using Multimedia to Advance the Scholarship of Teaching ." Carnegie Foundation for the Advancement of Teaching. Available: http://kml.carnegiefoundation.org/resources/resourcetext616.htm#2_2

8 Abbasi, Kamran, Michael Butterfield, et al. 2002. "Four futures for scientific and medical publishing." *British Medical Journal*. 325 no. 7378 (December 21). 1472.

9 Harman, Willis. 1979. *An Incomplete Guide to the Future*. New York : Norton.

10 Stephens, Kirby, Kamal, Ellis. http://www.pkal.org/documents/Vol4PoliticsAndProcessOfChange.cfm

11 Henning, Joanne. 2005. "Information Commons Study Leave: October 2, 2004–March 31, 2005. University of British Columbia. Available: http://jhenning.law.uvic.ca/

12 Stephens, Kirby, Kamal, Ellis. http://www.pkal.org/documents/Vol4PoliticsAndProcessOfChange.cfm

6

Tactical Planning: Managing the Conversation and Drafting the Project Documentation

Planning Template Step: Managing the Campus Conversation

In preparing for the final two steps of the IC planning template, *managing the campus conversation* and *drafting the project/program documentation*, it becomes important to revisit two basic questions: (1) does the situation now call for an Information Commons (adjustment, isolated change), or a Learning Commons or Collaboration Center (far-reaching change, transformation)? and (2) does the situation now call for building construction, expansion, or renovation? In Figure 4.4, the IC planning template was presented in a nominal framework with organizational planning steps laid out in parallel to building planning stages. In the real world, of course, things are not always so simple. Figure 6.1 repeats the nominal example in column B, showing the two planning tracks roughly synchronized. In column C, it shows an "IC Fast Build" example more typical of a first-floor library renovation, or perhaps a wing expansion near the front entrance. Here, the building planning stages are stepped up and proceed more quickly. In column D, the situation is an "LC Slow Build," more typical of an ambitious stand-alone building project where multiple academic support units will set up collaborative services and possibly themselves co-locate. In this case, the building planning stages are stepped down from the library's organizational planning effort and move at a more deliberate pace. As noted previously, the steps labeled "PKAL" refer to a "Project Sequence" described by Stephens, Kirby, Kamal, and Ellis in their Project Kaleidoscope (PKAL) essay on institutional building planning.[1]

In column B, the IC planning template will be wrapping up just as the building planning track is transitioning from the conceptual phase to the design phase. This allows both the campus conversation and project documentation steps to then inform the building design phase. By contrast, in an IC Fast Build situation, preliminary building design may begin even before the campus conversation step begins. In an LC Slow Build, managing the campus conversation may become part of the building conceptualization phase, and the project documentation becomes only a provisional draft, giving the library's portion of what

Figure 6.1 **The IC Planning Template: Theme with Variations**			
Column A	**Column B**	**Column C**	**Column D**
	NOMINAL	**IC FAST BUILD**	**LC SLOW BUILD**
Step	**A PKAL Building Planning equiv.**	**PKAL Building Planning stepped-up**	**PKAL Building Planning stepped-down**
Self-discovery	Preliminary: Project shepherd selection	Preliminary: Project shepherd selection, orientation	
Scenario-building	Preliminary: Project shepherd orientation	Conceptual stage: Perceived need, visions, goals	
Projecting the future commons among the scenarios	Conceptual stage: Perceived need Visions Goals	Feasibility study: siting, sizing, programming; Define scope, goals, and budget	Preliminary: Project shepherd selection, orientation
Managing the campus conversation	Conceptual stage: Feasibility study: siting, sizing, programming	Design stage: schematics, formal documentation, construction prep	Conceptual stage: Perceived need Visions, goals
Drafting and disseminating the project or program document	Conceptual stage: define scope, goals, and budget	Bidding or negotiation, Engage contractor, Construction begins	Conceptual stage: Feasibility study: siting, sizing, programming

will later become a larger document fleshed out in a campuswide vetting process. In any case, it is possible to make one general observation that seems valid across variations: at the very start of a major project, initial organizational strategic planning should precede any building planning. But sometimes there will follow a turnabout or tipping-point, where the unfolding building design and construction timetable begins to drive subsequent tactical steps in organizational planning.

Managing the Tactical Conversation: IC Presentation

This first example applies to the tactical IC campus conversation, under either a nominal or "fast-build" situation. A tactical IC presentation might be given in one central venue, as for a faculty assembly meeting, or, especially in a large university, the IC Planning Group might undertake traveling presentations for meetings of various academic departments and divisions. In either case, the presentation is "hitched" to the agenda of an existing forum. An alternative is to convene some type of special open or invitational forum that will deal entirely with the IC. In its manual on managing change, the American Council on Education (A.C.E.) addressed the issue of choosing the proper forum for presenting both tactical and strategic change initiatives.[2] The list is applicable for managing all types of IC and LC planning conversations, as summarized in Figure 6.2.

Figure 6.2 Choosing the Forum for IC/LC Planning Conversations		
Type of Conversation	**Length**	**Participants**
Focused dialogues	Two hours to two days	Representatives (10–30) from various on-campus groups
Retreats	One to two days	Representatives (20–100) from on-campus and off-campus groups
Seminars	Several hours	Varies from small, targeted teams to widely diverse groups
Symposia	Several hours	Entire campus or selected group
Town meetings	Several hours	Entire campus

To give a tactical presentation as part of a nominal or IC fast-build situation, a couple of hours spent in a focused dialogue or seminar may suffice. A fine example of an informational presentation that could be used in a concise IC seminar or focused dialogue is that prepared by the Information Commons Committee of the University of Maryland.[3] The narrative headings for their presentation framework seem especially well defined:

Figure 6.3 University of Maryland IC Committee Presentation
IC planning has involved . . .
What we hear from our users . . .
What is our role?
We hope to create . . .
Where are we now?
How will the IC look to our users?
View of floor plan
View of desktop
What are the issues?
Staffing. Training. Study Space. Noise. Food. Others?
Help us find the answers

The simple statements "What we hear from our users . . .," "What is our role?" and "We hope to create . . . " offer a succinct overview of a process that has already moved from discoveries to decisions, at least internally. The section "What we hear from our users" gives a thumbnail sketch of results from a typical discovery step in strategic planning (Fig. 6.4).

Whatever the local situation may be, the idea is not to hammer colleagues in other campus departments with theoretical jargon, but to pull key terms and concepts from theory and use the presentation (and project report) to invest them with local, practical meaning. A

Figure 6.4
IC Committee Presentation: "What we hear from our users"

- Need more computers, lines at both WAM lab and library computers
- Need one single method for printing
- Need more space for collaboration or group study
- Need to keep printers and computers up and running
- Need to work on a paper while researching
- Need to check email
- Need to print a paper quickly
- Want wireless capability

---

good example of shared language utilization can be found in a narrative description by Hester Mountifield. Though prepared as an article abstract, Mountifield's description applies key terms and examples from Strategic Alignment (boldfaced in the following example) in useful, concrete ways that cumulatively enable the creation of a shared terminology within the narrative.

> The newly constructed Kate Edger Information Commons, The University of Auckland's leading edge student-centred learning facility, provides a collaborative interdisciplinary environment where over 500 full-productivity workstations, electronic classrooms, and an additional 500+ flexible study and social spaces have been combined with proactive learning support. It presents the infrastructure for the **functional integration** of the information and technology services, learning support and language skills development offered by the University Library, IT Directorate, Student Learning Centre and English Language Self-Access Centre, consequently creating an enhanced learning environment that reflects the transformation of higher education, information resources and technology. The development of computer and information literacy skills is a key focus area of the Information Commons and opportunities for training are integrated into all aspects of service. The paper will look at the **key drivers** and **desired outcomes** that have guided the planning of the Information Commons building and facilities, the **strategic fit** of stakeholders resulting in the various collaborative arrangements and an integrated service model that provides a one-stop-shop for student enquiries.[4]

Another way strategic planning can flow into a coherent narrative, bolstering the campus conversation, is through the judicious use of scenarios developed earlier. Just as potential scenario-building examples ranged from global to local, scenarios can be used to animate the campus conversation in broad or targeted ways. As the earlier examples from the Case Western IC planning document also showed (Figures 5.1, 5.2, 5.3), targeted scenarios can dramatize in concrete, human terms the sorts of *learning outcomes* the IC is intended to achieve for real-life students in real-world situations. Especially useful is the fact that the first CWRU scenario addresses learning outcomes based on a specific project assigned by an instructor by way of a regularly scheduled course; the second offers a scenario for student independent learning based on research in an academic context, but outside of any assigned project for a course; and the third presents the IC's role of supporting group-process learning through IT tools and study rooms.

Managing the Strategic Conversation: Seedbed for LC Collaboration

If the situation clearly calls for far-reaching or transformational change, this managing the campus conversation phase will likely retain many strategic aspects, and may need to produce interdepartmental consensus that will inform an "LC slow-build" process. The campus conversation may need to extend over multiple seminars or retreats, and may need to interweave elements of building conceptualization and even early design. Major initiatives of this type can certainly bring a risk of overplanning, and a perception of becoming overly managed. On the other hand, unusually gifted key leaders sometimes emerge who seem to generate a sort of organizational alchemy and produce remarkable results with less management oversight or involvement than this text describes. But it is best here not to assume organizational alchemy. If the processes seem overly elaborate, the local manager is welcome to view them as simply an array of optional choices, and pick and choose accordingly.

In Chapter 5's scenario-building step, the following suggestion was offered:

> For LC planning initiatives aimed at far-reaching or transformational change, we recommend that planning group members review documentation of every other pertinent campus initiative that offers some potential relationship to LC services and resources. Take a close look at statements of justification, rationales for grant proposals, and especially *projected learning outcomes* for initiatives such as new writing centers, course management systems/virtual learning environments, smart classrooms, wireless laptop initiatives, corporate learning partnerships, teaching centers, pedagogical innovations, game/virtual reality environments, and even core curriculum revisions. Beyond reviewing documentation, we also recommend conversations with key managers, initiators, or champions of such projects and programs.

If that aspect of scenario-building was successful, the process should have identified, informed, and involved a key group of people who have served as initiators, managers, change agents, or champions of those other campus initiatives. Some or all of those people will now become the key stakeholders in a successful campus conversation aimed at development of a Learning Commons. Sometimes one key collaboration takes precedence over others and serves a model for later partnerships; in the case of UNC-Charlotte, it was the Center for Teaching and Learning. The campus conversation becomes the seedbed for a collaborative process that can begin within the library and extend outward, or can be the linchpin in a process already initiated by university leadership as part of a broader campus agenda. In either case, the campus conversation begins with the charting of a new course, and then identifies which boats in the flotilla will set that new course. The initial forum for this conversation should be suitably generous in scope—at the very least, an extended symposium, or perhaps one or more retreats. Properly accomplished, this process can have far-reaching impacts. Lizbeth Wilson of the University of Washington describes one real-world example that offers some interesting parallels.

> The transformation of the University of Washington's undergraduate library and collocated libraries are an outgrowth of collaborative design. In 1994, former University of Washington Provost Wayne Clough, now President of Georgia Institute of Technology, put together a team to "do something about technology in learning." At first blush it had nothing to do with space. Upon a closer look it had everything to do with space. The team was composed of representatives from the library, computing, and undergraduate education. Clough asked the team to address three

questions: (1) could technology be used to create learning communities; (2) could technology be used to encourage engagement among faculty, librarians, and students; and (3) could information and technology literacy be integrated into the curriculum? The team launched a small pilot called UWired. Sixty-five students were given laptops for a year, an integrated curriculum was developed, and 12 librarians and faculty were trained in the transformative use of new technologies. At the outset, space emerged as a problem. No existing classrooms were designed to facilitate collaborative learning in a networked environment. A different type of learning space had to be built, and would be situated, appropriately, in the library. Students, faculty, technologists, instructional designers, librarians, and an architect hammered out the design using a collaborative visioning process. At the time, there were few models to emulate and no common vocabulary to describe such a space.... The collaboratory is envisioned as an advanced, distributed infrastructure which would use multimedia information technology to relax the constraints on distance, time and even reality. It would support and enhance intellectual teamwork in both research and teaching. Since 1994, two more collaboratories, a Center for Teaching, Learning, and Technology, and the UWired Information Commons have been built using a similar collaborative design process. These collaborative spaces now occupy over 16,000 assignable square feet within the undergraduate library. The symbiotic relationship between traditional library functions and "nonlibrary" functions within the same physical structure has launched innovative services, realized significant benefits for learners and educators, and forged new relationships and administrative structures. The Program on Educational Transformation through Technology, UWired, a digital animation lab, Digital Copy Services, public art, multimedia student production, and a faculty development center now come together under one roof. While some may say these are "nonlibrary" functions, they represent the transformed library of the future, reshaped through collaborative design.[5]

We see many such examples of ICs marking developmental paths toward LCs, but the process is not easily generalized and heavily dependent upon local variables. Lizbeth Wilson's description provides a sense of the "carefully planned improvisation" and opportunistic entrepreneurialism that one finds in many such extended initiatives, though this in no way negates or trivializes the foresight and preparation involved. One should only add that to draw such a lengthy ambitious enterprise out of an initial modestly based IC project, care must be taken not to subsume the IC too completely within the mantle of the library's existing identity, lest the library's habits and routines artificially circumscribe possible innovations, and compromise the sensing and adaptive advantages to be discussed later.[6] Instead, one would hope that over time the opposite would occur, and that the IC could at least partially reshape the library's identity. This idea will be developed more fully in Chapter 8 as an aspect of a brand divergence marketing strategy for the IC/LC.

Whichever *type* of forum one chooses (focused dialogues, retreats, seminars, symposia, or town meetings), if the goal is to stimulate change and collaboration, the Planning Group should also give special attention to the problem of "mental models." Chris Soderquist describes the rationale for a process developed by his own consultancy, called, appropriately, "The Strategic Forum":

> ...mission, goals, and strategies...result from...individual and collective *mental models*. Mental models are the collection of assumptions, theories, anecdotes, and other mental facts and images used to make sense of complex systems (and most of life is complex!) and make decisions. Many...remain unspoken and untested—yet they drive the organization's behavior[7]

Soderquist's description is useful because faculty often carry with them their own idiosyncratic mental models of what libraries are, why libraries do what they do, and how libraries operate. These mental models are shaped by their own academic disciplines, and of course the pattern of traditional library support can vary significantly from one discipline to the next. The models are also shaped by their own positive and negative experiences with the existing campus library and with libraries previously used in their past educational histories. Such individual viewpoints, whether idealistic or iconoclastic, may facilitate or impede the strategic planning process for a Learning Commons. Sometimes inaccurate or inadequate mental models, if left unchallenged, result in negative attitudes, and push the process into misalignment. Faculty with flawed or outdated models of the library might also fail to envision the range of future possibilities being developed in other campus ICs and LCs. One goal of the forum, then, should be to constructively challenge idiosyncratic mental models of potential library futures that might impede the campus conversation, replacing them with shared models that facilitate change and collaboration. Techniques to accomplish this could be as simple as exhibiting the types of focus group scenarios and projections discussed in Chapters 4 and 5, or beyond this, arranging to bring in guest speakers (especially enthusiastic faculty) from peer institutions with successful ICs or LCs.

Outdated mental models are only one of numerous roadblocks that can crimp or compromise an LC's evolutionary development. As always, campus politics may play a crucial role, and if political obstacles do become apparent, consult the Project Kaleidoscope (PKAL) essay "Faculty and the Politics of Change," by Jane S. Halonen, Leonard W. ter Haar, and George Ellenberg.[8] Manager(s) may wish to convene the Planning Group, the project shepherd, plus (optionally) key external stakeholders, bring in a facilitator, and discuss the issues raised by Halonen, ter Haar, and Ellenberg. As an additional or alternative approach, see Figures 6.5 and 6.6, which list questions for reflection and discussion by the Planning Group. In the study on managing change report mentioned earlier, the American Council on Education (A.C.E.) studied campuswide change initiatives in the 1990s, including both initiatives that succeeded and those that failed.[9] They interviewed the campus teams that spearheaded the change initiatives and studied the types of questions these teams asked and the patterns of answers they recorded. The results of the A.C.E. study indicate that, in general, the questions were more important than the answers. In other words, while specific answers varied, the most successful teams tended to ask similar kinds of questions. The less successful teams tended not to ask the most probing questions. These question-adaptations are presented here in two sets, because the group may well want to meet and discuss the first questions—*Understanding Institutional Patterns of Change*, *Assessing the Climate for Change*, and *Preparing for Change*—in a preliminary session, then hold a follow-up session to deal with the second set of questions: *Assessing the Human Dimension* and *Articulating the Change Initiative*.

To understand how these questions and their potential answers may shape the campus conversation and subsequent decisions about a Learning Commons, you need to pause for a bit of theory. For a deeper understanding of how the campus conversation relates to collaborative, far-reaching, or transformational change requires a brief return to a diagram from Chapter 4, but with one important difference, as shown in Figure 6.7.

Figure 6.5
Key Questions Adapted from the A.C.E. Study on Managing Change

Understanding Institutional Patterns

- How loosely coupled is this institution?
- How does the pattern of diffused decision making facilitate or impede the IC/LC initiative?
- What possible strategies might the institution use to develop shared goals, common visions, and coherent institutional movement?

Assessing the Climate for Change

- Key questions: In what type of water is the institution: calm, currents, rapids, or waterfall?
- To what extent is this perception shared across campus?
- What strategies can be used to increase awareness of, and achieve consensus on, problems and opportunities?

Preparing for Change

- Key questions: In what ways does the IC/LC initiative fit in with the institution's mission and values [note concept of strategic fit]?
- Would the IC/LC initiative improve a core function of the institution? How might it impact teaching, learning, research, and service?

Figure 6.6
Shaping the Plan through Conversation and Narrative

Assessing the Human Dimension

- Who might be most likely to fear the proposed LC initiative? Why? What steps might be taken to alleviate their fear?
- How do other key people or groups view the initiative? Who are the institutional "have-mores" and might they resist the change? What might they have to lose and how might their support be gained?
- What steps can the IC planning group take to expand people's spheres of awareness and responsibility beyond the concerns of their own units?

Articulating the Change Initiative

- Remember the external and internal forces or pressures propelling change in other campus units. How can the LC initiative be articulated to appeal to faculty and staff spearheading other initiatives being propelled by those forces?
- If the initiative articulates an LC as a solution to "problems," which stakeholders might tend to feel targeted as responsible for those problems, and how can their potentially negative reactions be mitigated through consultation and conversation?

In the previous diagram, the middle box was a single unit labeled "Library." Now the middle box in Figure 6.7 represents an array of semi-independent subordinate units occupying the middle ground between the hosting institution and users. To understand this relationship we need to begin with Karl Weick's classic definition of educational institutions as loosely coupled systems.[10] A loosely coupled system can be compared to boats sailing in a flotilla, while a tightly coupled system can be described as railcars rolling along in a train (Figure 6.8). Both the boats and the railcars move purposefully toward given destinations.

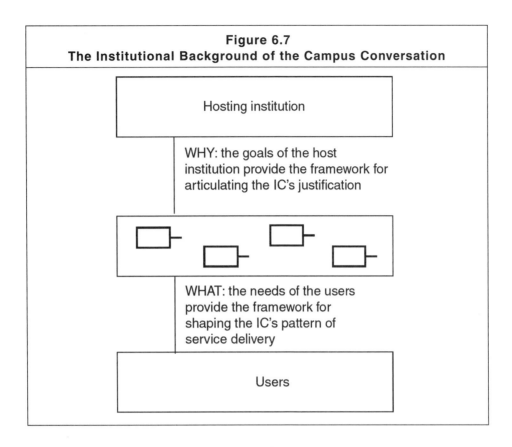

Figure 6.7
The Institutional Background of the Campus Conversation

Hosting institution

WHY: the goals of the host institution provide the framework for articulating the IC's justification

WHAT: the needs of the users provide the framework for shaping the IC's pattern of service delivery

Users

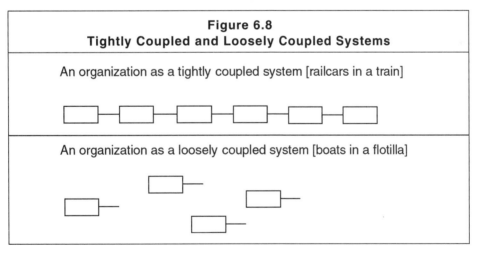

Figure 6.8
Tightly Coupled and Loosely Coupled Systems

An organization as a tightly coupled system [railcars in a train]

An organization as a loosely coupled system [boats in a flotilla]

But the path for the railcars is defined entirely by the tracks laid down by a command-and-control management regime. Workers within each railcar need only concentrate on their internal functions without regard to navigating in relation to other railcars. This type of tightly coupled system retains optimal alignment at all times, but lacks adaptability. By contrast, each boat in a flotilla must constantly exercise a degree of independent navigational control in order to maintain approximate relative alignment. This unit-level navigation is equivalent to the quasi-independent strategic planning functions within the many administrative and academic departments of a large university.

Weick's metaphor of a loosely coupled system forms the logical backdrop for the Strategic Alignment theory as a useful adjunct to use in support of IC/LC planning, as first outlined in "Conceptualizing an Information Commons" (1999), and adapted from original work by Henderson and Venketramen.[11] Though Strategic Alignment originated in the realm of corporate technology planning, it meshes with Weick's view of educational institutions for a number of interesting reasons. First, it proposes *strategic fit* to describe the complex relationship between an individuated unit and a larger loosely coupled system. The IC must find its optimal strategic fit within the library just as the library must find its own within the university. Second, it proposes *functional integration* to describe the interweaving of new technologies with patterns of service delivery. When properly deployed, these technologies enhance the sensing and data-gathering capabilities emphasized by Weick. And, third, its concept of *alignment* speaks to the issue of alliances between the IC and other units, such as the Center for Teaching, Computing Services, and Continuing Education, so important for successful adaptation.

How is alignment different from strategic fit, and why are both terms needed? Strategic fit is a complex, inclusive term that touches on the fully articulated role a unit plays within its hosting organization. Alignment (at least as used here) is the simpler, narrower term, and refers to the unit having its own goals aimed in the same general direction as the goals of its hosting organization. By one shorthand definition, alignment is the unit's direction toward the *goal* of the host; strategic fit is the unit's fulfillment of its *role* within the host. Sometimes the unit's role within its hosting organization may temporarily force it out of simple alignment. To return to the flotilla metaphor, for example, a fuel ship within a flotilla may depart from its simple forward course to periodically refuel the aircraft carrier at the heart of the flotilla. It moves temporarily out of simple alignment to achieve its proper strategic fit within the flotilla, as shown in Figure 6.9.

Imagine a scenario in which a small college wants to experiment with podcasting, at first on a relatively small scale. So the library plans for podcasting of information literacy sessions while the rest of the campus awaits the results of the library experiment. Here, the library departs from simple alignment in a way appropriate to its strategic fit within its hosting organization.

What applies to one unit may also apply to several in collaboration. A flotilla on a voyage of exploration might dispatch a small group of boats on a tangential course to explore a sighting of distant land. The exploratory boats achieve strategic fit by departing from simple alignment to play their proper role in the overall scheme. This contrasts with a tightly coupled organization, where an experimental change in course may require commitment of all

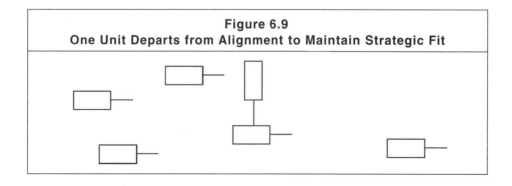

Figure 6.9
One Unit Departs from Alignment to Maintain Strategic Fit

organizational units and resources, and thus cause slower response time or a more cumbersome realignment. Figure 6.10 illustrates these different reaction patterns to change.

The difference between these two patterns in response to change can loom especially large when close cooperation between library and IT departments is essential, and where one department tends to be managed in a tightly coupled fashion while the other is loosely coupled. This can impact very specific components of decision-making and conflict resolution, also affecting more general compatibility of organizational cultures. These issues, which may have first surfaced in the focus group self-study stage, need to be resolved during the campus conversation so that a specific *Memorandum of Understanding* can be included in the next step of project documentation. More general issues of organizational culture between library and IT will be discussed again in the project management section of implementation.

Loosely coupled collaborative change may involve realignment to practices that are very concrete or goals that remain very abstract. In Figure 6.10, units X, Y, Z might be collaboratively exploring use of a course management system to develop hybrid courses, while units A, B, C, D retain their traditional patterns of classroom instruction. Or, X, Y, Z might reorient themselves as "communities of learning," while A, B, C, D retain their traditional identities as academic departments providing instruction.

Weick described the advantages of loosely coupled systems, three of which may be paraphrased as follows: (1) loosely coupled systems can contain subordinate units with sharply individuated identities, permitting a greater number of adaptations and mutations to a rapidly changing environment; (2) these units can then function as sensory mechanisms, feeding information up organizational channels and allowing the whole system to learn and know its environment more effectively; and (3) these units can also function as testbeds for

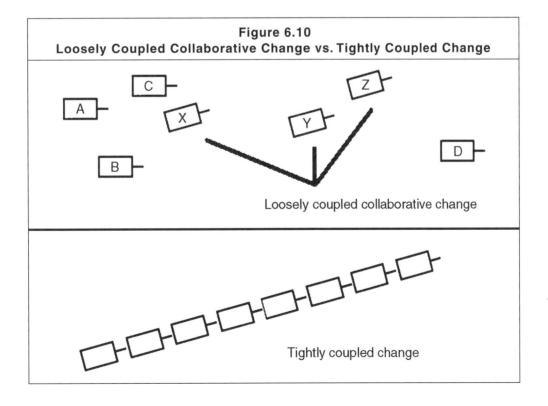

Figure 6.10
Loosely Coupled Collaborative Change vs. Tightly Coupled Change

Loosely coupled collaborative change

Tightly coupled change

experiments designed to prototype solutions without risking an immediate commitment of the entire organization's resources (such as the library podcasting example). Even though the IC is physically within the library, it can represent an experimental departure from alignment. In Figure 6.11, the IC is shown in a posture of isolated change: a subordinate unit reoriented to respond to new challenges.

By contrast, in Figure 6.12, we see an example of the definition of a Learning Commons, where the subordinate commons within the library is part of coordinated collaborative change with one or more campus units external to the library.

The Maricopa papers by Elsner and Tompkins (cited earlier) clearly reflect the philosophy of collaborative loosely coupled change. Commenting on the fact that old models of organizational leadership were typified by "the ruler ruling the ruled" (or what we would call railcars in a train), Elsner stated: "The technology environment Maricopa is used to operating under does not suggest rule, but it suggests empowerment of staff and the dominance of user groups in shaping the information environment."

An effort to manage this campus conversation must also surmount a number of the inherent *disadvantages* of spearheading change in a loosely coupled organization, evident in the general process of initiating academic change, and of particular concern in managing the campus conversation. Figure 6.13 summarizes how Eckel, Green, Hill, and Mallon describe these drawbacks.

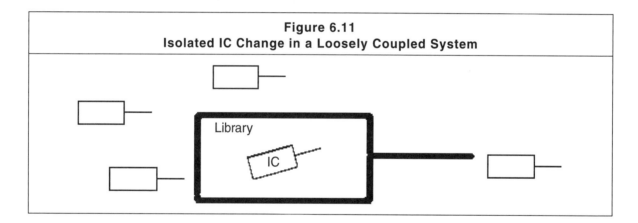

Figure 6.11
Isolated IC Change in a Loosely Coupled System

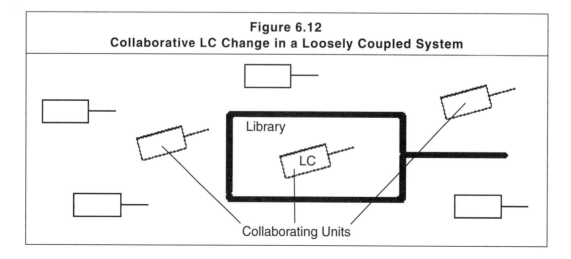

Figure 6.12
Collaborative LC Change in a Loosely Coupled System

Figure 6.13
Challenges to Change in a Loosely Coupled System
"Autonomy and independence complicate the change process, in that different offices and academic departments may operate independently of one another. Local improvisational change may override efforts at organization-wide planning."
"Decision-making can be diffused, with offices and departments not accustomed to the coordinated collaborative work that is sometimes necessary for comprehensive change."
"Effects can be difficult to attribute to causes. The untidyness of university management may result in delayed, confounded feedback, where outcomes of actions are only known after a lapse of time and only after other events have occurred that explain the actual outcomes."

Colleges and universities today face an extraordinarily complex climate of change involving demography, technology, economics, pedagogy, and social policy. Most universities host a number of individuated units that act as agents for interpreting and reacting to this change, including Academic Planning, Institutional Research, Computing Services, Continuing Education, Faculty Development Center, Center for Teaching and Learning, Writing Center, and the usual phalanx of task forces and committees. When turbulent changes in the environment affect the flotilla, one or more of these small boats can adjust course to explore possible options, which, as we have already suggested, might include information literacy across the curriculum, writing/authoring across the curriculum, cognitive immersion learning paradigms such as the "classroom flip," and learning object/IMS implementation, such as D-Space.

As shown earlier in Figure 6.11, the IC can be viewed as such a subordinate unit within the library, whose individuated identity permits special adaptations to the new digital environment. It can then further serve as a sensing mechanism for gathering data about that environment and how students and faculty are utilizing it. And, as shown in Figure 6.12, it can become an LC, a testbed for experimental collaborations with those other campus units supporting instruction and research. This last situation can lead to a very broad scope of IC/LC purpose, such as this proposed by James Duncan: "...a supportive service environment that provides a venue for experimentation, interaction, information and media access, assessment, teaching and learning."[12]

Planning Template Step: Drafting the Project Documentation

In drafting project or program documentation, good strategic planning includes the anticipation of, and even the preliminary integration of, implementation and assessment. Clearly defining the IC's identity from general concepts to specific examples will subsequently guide and shape the implementation process. Planning that has properly delineated such an identity creates a framework that anticipates and integrates implementation by generating statements of shared purpose and vision that in turn help define desired outcomes. These outcomes can then be linked to specific steps or tasks that can be mapped out through tactical planning onto an implementation checklist or timetable as shown in Figure 6.14.

| Figure 6.14 |
Possible Sections of Final Documentation
Institutional background; charge; approach
Mission statement; host organization goals and objectives
Survey results; conversations with users; focus group results
Scenarios drawn from the scenario-building exercises; extrapolate trends from these scenarios—both local and global
Project the commons in those scenarios; scale down the scenarios to envision individual students and faculty making use of resources and services
Broad outline of project budget and project calendar; collaborative structures and Memorandum of Understanding, physical facility plan, service delivery plan, staff training, IT infrastructure
Possible early schematics, draft floor plans, projection diagrams. Mapping the transition from strategic to tactical planning, through project or program management
Mapping the ongoing operational support, through project or program management

A good example of an IC mission statement or description can be found in Case Western Reserve University's planning statement for the IC in the Kelvin Smith Library.[13] The appendix that presents the Information Commons plan begins with a section titled "Concept:"

> An Information Commons environment is designed to foster continued learning outside the classroom. It is a collaboration-friendly environment that lends itself to instruction, consultation and group work. The Commons brings together library resources and research assistance with the latest technology in order to view, create, edit and produce finished products. It is an environment that encourages students to actively participate in and take responsibility for their learning. In the Commons, students have a human support system to help them solve problems, reach new solutions, contribute to a knowledge economy, and thus remain competitive in the changing marketplace.

This is classic "what and why" reasoning, but the CWRU IC plan does not stop there. Even in the "Concept" section, it proceeds to break out, in a preliminary way, certain key points that anticipate the "how and when" tactical planning elements of implementation:

In the Commons space, patrons need to:
- Have access to online and print information resources
- Receive instruction and assistance in selecting and using resources
- Have access to the latest hardware, software, and information tools
- Receive instruction and assistance with technology to produce finished products, whether they be electronic or print
- Have varied spaces for personalized instructional and collaborative learning.

In the Commons space, staff members work in a supportive, learner-centered environment. Across several service areas, they engage in a high degree of partnering and interaction, and need:
- Convenient access between staff areas to support a tiered service model, and to build relationships between staff, and with patrons
- Access to nearby information resources
- Ample space for a variety of information materials and services.

The "Concepts" section concludes with a renewed emphasis on alignment and strategic fit:

"In all, the Commons aims to provide the services, spaces, and staff for functional integration of content, technology, learning, and service delivery. In doing so, the Commons exhibits a strategic fit and alignment with Case and library goals, as well as with the rapidly evolving digital landscape.

The Case Western IC plan then moves to a section titled "How it Works." The "how" element still marks this as strategic planning, but it presents further details in a series of subsections that clearly anticipate the "what" topics of tactical planning: "Commons Activities & Services," "General Space Configuration," and "Visuals/Furniture." The entire "How it Works" section begins with a general overview:

On today's campus, the technology required to complete coursework has moved beyond e-mailing or downloading a file. Students and faculty must understand how to incorporate content and technology with skills in PowerPoint, Adobe Photoshop, web authoring tools, etc. Currently, resources and services necessary to navigate the many layers of electronic information resources and to receive help in using the software and hardware to create or edit work are scattered around the campus. The Information Commons model changes this. The Digital Library, Multimedia, and Language Resource Center provides sophisticated hardware and software, with staff that helps students and faculty make efficient and effective use of it. The Reference/Computer Consultation Desk is located near the Center, and is the focal point for assistance and instruction in using online and print information resources. Computer clusters for patrons are located near the desk so staff can easily move about to consult with and assist patrons while they work. Reference staff, in addition to advising and instructing patrons on selecting and using information resources, also provides basic assistance with many of the most popular computer programs (Word, Excel, PowerPoint, Photoshop, Acrobat, scanning). Student Assistants act as consultants for basic software and hardware issues and serve as back up to reference staff.

The "How it Works" section then becomes more specific and concrete, setting forth bulleted lists of physical and structural components, key interdepartmental adjacencies, staffing levels, and even comments about possible furnishings: "Computer clusters of various sizes (pods, half pods, 2,3,6-units) and shapes (circular, linear, concave, horseshoe, etc., for versatile group movements)." Such specificity may initially seem odd in a planning document, but the narrative moves with good coherence from "Concept" to "How it Works" and is a fine example of how good planning both anticipates and incorporates the basic framework of implementation in a meaningful way. In fact, the bulleted lists from the "How it Works" and following sections would form an excellent framework for a tactical planning document that then would proceed to address the specifics of "how" and "when."

Following implementation, the same feedback mechanisms built into the IC to allow its parent organization to learn about its changing environment can also, if properly designed, function as assessment mechanisms for the IC itself. The strategic planning framework anticipates assessment by proposing standards and benchmarks for those outcomes that can then be structured with feedback loops sending usage data back into the model. The idea is not to limit assessment to one-dimensional measurements. Tactical planning alone tends to result in assessments like the following (exaggerated only slightly for effect): "We said we would set up 200 workstations by July 1st. We actually set up 225 workstations by June 30th. Therefore, the IC has exceeded original specifications and succeeded beyond our wildest expectations." Such an assessment statement fails to tell us *why* 200 workstations were needed in the first place, because tactical planning doesn't normally address broader conceptual what-and-why questions. A good conceptual framework should force you to address the harder questions that cumulatively build to an assessment of whether those 225 workstations have created any measurable impact on desired learning outcomes, and why or why not. The Case Western Reserve University document states: "The social nature of learning and working plays an important role in defining the space and appeal of the Commons." This tells you *why* the IC should include "Computer clusters of various sizes (pods, half pods, 2,3,6-units) and shapes (circular, linear, concave, horseshoe, etc., for versatile group movements)." One can easily imagine a subsequent survey instrument aimed at measuring student use of these clusters that could both help university researchers learn more about social learning habits among students while also forming the basis of an internal IC assessment tool.

A very polished IC strategic plan that anticipates assessment criteria in a rather elaborate way can be found in the consulting report prepared for Pace University by consultants Jim Duncan and Larry Woods.[14] Titled "Creating the Information Commons: Connection, Community, Collaboration," the report first describes how the IC can align the library with Pace University's goals and objectives, as shown in Figure 6.15. This not only addresses the issues of alignment and strategic fit, but articulates how the library should align its resources and services with the priority goals of its hosting institution by meeting the needs of its users. It specifically links IC planning statements with core objectives from the University's Strategic Agenda, and anticipates the fact that these core objectives will ultimately be used to define measurable service-delivery outcomes for assessment and accreditation.

Figure 6.15
Alignment of New IC with Pace University Objectives

- Promote a student-centered environment by developing high-tech instructional settings, collaborative learning spheres, multimedia workstation clusters, and group study places that accommodate diverse pedagogical approaches and learning styles. [Strategic Agenda: Core Objective II—2, 4, 9 & 13]

- Integrate information technology and service delivery by generating a smooth continuum from initial research to document creation and final presentation in a holistic "one-stop service" mode. [Strategic Agenda: Core Objective II - 2, 4 & 9]

- Implement the primary objectives of the new Core Curriculum by facilitating development of students' critical thinking and problem-solving skills, oral, written and visual communication skills, information literacy skills, and technological fluency. [Strategic Agenda: Core Objective I—3a ii, 5b]

- Serve as an incubator for testing and evaluating new technologies, teaching and learning methodologies, and assessment practices. [Strategic Agenda: Core Objective I—1e, 3a ii & iii, 5b; Core Objective II—2]

- Provide a wide range of digital library resources, productivity software applications, and the synergistic expertise of a cross-departmental team of professionals and technical support staff. [Strategic Agenda: Core Objective I—1e; Core Objective II—2 & 4]

- Enhance the quality of the undergraduate experience, promote student retention, encourage interdisciplinary study, and spur recruitment of honors students in the Pforzheimer Honors College. [Strategic Agenda: Core Objective I—3a vii, 3d & e, 5b]

- Promote civic engagement, and cultural and global understanding, by creating a technology environment that ensures equity of access, independent thinking and diversity. [Strategic Agenda: Core Objective I—3a ii, 6d; Core Objective II—6]

The report goes on to identify key tasks such as building bridges among stakeholder partners, developing an IC advisory committee, and developing an IC project team. It also begins to anticipate implementation by noting "what and when" decisions that will need to be made about specific components of the existing library and IT infrastructure, including relocating microfilm collections, reference print collections, writing center offices, and systems offices. Finally it further anticipates assessment by including a statement on "Information Literacy and its Importance to Accreditation Standards," including references to pertinent sections of the Middle States Commission on Higher Education standards for accreditation, and a quote from the ACRL Competency Standards. Duncan and Woods present the following rationale for relating these competency standards to the continuum of services and resources within an Information Commons:

> The Commons offers opportunities not only to integrate focused information resources, research methods and tools into the context of a given academic subject area, it provides just-in-time resources for students to explore and learn in a variety of modalities. The Information Commons is a place where students can demonstrate growth in technical competencies, coupled with improved cognitive skills. These skills are among those required to successfully manage, integrate, evaluate, create, and disseminate new knowledge and information. Within the context of the Information Commons, students also will gain a deeper understanding and appreciation of the legal and ethical issues surrounding access and use of information. The overriding goal of the Information Commons then is to produce information-literate graduates who will be effective civic participants, productive workers, and committed lifelong learners.

The Project Documentation is also the place to present any formalized agreements between or among academic units necessary to the project's success. Chief among these would be a Memorandum of Understanding that sets forth mutual understandings and parameters between the library and IT departments. The following example presents one template that has been assembled and generalized from several specific examples:

MEMORANDUM OF UNDERSTANDING:
THE INFORMATION COMMONS

DEFINITION
A partnership to implement and operate an Information Commons for the University community is hereby established between the University Department of Information Technology, the University Library, the Center for Teaching, the Writing Center, and the Office of Media Services.

DETAIL & TERM OF AGREEMENT
This three-year pilot program includes staffing a central service desk to provide reference and research assistance [Library], support for software applications and hardware utilization [IT Department], and multimedia capture, conversion, and utilization [Media Services]. The agreement also provides for tutorial and instructional services on information literacy and database use [Library], writing composition [Writing Center], instructional technology [Center for Teaching], and technology access [IT Department plus Media Services]. The long-range goal will be to provide a single point of access and referral for all of the information access and instructional technology services students and faculty will require in the future.

GOVERNANCE
An Advisory Committee representing the major stakeholders will provide the Information Commons with general guidance and oversight. The Committee will include representatives drawn from departments specified in paragraph 1, along with representatives from the Faculty Assembly, and the Academic Computing Committee.

(cont'd.)

MEMORANDUM OF UNDERSTANDING:
THE INFORMATION COMMONS *(Continued)*

Direct management of the service will be the responsibility of the Coordinator of the Information Commons, however during the pilot phase, an IC Implementation Team will provide assistance on operational and management issues. The IC Implementation Team and the Advisory Committee will report jointly to the directors of the Univ. Library and the Dept. of Information Technology.

LOGISTICS

The Information Commons will be located in XYZ Library and funded (including salaries, equipment, furnishing, and various infrastructure) through IT User Support. The IC will be integrated into the Libraries' service environment. Staff from all contributing units will work together to provide a user-centered service. Guidelines will be specified to ensure appropriate referrals to related support services in the Library, the Department of Information Technology, and elsewhere on campus.

The Information Commons is projected to begin operation in September 200X with a three-year pilot phase.

ASSESSMENT

In addition to regular operational reporting, a review will be undertaken in spring 200Y and spring 200Z. These assessments will provide all campus stakeholders opportunities to gauge the effectiveness of the pilot, and work with the Advisory Committee in planning for the future of the Information Commons.

(SIGNATURES - SIGNED AND DATED)

Lastly, the project documentation should include at least a selection of any building design schematics and/or floor plans or programming diagrams that have emerged by this point in the process. The level of detail available at this point will certainly depend upon whether one is in a nominal, fast-build, or slow-build situation. In an IC fast-build example, where the commons may be inserted into a renovated first-floor library space that already exists, or perhaps in a wing expansion near the existing entrance, it may be possible to produce a floor plan with considerable specificity, such as the example in Figure 6.16. This example is from the University of the Sunshine Coast, in Queensland, Australia. Photographs of this IC are also included in the CD-ROM that accompanies this book.

In cases where the building conceptualization process is proceeding apace or in a down-stepped mode, more abstract graphical representations may be appropriate at this stage. The architect will likely have already taken the service point flowcharts and building-block diagrams from the projections stage discussed in our previous chapter, and produced more refined schematics. Figure 6.17 is a detail from the floor map produced for the Information Commons at the University of Calgary Library. The complete schematic, along with photographs of the Calgary IC, can be found on the CD-ROM accompanying this book.

Some very effective visuals use 3-D projections of building-block diagrams to impart a sense of space, traffic flow, work flow, and functional adjacencies. Figure 6.18 shows a detail of a floor plan schematic for the Kate Edger Information Commons at the University of Auckland, New Zealand. The complete schematic, along with full floor plans, photographs, and descriptions, can be found on the CD-ROM accompanying this book.

In addition to, or instead of, visual schematics, the documentation may include narrative statements about aspects of key areas projected for the IC. These need not be extremely elaborate at this stage. The goal for organizational planners is to set the parameters and then hire architects and designers to fill in the details. One IC planning report that offers exceptionally clear and concise building description statements is the *Porter Information Commons*

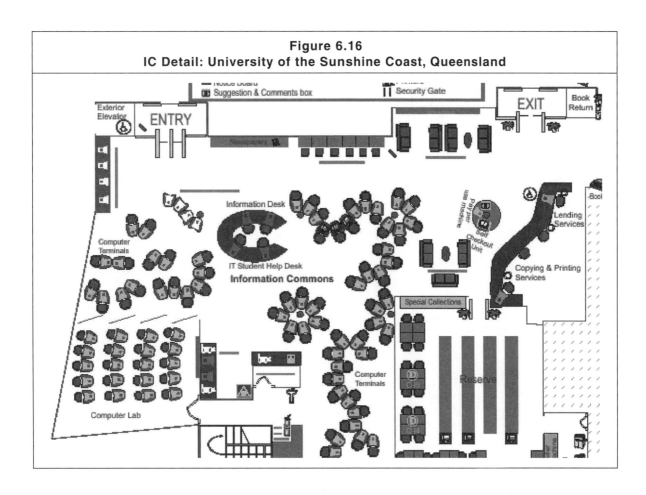

Figure 6.16
IC Detail: University of the Sunshine Coast, Queensland

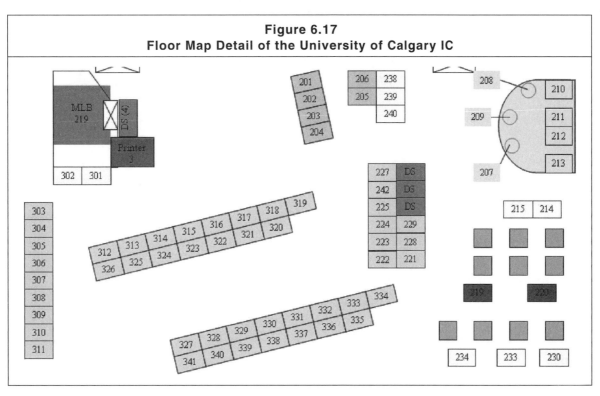

Figure 6.17
Floor Map Detail of the University of Calgary IC

Figure 6.18
Floor Plan Detail of the Kate Edger Information Commons

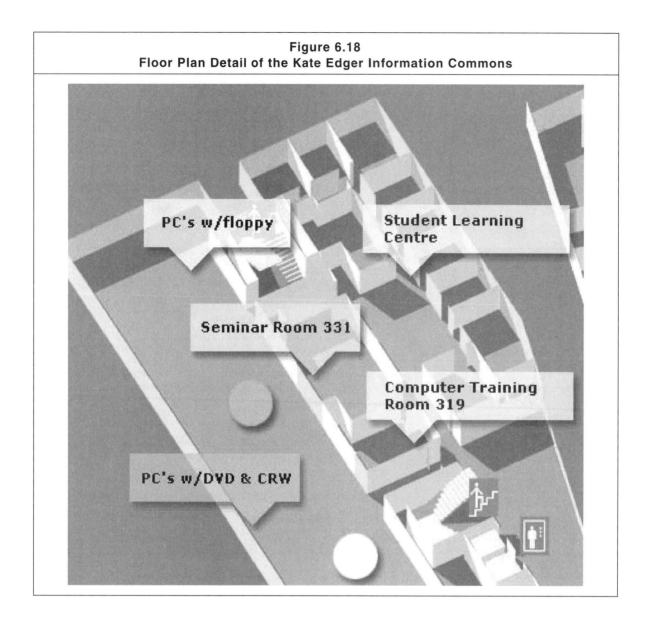

Planning Team Report for the University of Waterloo.[15] After a summary section of "guiding principles," the report lists key elements of their IC model, as shown in Figure 6.19.

After this summary, the report goes on to present more detailed space descriptions for areas 1–6, as excerpted in Figures 6.20, 6.21, and 6.22.

From Tactical Planning to Implementation

Tactical planning has remained a strength of the library community, so it is not necessary here to devise and explain an elaborate original template for moving through tactical planning. But there are some issues you should keep in mind.

Given a choice, it is better to use a tactical planning methodology that comes attached to a larger *project management* (PM) framework already accepted, practiced, or approved by university administration. Most likely, this would come in the form of project management

---

Figure 6.19
Summary of Key Elements of the IC Model: University of Waterloo

1. Computing Hubs with full-service capabilities: workstations (including software), computing peripherals (printers, etc.), carrels, chairs, and infrastructure

2. Express Terminals: workstations (including software), tables, stools, and infrastructure

3. Laptop Lending: laptops (including software), storage charging station/batteries, upgraded wireless

4. Information Desk area: relocation/redesign of the Desk, workstations, electronic notice board and software (for notices, availability of laptops and study rooms, etc.), and lighting renovations

5. Reconfiguration of the Alcove to form a Consultation Room and Printing Release Station Room

6. Group Study: tables, chairs, and electrical and network Single Study: tables, chairs, and electrical and network

---

Figure 6.20
Key Elements of the IC Computing Hub Area: University of Waterloo

- Provide for a minimum of 32 to 36 individual "full-function" computing workstations with sufficient space to accommodate computing hardware and personal accessories such as books, note pads, plug-in headphones, etc.
- This area will include an appropriate number of right- and left-hand workstations.
- Provide visual privacy from other workstations when seated but are still low enough to provide clear views through the area when standing.
- Assess and incorporate appropriate lighting in the area (both ceiling and local) to minimize glare and provide optimum task lighting.
- The area as located and arranged should be easily identifiable and provide for visual cues that advertise function.
- Provide for convenient and aesthetic electrical and network wire management to service workstations and provide for possible patron accessories that require power. (If possible this should be done without the use of power poles to improve visual appearance of the area.)
- Carpeting as required.

Figure 6.21
Key Elements of the Express Terminals Area: University of Waterloo

- Provide for a minimum of 20 to 26 individual computing "express" workstations.
- These workstations should by design provide for a little more space and privacy than the current installation. Use of flat panel displays may be desirable.
- This area will consist of an appropriate number of stand-up, sit-down, right- and left-hand workstations.
- A retractable swing-out seat for the stand-up workstations should be investigated and dependent on cost included.
- Provide for convenient and aesthetic electrical and network wire management to service workstations. (If possible this should be done without the use of power poles to improve visual appearance of the area.)
- Assess and incorporate appropriate lighting in the area to minimize glare.
- The area as located and arranged should be easily identifiable and provide for visual cues that advertise function.

Figure 6.22
Key Elements of the IC Info Desk Area: University of Waterloo

- Design and build new oval/round shaped information desk to provide for better traffic flow in and around the desk and to provide flexibility in providing service from multiple directions.

- Relocate desk closer to the main entrance and offset from center to be in direct line of sight from the entrance while still leaving adequate aisle space between the desk and the new books display.

- New workstations with flat panel displays and hidden system units to lessen visual barriers on the desk and reduce surface area required.

- Provide appropriate electrical and network connections.

- Provide appropriate lighting.

- Provide for a section of the desk to accommodate patrons in wheelchairs.

- Provide for the quick reference material shelving.

- Carpeting as required.

- Installation of large panel information display(s) above desk to provide information on study room and laptop availability as well as upcoming workshops, etc.

---

software that resides on a network server, such as Microsoft Project. PM is primarily concerned with project *implementation*, of course, but many PM products include widely utilized tactical planning components. While most of these PM planning components are not adequate for the type of "how and why" discovery and decision processes needed for IC/LC *strategic* planning, (and hence the reason for a custom IC planning template), they are adequate and practical for the "what and when" *tactical* planning phase that carries the process through to implementation. Most IC implementations involve significant reshuffling of people, workspaces, equipment, and furnishings that have scheduling and budgetary repercussions, and project management software offers appropriate toolsets for tracking and controlling these complex variables during implementation. It simply makes good sense that the tactical planning activities prior to implementation be carried out using the planning component of the *same PM product* that will be used *during* project implementation. In fact, the fifth step of the template, drafting the project documentation, may well include preliminary checklists, milestones, flowcharts, and summaries anticipating the tactical planning/project management framework.

An additional advantage of using PM planning components has been pointed out by Robert Favini, who makes the case that utilization of PM tools and techniques creates an effective way to bridge the institutional cultures of libraries and academic computing centers, which he contrasts in two tables shown in Figures 6.23 and 6.24.[16]

Much of the success of any IC/LC venture revolves around the relationship between these two units or equivalent units. Favini's recommendation to use PM to bridge these disparate cultures serves also as an excellent capsule description of the collaborative library/IT effort required in tactical planning for, and implementation of, an IC:

Improve leadership by adopting formal project management techniques. . . . The library and ACS can be viewed as functional units within the larger organization. . . . In the corporate world, projects are formed with team members from various functional units reporting to a single project manager. Team members are chosen based on how well their skills satisfy the needs of the project.

Figure 6.23
Robert Favini's Institutional Culture of Academic Libraries

- Emphasis on contact with people
- Technology used primarily to accomplish service goals
- Roles of organization members well defined and agreed upon
- The major functions of library work do not vary among institutions
- Librarians are products of a shared educational experience, MLS
- Staff turn-over relatively low
- Female-dominated profession
- Organizational power derived by formal job title
- Reward system is comparable across the industry
- The acquisition of technology driven by suppliers of information services rather than homegrown innovation
- Library traditionally under the Academic Provost with an emphasis on supporting Students and Faculty

---

Figure 6.24
Robert Favini's Institutional Culture of Academic Computing

- Technology is the main driver of services offered
- Change in organizational structure is frequent
- Use of formal project management techniques is common
- Male-dominated environment
- ACS under a Vice President of IT with an emphasis on supporting Administration, Staff and Faculty
- Salaries vary greatly throughout the industry
- Staff turn-over relatively high
- Team oriented focus to accomplish clearly defines goals
- Reward system is flexible, based on short-term performance
- People possessing technical expertise operate "behind the scenes"
- Pace of change is fast

By transferring the use of cross-functional project teams to an academic setting on a regular basis, the library and ACS will be better positioned, from an organizational standpoint, to work together effectively...It wipes out the uneven relationships as the common goals of the project become paramount. Formal written project documentation...can also serve to keep roles and expectations clear.

However it should still be recognized that PM planning software tends to be generic and oriented to commercial or corporate PM environments, not academic tactical planning. Hence some adaptation will be almost always be needed. One way to flesh out such an adaptation is to provide a crosswalk between PM/tactical planning modules and elements of planning documents drawn from existing IC initiatives. For example, a workshop on "Planning Collaborative Facilities in Libraries" prepared for an ACRL/CNI Preconference (Toronto 2003), facilitated by Barbara Dewey of the University of Tennessee-Knoxville and Betsy Wilson of the University of Washington-Seattle, included a "Planning Checklist" handout.[17] This "Planning Checklist" incorporates some strategic and tactical elements but is more directly suited to tactical application. In the examples to follow, brief headings excerpted from this "Planning Checklist" are crosswalked with pertinent content from the "Project Mapping" outline developed for the most widely used PM software package, Microsoft Project.[18] In certain cases where the Microsoft Project (MSP) schema seems unnecessarily cumbersome, such as its breakout of sections on "identifying project assumptions" and "identifying project constraints," key points are consolidated. The goal in these examples is to show how generic or corporate PM software, like Microsoft Project, can accommodate IC and library-specific planning by way of a crosswalk approach.

In Figure 6.25, Microsoft Project's project definition step is crosswalked to checklist sections on preliminary planning and project definition. The Microsoft Project text seems a bit clearer and more specific in its list of elements to be included, but it does not address the inclusion of key partnerships (or stakeholders) as effectively as the checklist. Crosswalking key points from both offers a particularly strengthened overview of IC/LC project definition.

In Figure 6.26, the Microsoft Project corporate lingo of "deliverables" can be misleading,

---

Figure 6.25
Define Project Objectives

ACRL/CNI "Planning Checklist"equivalent: **Preliminary Planning: Project Definition**

Microsoft Project "Project Mapping" key points:
Objectives may include:
a list of project deliverables
measurable results
outcomes
specific due dates
    —for both project completion
    —intermediate milestones
specific quality criteria deliverables must meet
cost limits that the project must not exceed
all project stakeholders must officially agree to the objectives.

---

as it sounds like the production of widgets, and may make a crosswalk to "collaboration agreements" and "service considerations" seem out of place. But in fact, collaboration agreements are most essential when partners envision the co-creation of a framework for deliverables. For example, the library and the academic computing center may agree that the IC will provide a service desk for work-study students acting as IT support assistants. There are two general types of deliverables in this example: (a) a service desk work area equipped and delivered by the library, and (b) student assistants trained and scheduled to be delivered by academic computing. Service considerations such as operating hours and access to facilities also become deliverables; key faculty stakeholders may support an IC/LC project expecting access to certain multimedia studios at certain hours. The suggestion of a crosswalk between definition of deliverables and partnership agreements should be approached in this context. The ACRL/CNI checklist also makes one key point by including "Integration strategies with adjacent units, partners (i.e., referral system, plan)." This is pertinent to the LC's positioning at the intersection of the strategic plans of multiple units, and also to the modeling of the "continuum of service" that is discussed under implementation.

Figure 6.26
Define Project Deliverables
ACRL/CNI "Planning Checklist" equivalent: **Collaboration/Partnership Agreements & Service Considerations**
Microsoft Project "Project Mapping" key points: **Defining the deliverables** tangible as well as verifiable must meet predetermined standards for completion, such as design specifications for a product or a checklist of steps that is completed as part of a service. Deliverables have stakeholders two kinds of stakeholders: —those who receive the finished product or service (students), —those who depend on the deliverable to do their own work (faculty, staff). **Deliverables have standards for completion:** stakeholders must agree on how deliverables will be assessed

There is not enough space to describe how this crosswalk approach works for an entire IC/LC project, so instead, here is a simplified example of a specific subproject: collaboration between the library and IT to provide student technology assistants at a central service desk within the IC. Planning consultant Rudi van den Berg describes how a tactical planning group meets to reach consensus on a preliminary project definition before anything is entered in Microsoft Project. He details a six-step process that is delineated under the following headings:

Step 1 Develop Work Breakdown Structure
Step 2 Develop Organization Breakdown Structure
Step 3 Develop Responsibility Assignment Matrix
Step 4 Define Tasks and Milestones
Step 5 Develop Network Diagram
Step 6 Develop Gantt Chart[19]

The first step of a work breakdown structure (WBS) is detailed in Figure 6.27. The group reviews the project proposal and discusses how to break it down into discrete deliverables. The bottom row in Figure 6.27 identifies six deliverables.

Figure 6.27						
Simple Work Breakdown Structure for Student IT Desk Project						
			Student IT Assistants Project			
Deliverables:	desk	IT install	IT training	orientation	scheduling	assessment

In the next step, the group discusses the organization breakdown structure (OBS). Which units will be principal leaders or collaborators on the project deliverables? Which other units might need to have some contributory input? The OBS should identify each of these units, and if possible, specific key individuals whose involvement will be needed. In Figure 6.28, the planning group has identified individuals in the principal collaborating departments, Library and IT, as well as contributors in the Human Resources office who oversee campus-wide work-study programs, Media Services whose staff will share the same central IC service desk, and the Faculty Center for Teaching who will on occasion also schedule these student IT assistants for their own projects.

Figure 6.28 Organization Breakdown Structure for Student IT Desk Project				
		Library Mgt. Connie Lagost		
HR W/S Office Sue Boylston	**IT Department** David Murphy	**Library/IC** Joe Jordon	**Media Services** Tanya Spelman	**Faculty Center** Howard Marks

The next step is the development of the responsibility assignment matrix (RAM), as shown in Figure 6.29. Here, responsibility for each deliverable from the WBS is assigned to units from the OBS. Furthermore, their levels of relative responsibility as Leader or Contributor for each deliverable is coded "L" or "C." In this example, any and all student orientation and scheduling plans need to be reviewed by the work-study coordinator within Human Resources, so HR is given a "C" role under the orientation and scheduling deliverables. Also, the HR office manages the campuswide assessment program for work-study students at this institution, so the HR office is given an "L" role under assessment, with library and IT listed as "C." The library takes leading responsibility for providing the desk, IC orientation and scheduling, while the IT Department leads in hardware/software installation and the in-depth IT training component.

Figure 6.29 Responsibility Assignment Matrix for Student IT Desk Project						
	desk	IT install	IT train.	orientation	scheduling	assessment
Library	L	C	C	L	L	C
IT Dept.	C	L	L	C	C	C
Media Cr	C	C	C	C	C	—
HR W/S	—	—	—	C	C	L

After deliverables are defined and their ownership levels assigned as "L" or "C," the project team can then detail all required tasks and milestones entailed by each deliverable. The planning group facilitator hangs up flip-sheets around the room, gives each team member a marker, and asks them to write every task and milestone they can think of related to each deliverable. The result will look something like the examples for three deliverables (IT Training, IC Orientation, and Scheduling) shown in Figure 6.30.

Figure 6.30 **Tasks and Milestones for Student IT Desk Project**		
IT Training	**IC Orientation**	**Scheduling**
Define skill-set Select problems and manuals Devise quizzes Post FAQ on website Set up IT 2nd tier help Schedule rolling sessions Assign students to trainers	Define referral expectations Select reference "orienter" Select media "orienter" Schedule IC overview Set up orientation calendar Set up "observer" chair Assign students peer helper	Monitor use levels for current ref desk, IT desk Determine peak IT needs Assign rovers and greeters Set up report-back system Confer with faculty center for out-scheduling

The next step is to lay out tasks and milestones in a network diagram. To design the network diagram, have group members write each task from the Task & Milestones List on a stick-up note. Each note should be placed on a large sheet left to right in the approximate order of initiation and completion. It may be helpful to draw a rough time line across the top of the sheet, ruler-marked for months, weeks, or days as desired. The task notes can then be aligned under the time line as deemed appropriate. Then use markers to diagram any relationships between or among the tasks, with special attention to tasks that have a cause/effect or completion/triggering relationship. Break out parallel line relationships for sets of tasks that can be ongoing simultaneously. Special tasks that represent triggering or completion of a defined deliverable (IT Training, IC Orientation, Scheduling, etc.) may be designated as milestones by aligning notes as diamonds. The result will look something like Figure 6.31.

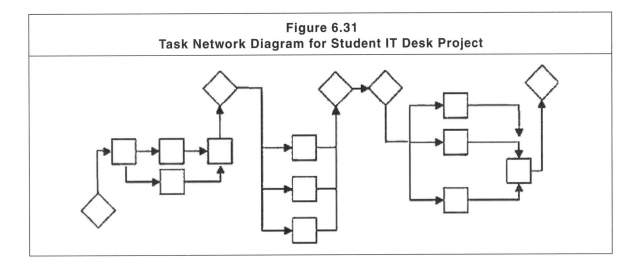

Figure 6.31
Task Network Diagram for Student IT Desk Project

The final step is to convert the network diagram into a more detailed GANTT chart using Microsoft Project or similar software. Each task and milestone is entered, durations are estimated, and start-completion relationships are set up. The result will look something like the screen print in Figure 6.32. This particular example assumes that student IT training continues on a rolling basis even after their desk assignments begin.

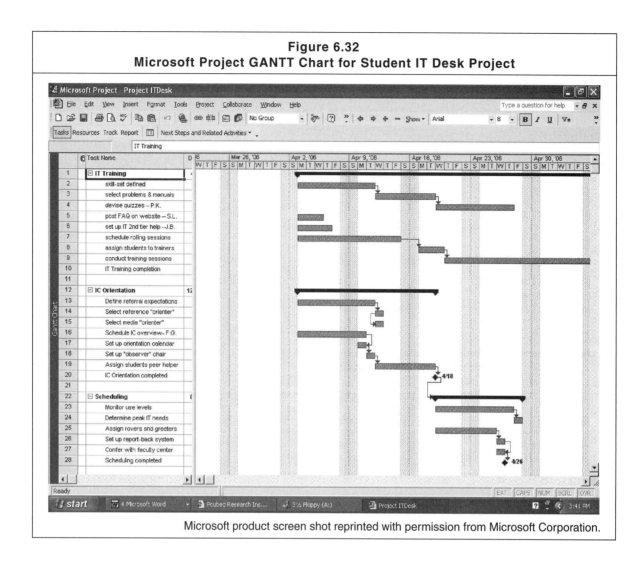

Figure 6.32
Microsoft Project GANTT Chart for Student IT Desk Project

Microsoft product screen shot reprinted with permission from Microsoft Corporation.

In addition to partnership agreements on key deliverables, there needs to be mutual understandings (and sometimes explicitly detailed explanations) of project assumptions and constraints. ICs sometimes involve shared space, blended personnel, and overlapping budgets. The Microsoft Project concept of identifying project assumptions and constraints seems especially important as crosswalked to the checklist sections on space, personnel, and budgets, as shown in Figure 6.33.

Achieving consensus on the specifications of space, personnel, and budget typically bring the project team to the end of tactical planning and to the start of project implementation. Before turning to implementation in Chapter 8, pause to check on special circumstances of institutional history that may confront particular campuses initiating IC/LC projects.

Special Case: IT/Library Administrative or Services Linkages

First, it is important to highlight cases where an actual marriage of library and IT administrative structures might be already in place (happily or otherwise), about to be initiated, or previously attempted and abandoned. There are too many possible permutations of this

---

Figure 6.33
Identify Project Assumptions and Constraints

ACRL/CNI "Planning Checklist" equivalent: Space; Personnel; Budget

Microsoft Project "Project Mapping" key points:

Resource availability and usage
—people
—materials
—equipment

When will key resources be available?
If project depends on collaborators, do they understand their roles and agree to the handoff dates?

Budget:
How critical is cost to project success?
If working toward a known deadline, can tasks be realistically completed with an acceptable level of quality?

Deliverables:
Does list of project deliverables match what students and other stakeholders expect?
If compromises must be made on a deliverable, have stakeholders agreed on what aspects would be compromised first?

Constraints: Schedule, Resources, Scope:
A change in schedule, resources, or scope usually affects the other two and can affect overall quality. Has a process for review of changing constraints been instituted?

---

circumstance to permit blanket recommendations, but it stands to reason (and accords with anecdotal experience) that the IC champion(s) and/or project shepherd will have smoother sailing in cases where there has been a happy marriage or collegial coexistence than where there is or has been a troubled marriage, separation, or divorce. If the institutional history in this area has been a difficult one, the following are recommended for either the focus group or campus conversation stage (or both): (a) personal one-on-one confidential interviews with key IT and library staff involved in previous joint or collaborative projects; (b) a thorough review of the literature discussing library-IT mergings, partnerships, and collaborations; (c) a structure to guide the strategic initiative with stakeholders drawn from both camps; and (d) a narrative in the project documentation that constructively confronts any difficult aspects of institutional history throughout the planning process, and includes lessons drawn from the literature review. Obviously, the Memorandum of Understanding already presented will be a vital part of the final project documentation. Beyond this, the arrangement may be depicted by visual schematics or flowcharts for clearer understanding. Two interesting examples of such diagrams can be seen in Figures 6.34 and 6.35, representing the functional IT/information service units and technical workflow management of the IKMZ-Cottbus, in Germany. Additional photographs of the IKMZ-Cottbus can be found on the CD-ROM accompanying this book.

To illustrate the problems that can arise when library/IT relations have experienced a difficult institutional history, here is the true case of College X, a private, mid-sized college that built a new library within the past ten years. The college planning group included representatives from the library and IT departments, as well as college administration, in meetings with the project architect and design team. As with most such endeavors, this process concluded with a "Library Facility Program" document; excerpts from this document are

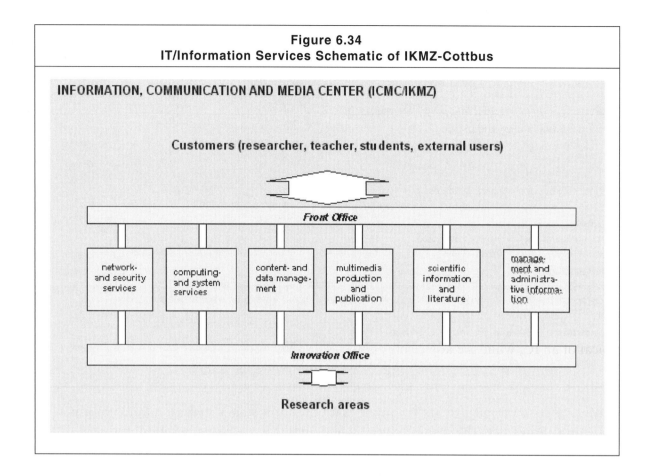

Figure 6.34
IT/Information Services Schematic of IKMZ-Cottbus

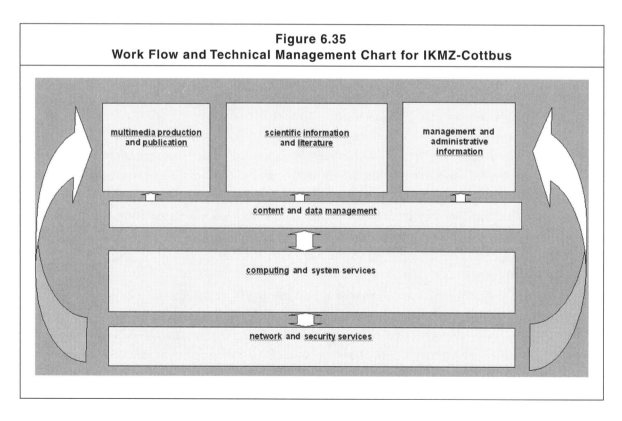

Figure 6.35
Work Flow and Technical Management Chart for IKMZ-Cottbus

abridged and paraphrased here. It briefly examined three models for accommodating the projected heavy traffic to and from student-access technology areas as contrasted with more traditional quiet study and research areas. In this case, an Information Commons option was reviewed and discarded for a very interesting reason: based apparently on a presupposition by the project architect and college administration, the IC model was believed to require an actual merger of library and IT management structures, or at least their complete co-location in the same facility. The particular institutional history of College X made them reluctant to follow such a path, and so the IC was discarded as an option very early in the process. However, the preferred floor-space model that eventually emerged included a so-called "collaboration area" placed midway between a student tech support desk and the library reference desk. Not equipped with technology at first, the area soon drew the attention of students wanting direct IT access near the library entrance, and over time, technology tools and network access points were added, together with an appropriate array of digital resources. Thus, even though an "Information Commons" was initially ruled out by library planners due to definitional issues that seemed to invite friction, the "Collaboration Area" of College X gradually (and rather informally) accrued the physical and digital resources typical of an IC, while the adjacent desks for student IT help and library reference gradually adapted their own patterns of service delivery to provide the human resources also characteristic of a full-fledged IC.

Special Case: TQM Implementation History

Special attention should also be given to cases where Total Quality Management (TQM) has been or is a focus of university or library management (happily or otherwise). While TQM principles actually originated as early as the 1940s, the TQM management movement gained widespread attention, and occasional application, in government and academia in the 1980s and 1990s, roughly coincidental with the emergence of the IC phenomenon. It emerged in a heyday of "management science evangelization" that recapitulated the marketing of earlier systems such as Management By Objectives (MBO). Some of the evangelical fervor was legitimately based on the fact that various management innovations developed within American corporations had sparked high-profile private sector success stories, and became topics of intense interest at home and abroad.

A perception of declining quality of products (such as American automobiles) and services (rude or inattentive behavior by public contact workers) in the 1970s had created a favorable climate for TQM, which stressed the adoption of a philosophy of total quality. Everyone, from top managers to entry-level employees, must "accept the quality challenge," acquire the necessary skills, and assume the responsibility for change to the new philosophy. TQM recognizes that human error is inevitable, but stresses systemization to ensure that poor quality should never reach the level of the customer. An organization should accept that imperfections may occur, but should work to ensure that defective products never reach the consumer.

Inevitably, there were attempts to apply TQM to nonprofit and public sector enterprises, including libraries. However, some researchers who followed the history of TQM implementation cautioned against the hasty application of "orthodox TQM" in public sector and service organizations, including governmental agencies and higher education. James E. Swiss authored a strongly worded article in 1992 that warned: "In its unmodified or orthodox form, TQM is strikingly ill-suited to the government environment. The use of TQM in government has several major problems: insufficient modification for services; insensitivity to the problems of defining governmental customers; inappropriate emphasis on inputs and processes; and demands for top-level intensity that can rarely be met by the governmental culture."[20] Specific objections cited by Swiss include:

Production oversight criteria: TQM originated in manufacturing environments and was applied to quality control systems for production. Swiss comments: "TQM remains much more difficult to apply to services because services are more labor intensive, and they are often produced and consumed simultaneously. This makes uniformity of output more difficult..." It also means that the consumer will evaluate the service in highly subjective ways that may not objectively measure its effectiveness. Throughout the Age of Print, book circulation has been the most easily identifiable service associated with libraries, and its repetitive quantifiable nature led to premature assumptions about the easy applicability of TQM to all aspects of library service delivery. An indirect result may be that in some cases, library-based TQM encouraged the very sort of reductive, just-the-facts-please view of reference service that the IC is intended to overcome, simply because serial fact-delivery was viewed as an aspect of reference work closest to the production of widgets, and therefore seemed a deceptively easy target for TQM oversight.

TQM's central principle is to delight the customer. But Swiss asks: "Who is the customer?... In business, the company can usually choose its own market niche, and thus define its target customers: luxury car buyers, for example, or price-conscious food purchasers. For many public agencies, on the other hand, defining the customer is a difficult and politically controversial issue. For the Bureau of Land Management (BLM), is the main customer the grazing interests, the mining interests, or the environmentalists? If some combination, how much weight should be given to each?" We know that students are delighted by the simplicity and speed of Google searches, and would be further delighted if librarians would do all their research for them. They may not be delighted by information literacy seminars that push them to engage more demanding databases, or by librarians who insist on teaching them "how to fish" rather than delivering (and cooking and serving) the fish.

Not all TQM initiatives in the academic sector failed, by any means, but some did, and it is our observation that when IC planning begins in an organization that has previously experienced a failed TQM initiative, nearly any subsequent management initiative, including the IC effort, faces special hurdles. In some cases, librarians with graduate degrees and years of experience may resent having been placed under the microscope of an intensely administered quality-control system, or harried and understaffed reference units may have been hit by a blizzard of additional paperwork meant to document incremental quality measurements. In some cases, university middle-managers did not use TQM to replace MBO or other earlier management initiatives but awkwardly piled it on top and overlaid them in contradictory ways, leading to an institutional culture of "the overmanaged." One can find a certain inherent hostility in staff who feel like marionettes and fear the IC initiative as yet another "management fad du jour." No magic spell can repeal this sort of unfortunate institutional history, but one reasonable approach is to include IC scenario-building and Potential Futuring narratives that stress the continuum of service and contradict simplistic oversight regimes that place undo emphasis on "delivery of fish." If the library's host institution remains firmly committed to TQM, IC champion(s) may wish to invest the strategic planning process with a recommendation for "Reformed TQM," a modified approach that Swiss and others believe to be more suitable to government and other nonprofit service organizations.

Planning Template Summary

In summary, the IC planning template calls on the planning team to:

1. Complete a self-discovery process, based on reference monitoring, survey questionnaires, and focus group interviews, reporting areas where (a) user needs are not answered or are answered insufficiently; (b) IT resources requested are not available or not properly supported; and (c) referrals are made beyond library walls with uncertain or inadequate results.

2. Complete a scenario-building process that characterizes possible futures, from local to global, that may result in new types of student and faculty information needs and learning initiatives, and that describes these needs and initiatives in the context of actual and potential library IC or LC service delivery.

3. Complete a Projecting the Future Commons exercise that projects a redefined set of library IC resources and services designed to meet the needs and initiatives deemed most likely to arise from one or more of the scenarios, and that maintains optimal alignment with goals and objectives of the hosting institution. Special attention may also be paid at this point to placement of an IC or LC within the matrix of adjustment, isolated change, far-reaching change, or transformation.

4. Complete a campus conversation that communicates the self-study, scenario-building, and Potential Futuring results, and that engages stakeholders in ways that invites their support and collaboration to whatever degree is needed while also replacing any constrained idiosyncratic mental models of libraries with shared mental models of enhanced IC services and resources.

5. Complete the drafting and dissemination of a project or program documentation that integrates the above findings 1–4, and that presents and describes the IC or LC envisioned as the conclusion of the process in a way that communicates the shared mental model and anticipates critical measures of implementation and assessment.

Endnotes

1 Stephens, Cahal, Charles Kirby, Leila Kamal, Kip Ellis. 2004. "The Politics and Process of Change: Institutional Building-Planning Teams." Project Kaleidoscope. Available: http://www.pkal.org/documents/Vol4PoliticsAnd ProcessOfChange.cfm

2 Eckel, Peter, Madeleine Green, Barbara Hill, and William Mallon. 1999. "On Change III—Taking Charge of Change: A Primer for Colleges and Universities." American Council on Education. Available: http://www.acenet. edu/bookstore/pdf/on-change/on-changeIII.pdf

3 "Information Commons Committee: Vision," University of Maryland Libraries. The IC Committee Web page is available at: http://www.lib.umd.edu/groups/infocommons/home.html. The PowerPoint slides are available at: http://www.lib.umd.edu/groups/infocommons/presentation.ppt

4 Mountifield, Hester. 2003. "Learning with a Latte. The Kate Edger Information Commons." University of Auckland. Available: http://www.information-commons.auckland.ac.nz/content_files/publications/educause_article.pdf

5 Wilson, Lizabeth A. 2002. "Collaborate or Die: Designing Library Space." ARL Bimonthly Report 222 (June). Available: http://www.arl.org/newsltr/222/collabwash.html

6 Note: A further issue worth discussion concerns the optimal degree of individuation for sub-units within the IC itself, in this case Media Services, Research Data Services, and Reference Services.

7 Soderquist, Chris. 1999. "The Strategic Forum." In *The Change Handbook: Group Methods for Changing the Future*, edited by Peggy Holman and Tom Devane. San Francisco: Berrett-Koehler Publishers. 77–78.

8 Halonen, Jane S., Leonard W. ter Haar, and George Ellenberg. 2004. "Faculty and the Politics of Change." In *Volume IV: What Works, What Matters, What Lasts*. Project Kaleidoscope. Available: http://www.pkal.org/template2.cfm?c_id=1453

9 Eckel, Peter, Madeleine Green, Barbara Hill, and Bill Mallon. 2000. *On Change III—Taking Charge of Change: A Primer for Colleges and Universities: Creating the Context*. American Council on Education Occasional Paper #3. Section I, [various sidebars]. Available: http://www.acenet.edu/bookstore/pdf/on-change/section_I.pdf

10 Weick, K. E. 1983. "Educational Organizations as Loosely-Coupled Systems." In *The Dynamics of Organizational Change in Education*, edited by J. V. Baldridge and T. Dea. Berkeley: McCutchan.

11 Beagle, Donald. 1999. "Conceptualizing an Information Commons." *Journal of Academic Librarianship*. 25 (March). 82–89.

12 Duncan, James. 2004. "Envisioning the Future of the Information Commons." University of Southern California, Teaching and Learning with Technology Conference. Available: http://www.usc.edu/isd/libraries/locations/leavey/news/conference/presentations/presentations_9-17/UIowa_Duncan1.ppt

13 "Whitepaper: Digital Media Services at the Kelvin Smith Library. Appendix B–KSL Information Commons Plan." Case Western Reserve University. (September 2004). Available: http://library.case.edu/ksl/admin/multimedia/

14 American Library Association, Association of College and Research Libraries. "Information Literacy Competency Standards for Higher Education," Approved by ACRL, 2000. Endorsed by the American Association for Higher Education and the Council of Independent Colleges (February, 2004).

15 "Porter Information Commons Planning Team Report." University of Waterloo. (October 9, 2003). Available at: http://www.lib.uwaterloo.ca/staff/infocommonsdpl/Report.doc

16 Favini, Robert. 1997. "The Library and Academic Computing Center: Cultural Perspectives and Recommendations for Improved Interaction." 1997. http://www.ala.org/ala/acrlbucket/nashville1997pap/favini.htm

17 Dewey, Barbara, and Betsy Wilson, "Planning Collaborative Spaces in Libraries: A Planning Checklist." In *Planning Collaborative Facilities in Libraries*. ACRL/CNI Preconference (Toronto 2003), Available: http://www.cni.org/regconfs/acrlcni2003/handouts.html

18 Excerpts quoted from: "The Project Map: your roadmap to project management." Available: http://office.microsoft.com/en-us/assistance/HA010745311033.aspx

19 van den Berg, Rudi. "Six-Step Proven Path for Schedule Development." Available at www.pcubed.com/Solutions/SolSixStep.asp

20 Swiss, James E. 1992. "Adapting Total Quality Management (TQM) to Government." *Public Administration Review*. 52 no. 4 (July/August). 358.

III
Making Vision Reality

In Part III, Chapter 7 explores public libraries and the Information Commons in relation to role-setting, service definition, and geodemographics. Chapter 8 discusses the IC implementation team, its relation to the director and the two critical tools both will utilize: the project budget and the project calendar. It includes a discussion of how satellite self-managed teams might handle the selection and organization of the physical, digital, and human resources necessary for the IC to open its doors and operate. A section on marketing and public relations presents the IC/LC as an opportunity for "brand divergence." In Chapter 9, Donald Russell Bailey discusses assessment and ideas for preventing certain key operational problems under the rubric "tragedies of the commons." Chapter 10 explores the IC's user community as a shaping force. Ethnographic research is presented as an additional tool for guiding the development of an Information Commons into a Learning Commons. The IC user community as a social network is then considered in reference to cultural commons issues of public domain, intellectual property, and public policy.

7

Information Commons and the Public Library: Special Considerations

Background

While primarily identified with academic settings, the IC movement has gradually gained momentum in the public library sector as well. Public library ICs, like their academic counterparts, have from the beginning looked beyond information retrieval to the larger rubric of "learning centers." But public library ICs face different types of strategic and tactical planning challenges, as their scope of coverage and user profiles are more variable and sometimes nebulous. College and university ICs are strongly shaped by curricula and academic disciplines, and their patrons tend to be sharply defined in their roles as students, faculty, and researchers. By contrast, IC justifications in public library planning documents include frequent references to the "digital divide," and broader descriptions of social demographics, often related to age and income. While public libraries certainly include students, faculty, and researchers among their patrons, the broad aggregate of their user community resists tidy compartmentalization and is probably better categorized by geodemographics. For this reason, IC planning in the public library environment has emerged from a long tradition of role-setting and service definition. Before discussing some practical aspects of public library IC planning, you need to place the issue in its larger social context.

Perhaps the best-known "flagship" IC in a public library is at the Toronto Public Library. Following is an excerpt from Barbara Tierney's extended description and case study of this Information Commons; and note its references to the digital divide and user group demographics:

> The goal of the Information Commons is to connect all Torontonians with access to electronic information. A specific objective is to address the digital divide among the City's population by providing access to computers for those who have no other access. . . . The Information Commons occupies approximately seventy-five percent of the public space on the main floor of 22,000 square feet. There is a total of 150 computers in this area including 42 in two User Education classrooms, 5 in a Digital Design Studio, 7 with adaptive technology in a Centre for People with Disabilities and 5 in bookable group study rooms. Approximately half the Internet access computers are bookable. The other half is first come/first serve.

Recommendations from the Service Model Review Report by the Randolph Group 1999 which looked at revitalizing and redesigning the Toronto Reference Library recommended the development of an Information Commons... The report stated: "There is an opportunity, through the consolidation of existing electronic resources and the addition of new ones, to create an exciting "Information Commons." The first Toronto Public Library Strategic Plan 2000–2003 "Creating the future; Treasuring the Past" included a strategic initiative:" To minimize barriers to access, especially for those separated by the digital divide." The goals were to "introduce more computers" and "Investigate and expand adaptive technologies both in the library and remotely to support access for people with disabilities."

In 2000, initial funding was obtained from the Bill and Melinda Gates Foundation for an additional 6 computers and 2 centralized printers to add to the main floor. In November 2000, an interdepartmental team of staff from all levels developed the concept and components of the Information Commons, including the staffing and operating models, and training. The IC was to be the electronic core of the library including:

- The "Information Connections" Electronic Reading Room providing a direct connection to the library's various databases, the Virtual Reference Library and the Internet. It is an area of approximately 80 computers with full Internet access, chat and e-mail.
- Centre for People with Disabilities with adaptive technology to enable people with disabilities to access library electronic information and collections.
- Personal Computing Centre to provide access to computers with a variety of office software applications for business, preparing presentations and reports, educational and recreation software.
- Learning Centre with two electronic classrooms to enable the public to acquire the skills to participate in the new knowledge-based environment.
- Digital Design Studio designed to offer the public access to leading edge software and computer equipment for applications such as Web design, image scanning and editing documents, photos, negatives, slides and other materials, preparing professional presentations, reports, newsletters and flyers.

The target audiences were:

- Youth primarily 16 to 24 years of age, particularly males who tend to be less frequent library users and senior high school students.
- Older adults and seniors who usually have less access to technology which separates them from the benefits of having access to the Internet and electronic resources of the library.
- Newcomers to Canada who need access to connect with "home" via e-mail and information sources.
- Tourists and visitors to the City of Toronto who need access to connect with family and friends through e-mail and stop at the library as a tourist destination.

In 2001, the Urban Community Access Program (UrbanCAP) grant program for libraries provided a significant addition of 72 computers and two centralized printers and funding for the Digital Design Studio that greatly advanced the implementation of the IC. The Urban Cap project was a Government of Canada initiative, administered by Industry Canada, that aimed to provide Canadians with affordable public access to the Internet and the skills they need to use it effectively to take advantage of the new global knowledge-based economy.

The consultants apparently did their research well; the Toronto Public Library IC has from the start been a resounding public success by any measure.

> The computers were fully occupied from the outset so a line-up system was initiated: A few years later a computerized booking system was instituted for the whole library system. All the computers were put on the booking system for half-hour periods, with the exception of 10 with 15 minute Express service and thirty-four computers on the terrace that remained on a first come/first serve basis with a line-up system for the next available computer. The computers are rarely unoccupied from the branch opening at 10:00 am to closing at 8:00 pm. There is usually a line-up of people waiting for the first available computer from noon to 6:00 pm daily. In 2004, 445,750 individuals accessed the computers in the Information Commons.

Why has the Toronto Public Library IC been so successful? Does its use level represent a successful bridging of the so-called "digital divide?" And if the digital divide is the central concern, might not local governments in times of tight public sector funding more efficiently set up minimally staffed computer labs and allow public libraries to wither on the vine? Or might IC growth and development reshape the future of the public library in America in unexpected ways? These are not mere theoretical questions, but eminently practical considerations that public library managers must confront. It is especially important to begin this part of the discussion with a brief historical review of how public libraries have tried to orient themselves toward independent learners.

Unlike some agencies of government, public libraries did not originate with an overt charge to organize their services by demographic categories. Instead, public libraries emerged with a broad mandate to serve the general population. However, even with the 1854 statement of purpose for a public library in Boston, some social motivations underlying library development hinted a level of demographic differentiation as well as an emphasis on *learning*.

> Why should not this prosperous and liberal city extend some reasonable amount of aid to the foundation and support of a noble public library, to which the young people of both sexes, when they leave the schools, can resort for those works which pertain to general culture, or which are needful for research into any branch of knowledge? . . . We consider that a large public library is of the utmost importance as the means of completing our system of public education.[1]

The statement suggested a linkage between a definition of service and one demographic group, with special focus on young people leaving the schools. This type of service definition clearly figured in early characterizations of the public library as "the people's university." It also conveyed an implicit socioeconomic message, for the people's university concept seems to have been aimed primarily at social classes unable to send their children to Ivy League schools. And the specific inclusion of "both sexes" clearly spoke to the dearth of higher educational opportunities for women during that period. This definition of service also distinguished tax-supported public libraries from the private subscription libraries, such as the Boston Athenaeum and the Charleston Library Society, that had already sprung up in eighteenth-century America.[2] By 1875 nearly 200 public libraries had been established, many with roughly similar service definitions.

However, after their doors were opened, these libraries came to be used by patrons who seemed more interested in reading popular fiction than the weightier works of philosophy, history, and science that would have validated the original service definition. Librarians responded by redefining their service as a gradual process of elevating popular taste. Their reasoning suggested that once patrons came to the library they would be exposed to works of greater merit, a redefinition that reinforced the original socioeconomic concept of the people's university. But by the 1890s, the taste elevation theory had been largely cast aside. There was scant evidence that people reading popular fiction were cultivating a taste for Aristotle. The debate grew about whether public libraries should exclude "inferior" popular fiction, or simply accept entertainment as having social value. Over time, a consensus formed that public libraries should supply readers (re: taxpayers) with what they wanted, a stance that actually represented a significant broadening of the scope of service delivery in response to community input. Over time, this led to a frequently used tripartite definition of public library service: *education*, *information*, and *recreation*. This service definition is still seen in modern public library planning documents, such as the 1995 Mission Statement of the Carnegie Library of Pittsburgh.[3]

What accounts for the persistence and popularity of this seemingly simplistic definition? It is worth noting that these three words have concisely captured both internal structural and external demographic realities. First, the three terms roughly parallel the traditional division of public library print collections into reference (information), nonfiction (education), and fiction (recreation). And as the century progressed, the rise of an information economy and a new retirement class seemed to create further parallels with definitions of service delivery along external demographic lines: educational services for youth, informational services for adults, and recreational services for seniors, as shown in Figure 7.1.

Figure 7.1 Roles and Divisions of Public Library Service Delivery		
Role	**Traditional divisions**	**Demographic**
Education	Nonfiction collections	Children and young adult learners
Information	Reference collections	Working adults; the "information economy"
Recreation	Fiction collections	Seniors

However the inherent fuzziness of these categories complicates their use as effective library planning parameters, due to inevitable overlaps and inconsistencies related to lifelong learning (education for adults and seniors), children's summer reading (recreation for the young), and the explosion of digital information transcending age-group differentiation. Clearly the linkage between role-setting, service definition, and community demographics would need to become more sophisticated, more data-driven, and more analytically complex.

Major steps in this direction were taken in the 1980s with the Public Library Development Program (PDLP) and its work on library role-setting, which culminated in the publication of *Planning and Role-Setting for Public Libraries* in 1987.[4] Designed to guide librarians through the planning process, this manual stressed the relationship between community analysis and the redefinition of library services in the guise of nine possible roles. "Libraries reflect the diversity and character of the communities they serve. Excellence in library service is not a simple matter of numbers. It lies in the 'fit' between the library's roles and the needs and expectations of the community it serves. As communities change, so do their libraries." To achieve this fit, the manual suggested "looking around" activities to gather community information related to demographics, economic conditions, social conditions, and other informational and educational services. The resulting community profiles were then to be matched with one or more roles for the library to undertake. The nine potential roles were conceptual definitions, each of which included a cluster of characteristic services. But interestingly, only one of the roles, *Preschoolers' Door to Learning*, was clearly tied to an identifiable population demographic.

The 1970s saw other trends of significance to this discussion. First, the publishing industry nurtured a growing market for popular nonfiction books, including areas such as self-help, popular psychology, home improvement, health and nutrition, consumerism, and so forth. This wave of popular interest washed over libraries, and in an ironic twist, partly validated the old notion that patrons habitually seeking fiction might someday expand their reading to other subjects. It further suggested that the whole original notion of "taste elevation" may have been a rather silly artifact of Victorian culture. The attention given to the failure of the taste elevation schema may well have masked the fact that a very real pattern of self-directed learning had indeed established itself in public libraries, often on the part of poor urban immigrants. Apocryphal stories began to emerge of anonymous individuals spending years in the business and investment reference rooms of public libraries, and upon their deaths, bequeathing vast fortunes gained through years of library-based self-directed *learning*. Some of these stories were urban legends, but the pattern was unquestionably rooted in actual experience.

The 1980s saw the rise of the movement toward community I&R centers, captured in the PDLP planning process through the role of *Community Information Center*. Library-hosted I&R centers established several critical precedents: (1) they became vehicles of collaboration between public libraries and other agencies; (2) they broadened the use of information resources from the traditional reliance on facts found in books to an awareness of knowledge resources in the wider community; and (3) they reinforced the need for library managers to study the characteristics of their users through a variety of statistical tools, most importantly the U.S. Census.

And of course, the 1980s also saw the mass-market introduction of personal computers, which eventually led to the introduction of geographic information system (GIS) software and geodemographic analysis in library settings. GIS was originally introduced to managers as a tool for studying potential branch locations. This met an important need brought about by the suburbanization of post–WWII America that forced libraries to develop systemwide branch-building projects across entire metropolitan regions. This use was best articulated by Christine M. Koontz, whose work with Dean K. Jue of Florida State University's Spatial Analysis Research and Training Program led to the publication of the *Library Facility Siting and Location Handbook*.[5] But even in a book as specifically premised as this one, Koontz suggested related applications for GIS, especially market analysis to track census data categories that can be associated with library use, including population, sex, race, age, family life cycle, owner-occupied housing, income, education, and vehicles per housing unit.[6]

Public librarians soon felt the ground shifting beneath their feet with the introduction of the Internet. A movement for the establishment of community information networks, or "freenets," rapidly accelerated as a new incarnation of the I&R phenomenon, but with libraries mostly disintermediated; with e-mail and hypertext links among agency Web sites replacing the old laborious processes of telephone referrals through printed interagency directories.[7] Civic network pioneer Frank Odasz, founder of Big Sky Telegraph, provides a retrospective:

> In 1986, the Cleveland Freenet, lead by Dr. Tom Grundner, presented a text-based menu of community information and service options; and offered free text-based Internet access over phone-lines...people could now extend their impact on their communities with the convenience, inherent efficiencies, and the social safety of online communications from their own homes. High quality information from worldwide sources could now be accessible to all, to meet local needs.... Over 100 community Freenets soon appeared with the National Public Telecomputing Network (NPTN) as the non-profit lead organization. But, for NPTN, and most of these Freenets, the grant funding ran out and the lack of a sustainable income caused them to close down.[8]

In spite of the NPTN collapse, the Web brought a new wave of initiatives and "...five main models of community networks appeared, with a certain confusion regarding just what defined a community network, and which emphasis, or combination of features, any given community network represented." Here are Frank Odasz's capsule summary descriptions of the five models.

1. The Freenets

Freenets began with the mission of providing free local dialup Internet access, and creating a public forum for online discussions, to those who would otherwise go without such access. Freenets were community networks dedicated to providing Internet access to citizens in a day when this access was very new and otherwise not available to most citizens. As Internet access became less expensive and more commonplace, Freenets were challenged to refocus their mission from bringing Internet to have-nots, to that of providing some enhanced form of community value and collaborative capacity.

2. The Community Web site

When the WWW appeared, bringing easy-to-use graphical web pages, many people viewed the collaborative text-based Freenets as obsolete text-based systems. The new model of a community network was a community-sponsored web archive of graphical web pages, with hyperlinks to resources from community organizations and businesses, and it made great sense! But one-way billboards of information had little impact on community collaborative capacity. It was not unusual to have a community network with no specific communications component, except for posting e-mail addresses, despite the availability of free web conferencing tools. Confusion often resulted from multiple city Web sites appearing in a single city, as to which was the official city Web site.

3. Community Learning Centers, also called Community Technology Centers

These consisted of a physical computer lab for training community members on the use of computers and Internet by providing computers and Internet access to those who would otherwise have access to neither. While such centers were, and are, certainly necessary, often there was/is no real online community network, community interaction component, or use of online learning. Many community networks, however, created such centers to provide training for citizens. Opinions differed as to what "community curriculum" would most benefit citizens.

4. The Community Education Network

School, or college-based, systems were created to specifically provide online training and instruction regarding use of computers and Internet, and other topics. Such systems attracted primarily educators and perhaps an educated subset of the community. It was presumed that developing online collaborative skills was something that needed to be learned. Issues surrounding the appropriate role for, and effectiveness of, online learning, continue to be debated!

5. The Community Public Forum

After the WWW appeared, this was the rarest model, ironically the model of the original Freenets, dedicated to creating a public forum for discussion and was based primarily on supporting civic collaboration through Web-based text systems, or a combination of both Web-based and older text-based systems.

However, the commercialization of the Web during the 1990s, and the entrance of major corporate players undercutting small local Internet Service Providers (ISPs), eventually caused the freenet movement to lose much of its initial social and political momentum. At this juncture, public library managers found themselves seemingly adrift in a newly competitive information marketplace. Yet, at the same time, the decline of the independent freenet movement appeared to offer public libraries an important window of opportunity. With the Web facilitating the formation of virtual communities of interest independent of any geographical location, the need for library service redefinition seemed more acute. But would geodemographic analysis be of any further use in this environment, as the information-seeking behavior of users appeared to migrate from physical to virtual environments?

During this volatile period, two significant research projects attempted to chart the potential future course of public libraries. With funding from the W. K. Kellogg Foundation, the Benton Foundation undertook a major opinion survey targeting both library managers and the public.[9] The results reinforced the continued importance of geodemographic analysis on two fronts. First, the library manager respondents stressed the importance of sharpening the library's competitive edge, suggesting that libraries must evaluate their roles and functions like businesses, sizing up the competition and opportunistically seeking out niches. Second, it was found that public respondents' expectations of libraries varied significantly, and these variations were found to be *strongly related* to demographics of age, race, education, and income, confirming that the typical public library does not serve a monolithic community but serves multiple constituencies. Service definition is vital in such an environment, since the information needs and interests of multiple constituencies may evolve, grow, and mutate independently of one another, sometimes converging or diverging, requiring continual recalibration of public awareness and programming.

The public library community was also influenced by a summit conference of invited library decision-makers and technology experts from throughout the United States and the United Kingdom convened by the 3M Corporation. Dubbed "Vision 2008" by 3M, the group served as an industry think-tank during a three-day meeting where summit attendees attempted to map the next 10 years of the library industry and develop a shared vision for possible end-states representing the library of the future.[10] According to their rankings, participants at the November 1998 summit concluded that the "best" future for the library industry would be a combination of end-states, where libraries would be the information managers for the public offering a wider diversity of services, defined by market analysis. Service diversity would parallel an increased acceptance of social diversity, again as an acknowledgement of multiple constituencies within a physical community. Fees might be charged for certain services, and revenues generated would be reinvested in facilities, staff and services, making libraries less dependent upon tax revenues. The success of this library of the future would be measured both in terms of growth in patrons and services. Here again, library managers addressed the topic of service redefinition, and the issue of selective fee-based delivery added urgency to the need for demographics related to income and education, community market niches, and ongoing assessment of private sector competition.

Lastly, unexpected conceptual support for geodemographics surfaced through the very manner in which the corporate cyberspace boom temporarily turned into a partial bust, as major corporate players suddenly found their e-commerce endeavors to be on uncertain footing. Merrill Lynch, for example, ran advertisements touting the use of their walk-in offices even as they still pitched online investment trading. It came to be called the "clicks-and-bricks strategy," where virtual and physical locations served to leverage one another, and where the key to success appeared to be strongly defined services that were clearly branded and identifiable to customers across that conceptual boundary.[11] Suddenly, geodemographics became relevant again in an entirely new context, as information providers studied the socioeconomic characteristics of the digital divide. If "clicks" pertained to constituencies and "bricks" pertained to communities then the charting of potential relationships between the two became crucial. And of course demographics played a prominent role in the selection process for new library-based computer learning centers sponsored by the Gates Foundation.[12]

The Gates Foundation and the Digital Divide

In the report *Toward Equality of Access*, sponsored by the Bill and Melinda Gates Foundation, it was reported that

> ... public access computers are now available in more than 95 percent of the nation's public libraries. More than 14 million Americans ... regularly use these computers. ... Between 1996 and 2001, library visits increased more than 17 percent, a trend partially attributable to the availability of computers with Internet access.[13]

These sorts of numbers dramatically outpace the quantifiable outcomes of earlier independent freenet initiatives described by Odasz. In a sense, this sequence of events parallels what we saw in our discussion of the original visions of the virtual commons advanced by Harlan Cleveland and Robert Lucky, and the later growth of the physical commons in academic libraries. Independent freenets initially reflected the assumption that the virtual commons would need no meaningful physical component or counterpart. But just as academic libraries began repositioning themselves to fill the growing need for the physical commons, so to it became increasingly clear that community needs for online learning "anchors" gave public libraries an important role to play in hosting the physical commons as an access point and *learning conduit* to the virtual commons.

But why have physical commons prospered in public library environments, rather than taking the form of the stand-alone "public access terminals" envisioned by Robert Mingioni, or the independent Community Technology Centers described by Odasz? The answer can be found in a deeper understanding of the digital divide provided by Warschauer's reasearch, and its unexpectedly subtle and complex linkages to the nature of situated learning. Early studies of the digital divide were starkly drawn and, in retrospect, simplistic. A 2003 study from the Pew Internet & American Life Project provides a more nuanced description of the divide today:

> ...a large number of responses indicate that *barriers to access* and *lack of skills* are perceived as obstacles to Internet use. Forty-six percent of non-users indicated that "the Internet is too complicated and hard to understand," while another 48 percent indicate "cost" is a reason they are not online.[14]

We would agree that the Pew findings suggest that the digital divide cannot be addressed by the simple infusion of IT onto a blank canvas; the skill and cost barriers show that physical, social, and human resources supporting IT introduction are all critical. As shown by this brief historical review, the public library began in America as an idealistic movement to enable a "people's university," and while it has gone through periodic adaptations, this theme has continued to underlie its emerging role as host for the physical commons. And just as the IC continuum of service has paralleled ICT literacy in academia, so too the data suggest that ICT literacy skills must converge with the physical commons in any attempt to bridge the digital divide among the general population.

In his article "Reconceptualizing the Digital Divide," Mark Warschauer offered case studies of failed attempts to "plunk down" stand-alone computer labs in India, Ireland, and Egypt.[15] In each case, the IT infusion occurred a priori, set apart from existing social systems of interpretive coaching or content. In spite of the widely different cultural environments, the three projects failed in notably similar ways, and Warschauer links their failures to a failure to integrate IT access with ICT literacy and learning. He finds parallels between ICT literacy and print literacy, a comparison that holds significant implications for libraries. He suggests that literacy needs to be understood as a set of social practices rather than as a narrow cognitive skill.

The stand-alone public computer lab, deprived of the library's uniquely supportive culture of service delivery, its assembled knowledge of media resources, and its I&R linkages to social resources, risks the very type of failure Raschauer documents in India, Ireland, and Egypt. "Simply providing an individual with access to computers is not enough to bridge the digital divide," agrees the Gates Foundation report; "the skills and knowledge to use information technology effectively are equally important."

Discussions of IT-centered library facilities seem invariably to focus on the specifics of the technology, but the specific technology baseline has become relatively well established and even, in many respects, standardized. The key questions now revolve around how the library assembles and organizes (or reorganizes) its physical, digital, human, and social resources in support of those who, within specific virtual constituencies of interest or specific geographic communities, use its technology in pursuit of learning and knowledge. Public library environments, through their legacy as institutions of public education, are uniquely well positioned to provide these contextual resources, either directly through librarian consultation, or indirectly through interpretive knowledge media. "Americans are accustomed to asking librarians for help and answers," concludes the Gates report.

> Nearly two-thirds of computer-using patrons report that they ask librarians for help when they have a problem with library computers. Importantly, the emotional barriers to Internet use referenced in the Pew study—such as fear or misconceptions about difficulty—can be overcome with a helpful, trained librarian.[16]

Yet the potential is even greater for, as the Toronto Public Library's Digital Design Studio shows, libraries can host centers for community learning that reach well beyond basic skills instruction. Collaboration between public and academic libraries may prepare the way for a time when motivated self-directed learners at public library ICs may consult with library staff to access and download multimedia learning objects from academic repositories like D-Space or MERLOT. That type of collaboration again moves beyond the transition from Information Commons to Learning Commons.

If you agree that that ICT literacy instruction "...is most effective when it involves content that speaks to the needs and social conditions of the learners," then it becomes vitally important to understand the characteristic needs, interests, and social conditions of the communities utilizing libraries that host ICs and LCs. The following case study clarifies how geodemographics can be used in this way.

Case Study: The Charleston Project

While GIS is most frequently used for new facility siting, the Charleston County Public Library GIS project actually began after a library building program was well under way. Charleston County had operated a main library and small neighborhood branches for decades, but surging economic and population growth dictated further systemwide expansion. A consultant had been hired and worked with library administration to develop a plan for building four large regional branch libraries at carefully selected locations around the metropolitan area. Service redefinition was part of the concept, as a tiered model of service delivery was viewed as most appropriate to a system encompassing one main library, four proposed regional libraries, and numerous existing neighborhood libraries. The new regional libraries were seen as offering an intermediate level of service between main and neighborhood libraries. But how would these tiered services be defined?

Regional branch managers, hired well in advance of branch openings, worked with the consultant's report to compile and evaluate a large body of community and demographic data for analysis. The facility siting process proved to be highly successful, with all regional branch libraries meeting immediate and widespread public acceptance within their respective communities. However, forecasting levels of staffing proved more problematic, as introduction of new technology brought new complexities to old position descriptions.

Levels of complexity are closely related to the particular information needs and expectations of residents being served. You need to further explore the distinction between facilities oriented toward *communities*, and services oriented toward *constituencies*. This distinction implies that while facility siting might well be based on community analysis, service definition and staffing projections should be based on *constituency analysis*. As the Benton Foundation study indicated, patron needs and expectations vary significantly based on demographics, reflecting a complex and variable mixture of constituencies within any given community. Any best-case staffing scenarios generalized from multiple unidentified physical locations must inevitably gloss over crucial details and differences. In summary, regional branches will see greater proportional workload due to their role in a tiered system involving referrals from neighborhood branch libraries, because their larger service areas by definition will encompass a wider variety of constituencies with varying needs.

As library managers reviewed the population data that had been gathered by and for the consultant, they determined that further GIS analysis was in order, and that the study would attempt to calculate ratios of library users and nonusers by comparing household addresses found in the library patron registration file to all valid household addresses derived from local government property records. Because the four new regional library openings had sparked great community interest and many new patrons, the goal was to see what might be learned about library users and information constituencies from a mass review of library registration records contrasted with known demographic data about regional and local population subgroups. GIS would be the tool of choice to relate the library users to the demographic characteristics of the population at large.

First, GIS consultant Fred Phillips, then with the Office of Applied Technology at the College of Charleston, selected and captured 250,000 library patron records and matched them against the transaction file, selecting all library cards issued in the prior three years, as well as all those issued in earlier years that had been used at least once after 1995 and were therefore "active" in the library patron roster. Personal names were replaced with random variables to protect individual privacy. It was decided to exclude records that could not be assigned to full-time residents: nursing homes and hospitals, ships at sea, fire stations, college dormitories, etc. Since more than one library card could be issued within a household, or to different tenants at the same location, a file of unduplicated addresses was then created. Address fields were standardized and matched to census master address files to identify addresses in neighboring Berkeley and Dorchester Counties. Remaining addresses were taken to be residents of Charleston County.

But the available census master address file was from 1990, already years outdated. Therefore Phillips later matched addresses against an updated Charleston County street address file based on the Assessor's parcel identification system. Using the land use codes from the Assessor's parcel file, he (1) eliminated nonresidential addresses (people taking out library cards and using their business address); (2) matched residential addresses to Assessor's property code fields to account for multiple units at the same street address (apartment complexes) or other residences that do not appear on the real property rolls (public housing which is not taxable, mobile homes which are considered personal property because they can be transported from place to place, etc.); and (3) developed and mapped ratios of utilization comparing number of library cards to number of residential units. What emerged was a database of active library users that offered both greater granularity of detail and greater sensitivity to changes in population patterns than the census itself. Maps could be generated from this database in response to specific queries related to management needs.

The justification for using the Assessors' file was based on a simple assumption: In our culture, a person's principle residence is typically seen as the single most telling statement of that individual's station (or transitional phase) in society. For most people, home ownership is the principle vehicle of investment and financial stability. And persons investing in homes typically do so through the offices of professional Realtors, who share a national industry-wide consensus that the three most important elements of housing value are "location, location, and location." In this environment, the continued importance of geodemographic analysis as a tool to understand the distribution of constituencies among the communities that are served clearly deserves further exploration.

Library use of market research tools such the PRIZM Lifestyle Segmentation System by Claritas can unearth interesting generalizations about constituency and community characteristics. For example, entering the zip code for the Charleston suburb of Mt. Pleasant, S.C., resulted in retrieval of five characteristic lifestyle segments from PRIZM, as shown in Figure 7.2. (details not updated from the 1990s).

Figure 7.2
PRIZM Lifestyle Segmentation for Mt. Pleasant, S.C.

Description	Age	Income	Watches	Reads
Boomtown singles	18–44	$36,600	*X-Files*	*Rolling Stone*
Low income retired	65+	$20,000	*700 Club*	*Discover*
College town singles	18–34	$19,700	*Friends*	*Glamour*
Affluent sunbelt retirees	55+	$41,800	Travel Channel	*Modern Maturity*
Upscale executive families	45+	$67,800	*Frasier*	*Bon Appetit*

Because PRIZM retrieves such data based upon census characteristics, the generalizations it draws must inherit certain weaknesses of census methodology as well as its strengths. Obviously, the 10-year data cycle results in a downward curve of reliability past the midpoint of each decade. And census tracts themselves can be blunt instruments for geodemographic analysis related to focal points of service delivery, such as outreach programs, kiosks, and bookmobile routing. The methodology addressed both of these weaknesses by incorporating local records based on the annual tax collection cycle for greater currency, and maps generated from a parcel-level GIS system for greater granularity.

Such granularity becomes important when one recognizes the very different service definitions appropriate to segments such as "college town singles" and the "low income retired." These two lifestyle segments show an almost identical income level, and therefore similar purchasing power for residential property. But their demands upon libraries clearly must be differentiated, with service definitions varying accordingly. Similarly, the analysis indicated that the one small neighborhood branch already located in Mt. Pleasant was situated in an area serving both "upscale executive families" and "affluent sunbelt retirees." This overlap is not unexpected, given their equivalent purchasing power, but clearly these are two constituencies whose interests in children's services might diverge significantly. And to the immediate point of our discussion, the most likely segment of the Mt. Pleasant community to be on the far side of the digital divide would be "low income retired."

Beyond the issue of the actual Charleston database lies the broader issue of what *could* be gleaned from a library registration file if library managers made a concerted effort to build such files as part of an ongoing feedback mechanism for planning services and collections. What questions might be included? How would privacy be protected? What about optional user preference profiles similar to those created by Amazon.com? What can be learned from other niche marketing initiatives in the private sector? Such questions need to be asked in the context of a systems analysis approach to the entire spectrum of community information resources.

The Age/Service Grid

Along with the database project, several regional and neighborhood branch managers both within and beyond the Charleston system were queried to gain their subjective insights into levels and definitions of services at their locations, and for any intuited or perceived relationships to demographic characteristics. The sample was too small to constitute a scientifically valid study, but the results were interesting and pertinent to this discussion.

While comments were made about perceived relative levels of income, education, and home ownership as related to overall library use, none of the respondents readily correlated these factors with specific definitions of service delivery or library roles. Only one demographic factor correlated consistently with service definition across all branch locations, and that factor was age. This correlation emerged from interviews even more strongly than anticipated, and resulted in a draft of what came to be called the Age/Service Grid. Figure 7.3 shows the Age/Service Grid as formulated through branch head interviews. It is not an exhaustive list, but represents both real and potential services that branch heads listed as being "likely to succeed" within age-group categories. It deliberately is presented in an unrefined state, because the goal was to capture the intuitive insights and spur-of-the-moment thinking of library managers.

These interview results also led us to conclude that the tripartite service definition of education, recreation, and information still held significant meaning and perceived value for library branch managers, but needed to be elaborated within a framework of service priorities. The result of this elaboration is shown in Figure 7.4. It effectively summarizes the fact that all three broad age groups use public libraries for all three service categories, but that (in the experience of library managers) the three service categories tend to shift in relative importance from one age group to the next.

In summary, the library managers we interviewed tended to agree with the PRIZM approach that generates lifestyle segments based primarily upon age, but seemed ambivalent about secondary or tertiary segmentation based upon income, education, etc. While income may be a strong demographic predictor of overall library usage, our study found some reluctance to use it as a framework for service definition in the minds of library managers. We

Figure 7.3 **The Age/Service Grid**	
0–4 yrs	**5–14 yrs**
Preschool story time	Computer literacy: Internet, IT
Links to daycare center activities	Links to school libraries
Programs: children w special needs	Early Science projects
Programs: HeadStart in reading skills	Statewide summer reading programs
Reading is Fundamental	Links to TV and movies
15–24 yrs	**25–44 yrs**
Gifted & talented, special needs	Skills/job change/career planning
Study skills, homework helpline	Distance learning/recertification
College planning, test taking (SAT)	Business & consumer reference
Multimedia, CD, video	Investment seminars
Dropout prevention, GED	Tuition & retirement planning: 401 k
Link: public & academic libraries	Parenting/family law/divorce
45–64 yrs	**65+**
Retirement planning	Health care/medical information
Financial planning/estate planning	Wills, insurance, power of attorney
Readers advisory service	Genealogy
Hobbies/recreation	Travel-related programs
Travel-related programs	Hobbies
Tax assistance	ElderHostel, continuing education
Community activism	Political activism

Figure 7.4 **Service Definitions and Demographics: Perceived Priorities**			
	Children & youth	**Working adults**	**Retired seniors**
Priority 1	Education	Information	Recreation
Priority 2	Recreation	Education	Information
Priority 3	Information	Recreation	Education

reached similar conclusions, for the most part, about ethnicity and education. While library branch managers tended to *implicitly* acknowledge and accept the significance of income segmentation, their reluctance to *explicitly* factor it into their planning may be due to historically egalitarian definitions of public library service delivery. We also interpreted this to mean that the broad age-group prioritization of service definitions would be seen as holding across income categories, but that the particular *types* of educational, informational, and recreational resources favored within each category might secondarily correlate with income. For example, "low income retired" and "affluent sunbelt retirees" occupy the same general age category, with both constituencies sharing habits of recreational television viewing. But their specific recreational viewing preferences appear to differ (*700 Club* vs. Travel Channel) in ways roughly correlated with income.

Future IC Models in Public Libraries

The successful installations at Toronto and elsewhere suggest that ICs and LCs do have great potential in public libraries. But because the user community is more diverse and amorphous than in academic libraries, the positioning and branding of public library ICs may become even more significant. Building on the success of the Gates Foundation initiative, it may be that the public library community should continue to look seriously at three of the five original models of the "community information network" as described by Odasz in *The Community Technology Center*, *The Community Learning Center*; and the *The Community Public Forum*. The reason these original models failed to take hold to the degree their proponents originally envisioned was arguably due to the fact that they were simplistically forecast as purely virtual entities. In other words, the public freenet movement replayed the same script that Harlan Cleveland and Robert W. Lucky had written for the virtual Information Commons, and assumed that there would be little or no need for physical, tangible anchors or access points to this new digital world. However, one can see potential for a library-based *physical commons* that combines the functions of Community Technology Center, Community Learning Center, and Community Public Forum, with public librarians selecting, organizing, and interpreting the physical, digital, human, and social resources necessary to support them. Figure 7.5 matches resources to roles in IC community-building models.

Some specific examples follow. In my experience, there is a sizable population of adults still uncomfortable with, yet very curious about, many areas of modern technology, with examples including digital photography, digital video recording, audio and video downloading, and a confusing array of optical media formats. ICs that function as Community Technology Centers can play a role both by loaning devices, hosting user groups, and holding new technology overviews. ICs embracing the role of Community Learning Centers can collect a wider range of knowledge media, hosting educational gaming events, and explore ICT literacy volunteer networking following a model roughly akin to that established by Laubach adult literacy volunteers for peer teaching in basic adult literacy. And while many hold the superficial opinion that every community organization that wants a Web site can easily produce one, anecdotal evidence suggests that this is often not the case. Small volunteer

	Technology Center	Learning Center	Public Forum
		Figure 7.5 **Matching Resources to Roles in IC Community-Building**	
Physical	Powerful CPUs Loanable devices	Knowledge media; guides to online curricula	Audience feedback devices; meeting rooms
Digital	Advanced productivity software	Online user guides Curricular navigation; learning objects	News sources, community-building
Human	IT tour guides; peer networked troubleshooters	Coaches, tutors, guides	Guest speakers; Current awareness programs
Social	User groups; community IT outreach;	Peer learning & support, fashioned around adult literacy models such as Laubach	Advocacy contacts; Local history digitization

organizations, such as community garden projects, frequently struggle to design, produce, and upload functional, attractive Web sites. Library-based ICs can engage in community-building by hosting skills sessions in small-organization Web site production, and in some cases, perhaps even make server space available.

The adjacency or fusion of a Community Technology Center and a Community Learning Center could be organized around the modalities of Mobile Learning, Connected Learning, and Visual/Interactive Learning, as follows:

Mobile Learning
Tablet PCs
Laptops
Mobile phones
Wireless keyboards/mice
PDAs/iPods
Digital cameras

Connected Learning
Wired computing
Wireless-enabled laptops/tables PCs
Internet-enabled PDAs
Mobile phones
Assistive technologies

Visual and Interactive Learning
Video conferencing
Video streaming
Image projection
Interactive whiteboards
Voting devices
Plasma screen information points[17]

Public access to such a rich array of conduits and devices requires careful application of policies and procedures. Following are the pertinent policies and procedures applied by the Virtual Village in the headquarters building of the Public Library of Charlotte and Mecklenburg County.[18]

Figure 7.6
Public Library of Charlotte and Mecklenburg County Virtual Village Use Policies

Virtual Village Use Policies

The following policies for use of the Virtual Village have been established to insure that all our patrons will have equal opportunity to use these resources:

1. For young adults, ages 13 to 18, computers are available with prior written permission from the parent. Children 12 and under may use the computers located in the Children's Department.
2. Computers in the Virtual Village are available for same day reservations or on a walk-in basis as space permits.
3. Patrons may stop in or call to reserve a computer for a one-hour time slot. Patrons may use a station for one 1 hour period per day, either walk-in or reservation, which must be in one consecutive session.
4. If a one-hour period does not exist, the patron will be offered whatever space is available as their turn for the day.
5. There is a 10-minute grace period for reservations. If you do not arrive within this period, your computer will be offered to someone who is waiting.
6. Installation and use of outside software, CD-ROMs, diskettes and other items is prohibited. The only exception is the Software Exploration Station.
7. **Copy Charges:**
   - Black & White prints are ten cents each.
   - Color prints are $1.00 each.
     Only Library supplied paper may be used.
8. No documents or files can be saved to the hard disk or network server. Patrons should save to their floppy or print out their work each day.
9. **Preformatted disk Charges:**
   - Floppy diskettes are $1.00 each.
   - CD-Rs are $1.00 each.
   - CD-RWs are $2.00 each.
10. Staff is available to advise patrons in the use of the equipment and most applications. Many applications require the user to have extensive training or experience to use. Reference books are available for patrons wishing to use these applications.
11. The copyright law of the United States (Title 17 U.S. Code) governs the making of reproductions of copyrighted materials. Persons using Library scanners or CD burners will be liable for any infringement. The unauthorized scanning, altering, or copying of documents, licenses, or currency is against Library Policy and in most cases is illegal. Violators will be subject to arrest.
12. Virtual Village may close for workshops & maintenance. Notice will be posted in advance for these times.

In summary, the Charleston GIS study reached a conclusion similar to Waschauer's: A mix of physical, digital, human, and social resources will be needed to serve the public's information and learning needs, and each different constituency within a community will require a different mix, or in many cases, *multiple mixes*. A community as defined by physical boundaries can include needs as varied as those of college town singles, upscale executive families, and the low income retired. If the computer lab in the library remains a mere computer lab in a library, it will fail to reach its potential value to these constituencies, no matter how efficiently it is tended. If the proper mix of physical, digital, human, and social resources are assembled and organized around it, it becomes the sort of Information Commons that we see at the Toronto Public Library.

These findings lead to the conclusion that future public library IC/LC development should be closely linked to community-building partnerships built upon collaborative geo-demographic research. The problem seems to be that assembling and organizing the necessary physical, digital, human, and social resources requires an analytical scope and framework broader than any strategic planning template aimed at the needs of a given institution, and may ultimately require collaboration between public library and academic library sectors and interests. Some colleges and universities, of course, have already begun using GIS analysis to supplement market research for their own educational and community outreach services.[19]

Such collaboration would facilitate an important future step for public and academic libraries alike, especially in the face of increased private sector competition for both informational and educational services. This would be an effort to move community analysis and strategic planning to an expanded model, well beyond the "looking around" activities of an earlier generation. It could involve conceptualizing an entire metropolitan region as an *information system*, with geodemographic analysis contributing highly focused portraits of multiple constituencies with their complex and variable information needs, preferences, and expectations. It would also nudge library managers toward a clearer awareness of other agencies, businesses, and community groups as potential *institutional customers* for library information and data services. New Web-based and wireless technologies, residential satellite, and optical cable networks offer libraries a toolset for delivery of an unprecedented diversity of services and content packages to institutions as well as constituencies, with corporate and institutional service delivery also offering the potential for future library revenue growth, as foreseen in Vision 2008. What seems to be needed for the realization of this vision is a conceptual schema that can be applied by local government and academic planners to map out the information environment within a comprehensive systems analysis framework.

One promising candidate for this type of framework may be found in the literature of GIS itself, having originated in an article by environmental designer Carl Steinitz.[20] Described as a working shell for understanding and organizing the process of environmental design, the Steinitz framework proposes a planning process oriented around the generation of six models, which is shown here in Figure 7.7, provisionally adapted to the systems analysis of an information environment.

A thorough exploration of this adaptation of the Steinitz framework is beyond the scope of this book, but a few preliminary thoughts bear mentioning. The Representation Model is the most crucial step, as all subsequent models are derived from it, but also the most challenging. Representing an entire city or region as an information system may seem an impossibly ambitious undertaking. However, for many areas of the country, local government planners have probably already done at least some initial work. For example, a nascent representation model was built by Fred Phillips during his tenure as city manager for Stockton, California. Laid out as a grid or matrix, the model was an inventory of all governmental services pertinent to the individual and social needs of residents at every stage of their lives from birth to death under general headings such as education, transportation, public safety, housing, and so forth. Elevating this type of service/needs inventory to a Representation

Figure 7.7 The Steinitz Framework for Systems Modeling	
Representation Model	How should the state of the information environment be described in terms of boundaries, space, and time?
Process Model	How does the local information system work? What are the functional and structural relationships among its elements?
Evaluation Model	How does one judge whether the current state of the system is working well? The metrics of assessment may include accuracy, currency, cost, applicability, user satisfaction, etc.
Change Model	By what actions might the current information system be altered: what, where, and when? This level of inquiry leads to *Change Models*. At least two important types of change should be considered: how the system is likely to evolve through current trends, leading to *Projection Models*; and how it might be changed by implementable action, leading to *Intervention Models*.
Impact Models	What predictable differences might the changes cause? This level of inquiry shapes Impact Models, in which the Process Models are used to *simulate* change.
Decision Models	How is a decision to change the system to be made? How is a comparative evaluation to be made among alternative course of action? This level of inquiry leads to a *Decision Model*.

Model requires (1) that each service/need be linked to the geodemographic canvas of population subgroups; and (2) that each of these service/needs be further linked to the cluster of information predicates (who, what, where, when, why, how) that are associated with it.

For example, a local government dropout prevention program is responsive to a very real individual and community need, and this need can be associated with a cluster of characteristic information needs on the part of teens, teachers, and parents. Where do parents of dropouts or potential dropouts typically turn for information? What responses do they typically receive? Through the application of studies of information-seeking behavior, the Representation Model would thus evolve into a Process Model, and lead to an understanding of how the information system actually functions. Data from this Process Model, when subjected to qualitative assessment tools and techniques, would then lead to an Evaluation Model. It is at this juncture that collaborators in the analysis (library, university, regional planning office) could begin to apply new service delivery scenarios to generate corresponding Change Models. From here, forecasting and extrapolation techniques would lead to the construction of Impact Models. And finally, the entire collaborative process would then be moved into the political and budgetary arenas in the form of one or more Decision Models.

Based on this project, one can contend that a database built around the Assessor's parcel file and tax records can not only bring greater granularity to current GIS analysis, but could also contribute to the generation of representation and process models in the Steinitz framework, thus facilitating a more comprehensive systems analysis view of the community's information environment. Such analysis, in turn, could relate geodemographic studies to a number of other significant trends and initiatives in current library literature, including new attention to the role of public libraries in the processes of community-building,[21] and a recent proposal to move academic library information services away from a resource-based model to a constituency-based model.[22]

Endnotes

[1] Williams, Patrick. 1988. *The American Public Library and the Problem of Purpose*. New York: Greenwood Press. 4.

[2] "Charleston Library Society: Founded 1748." Available: http://www.sciway.net/lib/cls_home.html

[3] Carnegie Library of Pittsburgh. "Meeting Carnegie's Challenge, The 1995–2000 Strategic Plan." (1995). Available: http://www.carnegielibrary.org/clp/mission.html

[4] McClure, Charles R., et al., 1987. *Planning & Role Setting for Public Libraries: A Manual of Options and Procedures*. Chicago: American Library Association. 117p.

[5] Koontz, Christine M. 1997. *Library Facility Siting and Location Handbook*. Westport, Conn: Greenwood Press. 206p.

[6] Ibid. 116–119

[7] "Community Networking '96: Bringing People Together." LaPlaza de Taos Telecommunity. 1996. Available: http://www.laplaza.org/about_lap/archives/cn96/

[8] Odasz, Frank. "What Is A Community Network? A Short History of Community Networking Models." From *The Good Neighbor's Guide to Community Networking*. Lone-Eagle Consulting. Available: http://lone-eagles.com/cnguide.htm

[9] Benton Foundation. "Buildings, Books, and Bytes: Libraries and Communities in the Digital Age." (December 16, 1996). Available: http://www.benton.org/Library/Kellogg/buildings.html

[10] "Vision 2008: Mapping the Future of Your Library." 3M Library Systems. 1998. Available: http://www.3m.com/market/security/library/whatsnew/1998vision2008report.pdf

[11] Knox, Noelle. 2000. "Online Brokerages Go from Clicks to Bricks: New Offices Provide Personal Touch Some Customers Crave." *USA Today* (January 29).

[12] "U.S. Library Program." Bill & Melinda Gates Foundation. Available: http://www.gatesfoundation.org/libraries/uslibraryprogram/default1.htm

[13] "Toward Equality of Access: The Role of Public Libraries in Addressing the Digital Divide." Bill & Melinda Gates Foundation. Available: http://www.gatesfoundation.org/nr/Downloads/libraries/uslibraries/reports/TowardEqualityofAccess.pdf

[14] Ibid.

[15] Warschauer, Mark. 2002. "Reconceptualizing the Digital Divide." *First Monday*. 7 no. 7 (July). Available: http://firstmonday.org/issues/issue7_7/warschauer/index.html

[16] "Toward Equality of Access: The Role of Public Libraries in Addressing the Digital Divide." Bill & Melinda Gates Foundation. Available: http://www.gatesfoundation.org/nr/Downloads/libraries/uslibraries/reports/TowardEqualityofAccess.pdf

[17] Joint Information Systems Committee. 2006. *Designing Spaces for Effective Learning*. London: Higher Education Funding Council. Available: http://www.jisc.ac.uk/uploaded_documents/JISC%20learning%20spaces.acc.pdf

[18] "Virtual Village Use Policies." Public Library of Charlotte & Mecklenburg County. 2005. Available: http://www.plcmc.org/aboutUs/policiesVirtual.htm

[19] Blough, David. "How GIS Enhances Survey Research: Examples from Marketing Higher Education." Available: http://www.esri.com/library/userconf/proc01/professional/papers/pap378/p378.htm

[20] Steinitz, Carl. "A Framework for Theory Applicable to the Education of Landscape Architects (and Other Environmental Design Professionals." Available at: http://www.gsd.harvard.edu/studios/brc/framework/framework_treatise.html

[21] McCook, Kathleen de la Pena. "Libraries Building Communities." Available: http://www.cas.usf.edu/lis/a-librarian-at-every-table/libraries.html

[22] Barth, Christopher D., & Janet R. Cottrell. 2002. "A Constituency-based Support Model for Delivering Information Services." *College & Research Libraries* 63 (January). 47–52.

8

Implementing an Information Commons, Growing a Learning Commons

In building traditional libraries, implementation frequently involves project management (PM) tools and techniques, which tend to be wrapped up and set aside on opening day. After the door opens and books begin circulating, operational management (OM) of traditional libraries tends to be quite distinct from the PM techniques used for implementation. The Learning Commons or Collaboration Center, by contrast, may well involve a constant sequencing of interdependent collaborative projects and activities managed in coordination with other campus units; this may also be true to a lesser extent for the Information Commons. Day-to-day operational management of an LC may require the ongoing use of project management or even program management tools and techniques to a degree not familiar to traditional library managers. So the emphasis on a PM approach for tactical planning, introduced in Chapter 5, is carried through here to implementation, and is also intended as a transition to what may become a normal course of operational project or program management once the IC/LC is running.

The Implementation Team

Many successful implementations begin with the establishment of an implementation oversight group or team, designated to meet regularly to guide, coordinate, and oversee the implementation task calendar. Such a team may be a renaming of the IC Planning Group itself, but we present it here as a newly constituted self-managed team drawing upon key internal areas of the library organization chart with perhaps some representation from the earlier planning team. Figure 8.1 is a brief composite narrative assembled from several specific descriptions of IC implementation teams, giving a sense of the typical workflow:

There already exists a strong tradition of self-managed teams within academic library administration. Charles B. Lowrey, Dean of Libraries at the University of Maryland, posted a representative working paper titled "The Vision of a Team-Based Learning Organization."[1]

Figure 8.1
IC Implementation Team Overview, Part 1

The implementation team was initially called together by the Library Director, who was the overall supervisor for the IC project. The Director convened a group that she felt best suited to oversee implementation of the IC. That implementation team would include appropriate representatives from the library, and would also require representatives from the appropriate support offices as identified in the master Work Breakdown Structure (WBS) laid out by the Planning Group.

The implementation team formalized its approach very quickly in the process, and the Associate Library Director and the Associate Director of Computing Services became the co-chairs. The Associate Library Director managed the support groups represented on the library team, i.e., reference, instructional services, library systems, and data services. The Associate Director of Computing Services managed the collaborating group, including representatives from Instructional Technology, Media Services, and the Writing Center. The implementation team quickly placed its focus on task coordination and information exchanges as a project calendar unfolded.

The model presented here encourages the Library Director to tap into this tradition, because of the usefulness not only of a self-managed team at the core of the IC/LC implementation, but the possible further spinoff of its operational work to four satellite self-managed teams for the selection and organization of physical, digital, human, and social resources respectively. Under this model, the IC/LC initiative presents library managers with a crucial choice. If the traditional library has been managed under a vertical coordinator/unit-head regime, the IC/LC may offer a significant opportunity to verge off with the new management approach of self-managed teams. On the other hand, there may be situations where the IC/LC initiative in itself presents such a management challenge that taking on the additional stress of initiating a new team-based management structure could become overwhelming. As always, the local manager is best positioned to make this judgment call. Certainly an IC or LC can function effectively either under vertical line-management or as a team-based learning organization. The examples that follow also allow for a middle course: self-managed teams can be set up to oversee implementation, but if operational management after implementation requires oversight by traditional unit coordinators, the self-managed teams could then be steered into assessment oversight responsibilities. The team-based assessment experience at the University of Arizona Library offers a precedent, as Carla Stoffle and Shelley Phipps describe:

> ...teams engage in discovering what is most important to their customer groups about the services they provide. They use this information to formulate standards or performance targets for the particular service activity. They gather data on progress toward these standards and report periodically....[2]

Stoffle and Phipps describe their use of certain LibQUAL+™ measurements as well as internally-generated metrics. We will discuss LibQUAL+™ specifically in the next chapter, but we begin including some references to assessment at this early point in our section on implementation because of the importance we attach to following the lead of Amos Lakos in creating a culture of assessment within the IC/LC organization.[3] The crucible of implementation tends to shape organizational culture even more than the experience of planning, and so interjecting the basis for an assessment mechanism at the earliest stages of implementation becomes important.

Lines of authority and communication for IC implementation first center on the relationship between the Library Director and the Implementation Team. This line of authority determines execution of the strategic and tactical plans, because these two offices hold control over the two essential tools of any implementation: the project budget and the project calendar, as shown in Figure 8.2. The project budget may be controlled by the Library Director, with key aspects delegated; the project calendar will likely be delegated to the IC Implementation Team, with a few key aspects (milestones) controlled or closely overseen by the Director. There are many good project management (PM) guidebooks to project budgets and calendars, as well as useful discussion of both in Microsoft Project software documentation and user guides. There is no indication that IC implementation should require departing from such widely available resources, and so, in the interest of space, we will not offer custom budget or calendar templates here. However, LC implementation may well entail a shift from *project management* to *program management*, either before or after opening day, and this may present special issues for the budget and calendar that we will discuss at various points.

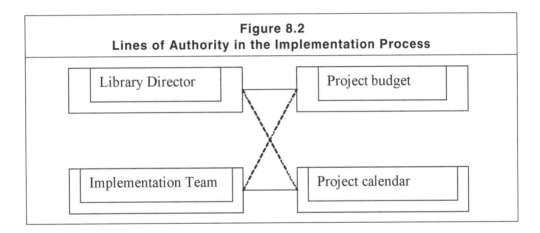

Figure 8.2
Lines of Authority in the Implementation Process

Library Director

Project budget

Implementation Team

Project calendar

Project Budget and Breakout Program Budgeting

The master IC implementation and operations budget may well be a line-item budget, the most widely used of all budgeting systems. Line-item budgeting offers some advantages in that such budgets are relatively easy to prepare and do not demand sophisticated financial skills. The line-item budget is straightforward, relatively simple to administer, and understood by campus administration and library middle-management. Moreover, the simplicity of the system makes it easier for the Implementation Group and and Library Director to monitor revenues and expenditures. Assuming that Microsoft Project has been used for tactical planning, the preparation of GANTT Charts for the project may also have spun off linked Microsoft Excel worksheets that will detail the best predictions of budget parameters. While the basic line-item format is well-established, one also finds many examples of "modified" line-item budgets that include certain elements of program or cost-center budgeting. Greatly abbreviated capsule views of "master" project budgets for IC personnel and equipment are shown in Figures 8.3 and 8.4:

	Librarian (FTE)	PA (FTE)	Hourly Assistance (hrs/wk) $8/hr	Estimated New Annual Costs
Figure 8.3				
Sample Information Commons Master Budget: Staffing				
Area				
Information Desk Reference				
Statistical Data Librarian	1			$ 55,000
General Reference Librarian	4			$220,000
Media Services				
Digital Library Services		1		$ 52,400
Digital Imaging Technician			40	$ 16,640
Network Administrator		1		$ 51,300
Media Collections Librarian	1			$ 58,450
Collaboration and Visualization				
Visualization Senior Staff		1		$ 64,500
Data Analysis				
Research Data Consultant			40	$ 16,640
Software Support				
Computer Support		1		$ 54,500
Staff Coordinator			40	$ 16,640
TOTAL	**2**	**4**	**70**	**$606,070**

The major drawback of line-item budgeting, pure or modified, is that the laundry-list format of the method can make it difficult to determine the extent or impact of a particular subset of IC resources or services produced by a given level of spending. Also, the broad expenditure categories used in a line-item budget make it difficult to set service priorities because there is no subsequent way to readily calculate the quantity or quality of services that would result from various expenditure levels.

Unlike the line-item budget per se, which lists total departmental appropriations by items for which the library will spend funds, a program budget displays (or breaks out) a series of "mini-budgets," which show the cost of groups of services and resources under key programs or subcategories. In the case of the IC, for example, a breakout mini-budget could be established for digital resources and services (software licensing, Web interface design, etc.) and another for physical resources (fixtures, furnishings, equipment, etc.) within various IC/LC programs. This type of breakout budgeting may be especially useful if the planning group and implementation team are following a Work Breakdown Structure, where deliverables

Figure 8.4
Sample Information Commons Master Budget: Equipment

Equipment	Initial Cost	Annual Replacement Costs*
50 public workstations and associated servers and equipment	$ 60,000	$ 15,000
12 multimedia/GIS workstations (with flatbed scanners, large flatscreen monitors)	$ 75,000	
4 public OPAC/e-mail standup workstations	$ 3,200	$ 800
4 black & white laser printers	$ 8,000	$ 2,400
3 42" plasma displays	$ 12,000	$ 1,200
1 48" bed freestanding plotter	$ 5,000	$ 1,500
1 color printer	$ 4,000	$ 1,200
DisplayWall and AccessGrid for seminar room	$250,000	$ 68,200
Workstations & displays for presentation rehearsal studios (4)	$ 12,000	$ 3,000
Workstations & displays for gaming/VR studios (2)	$ 8,000	$ 2,000
TOTAL	**$437,200**	**$102,500**

are assigned under the four resource categories. The sample in Figure 8.5 shows the budget for Digital Resources & Services for multiple projects of an Information Commons program. Each of the other resource areas undergirding the program—human resources, physical resources, and social resources—could have a similar, breakout mini-budget.

Program budgeting enables the Library Director and IC Implementation Team to identify the total cost of each subclass of resources and services and set spending levels and priorities accordingly. The downside to the program budget approach is that significant time and effort are required to establish and maintain the breakout subsystem. Also, programs tend to

Figure 8.5
IC Breakout Program Budget for Digital Resources and Services

Expenditure Classification	Previous Fiscal Year 2005–06: Actual	Current Fiscal Year 2006–07: Budgeted	Next Fiscal Year 2007–08: Request
Project 1 **Desktop**	$	$	$
Project 2 **Academic software**	$	$	$
Project 3 **Multimedia**	$	$	$
Project 4 **Gaming studio**	$	$	$
Program subtotals	$	$	$

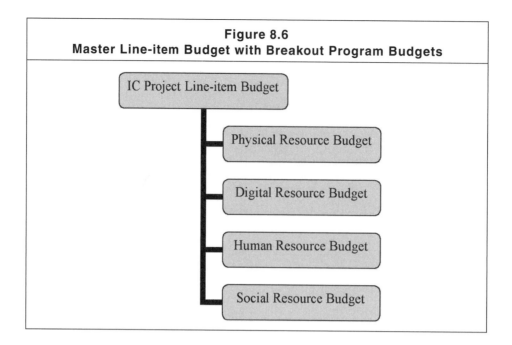

Figure 8.6
Master Line-item Budget with Breakout Program Budgets

overlap, both between departments and within the same departments, which can make collecting data and tracking progress more difficult.

Another option for breakout mini-budgets is the "cost-center budget," shown in Figure 8.7, where constituent activities may even be broken down into percentages of staff time, and accordingly, percentages of salary expenses, along with equipment, supplies, and associated contract services (as for maintenance or service contracts).

Figure 8.7 **Cost-Center Budget for Media Services**				
MEDIA SERVICES COST CENTER	**STAFF**	**EQUIPMENT**	**CONTRACT SERVICES**	**SUPPLIES**
Media Acquisition Digital Audio Production Digital Video Production Scanning Slide and Photograph Scanning Digital Photography Media Conversion				
Media Production Macro. Flash Animation Interactive DVD Production Custom PowerPoint Presentation 3D Animation Digital Video Editing WWW Site Production & Design				
Distribution/Technical Support Streaming Audio and Video Tape, CD and DVD Duplication System Administration				

Master Project Calendar with Breakout Subcalendars

In some cases, the Project Calendar is laid out by the Director in some detail and handed to the Implementation Team upon its first meeting. More often, a very general time frame is laid out with a few key milestones, and the first task of the Implementation Team is to flesh out the framework into a fully articulated Project Calendar.

The depiction of scheduled phases and subphases of implementation in Microsoft Project will ultimately be represented by a GANTT chart, with subphase durations extended across a calendar table. In Figure 8.8, the completion phase of an IC implementation calendar is depicted with wrap-up subphases broken out by tasks assigned to resource teams designated physical, digital, human, and social resources:

The master calendar may well be supplemented by breakout mini-calendars for subphases of the project. The breakout of mini-calendars for project subphases may or may not reflect the same headings as the program budget breakout of digital, physical, human, and social resources. While it is true, for example, that workstations and servers (physical resources) must be installed before software packages (digital resources) are loaded, there will normally

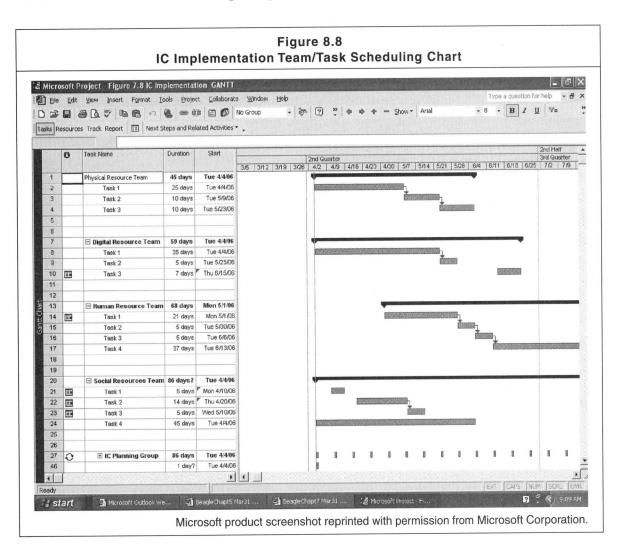

**Figure 8.8
IC Implementation Team/Task Scheduling Chart**

Microsoft product screenshot reprinted with permission from Microsoft Corporation.

be significant, intermittent, and sometimes unexpected overlaps between implementation activities pertaining to all four resource groups. However, it is possible to break out the implementation team effort into smaller subteams organized around the four types of resources, as shown in Figure 8.9. In such cases, each self-managed satellite team may be given the initial task of assembling a detailed calendar for its piece of the implementation, under the oversight of the IC Implementation Group. The specific way the Implementation Team breaks out and further delegates its authority to subteams is very much dependent upon the judgment of managers at a given institution and in a particular situation.

Figure 8.9
IC Implementation Overview, Part 2

As IC implementation progressed, the team expanded to include smaller working groups within each area: a Digital Resources Team, Physical Resources Team, Human Resources Team, and Social Resources Team; the work of each of these teams was summarized and explained to the larger group at each meeting. These groups concentrated on specific processes and functions, identifying how those would work and what further analysis needed to be done by the larger group.

Each of these teams will probably begin to meet on its own, sending a representative to report back periodically to the Implementation Team. The teams need not be large groups; in some cases, these four areas of responsibility might simply be delegated to four key members of the Implementation Team, who would recruit a specialized assistant or two if/when necessary. Regardless, each individual or team will use as its starting point the documentation that emerged in the last step(s) of the planning template, but each will also need to have sufficient delegated authority and flexibility to propose additional resources or necessary revisions as their work proceeds. Lowrey has described in general terms the scope of work for self-managed teams, two of which seem especially pertinent to the four resource teams:

- ...a planned (usually permanent) collaboration expressed through a formal organizational structure intended (in our case) to support a library service or technical function; and
- a problem-solving group that uses well understood tools (e.g., CQI process re-engineering) to assure that the whole organization remains flexible and responsive to its environment.[4]

In this example, of course, the breakout teams operate in parallel to the areas of the breakout program satellite budgets discussed earlier, and develop their breakout satellite calendars accordingly. This level of parallelism can bring significant clarity and coherence to monitoring the overall implementation effort. Quite frankly, the use of such teams may also have advantages in the context of campus politics in cases where a Learning Commons is implemented around interdepartmental collaboration. The Digital Resources Team may be an effective mechanism to gain the involvement of a key software specialist in the Business School, for example, or a Human Resources Team may secure the active participation of a highly regarded training specialist in the Education School, and so forth. These are not trivial considerations, because if one develops an LC with high-profile collaborative projects, each campus unit with an interest in project outcomes may need to have a structured mechanism for management input and oversight. The self-managed satellite resource teams offer one possible inclusive mechanism. Given that such collaborative projects are sometimes initiated with grant funding, the parallel breakout budgeting scheme may also prove especially useful in tracking and reporting discrete bundles of grant revenues and expenditures.

The need for, and effectiveness of, such resource teams may need to be balanced against the degree of line authority to be established within the IC/LC staff. Such teams may be given "peer-supervisory" decision-making roles in an IC that functions around a single omnibus service desk with numerous floaters, rovers, and flexible referral patterns. Or, the LC may be given a more highly articulated and traditionally structured internal organization chart, in which case the role of resource teams will be advisory. In some cases, the teams may be deemed useful for initial implementation but then phased out of existence after opening day. Or, as mentioned previously, they may be turned into assessment oversight teams with evaluation responsibilities in their respective resource areas. Suppose, for example, that an LC such as Indiana University's Research Commons were staffed so that each service unit had its own coordinator, as shown in the following list.

Hypothetical Unit Coordinators for LC Service Units
- Coordinator of General Information Services
- Coordinator of Reference and Research
- Coordinator of Digital Media Production
- Coordinator of Research Compliance & Intellectual Property
- Coordinator of Data Analysis and Advanced Computation
- Coordinator of Collaboration and Visualization
- Coordinator of Software Support and Distribution

Such coordinators would presumably be expected to assume front-line implementation responsibility for their respective units. However, in a large complex LC, top managers would still want to see continuity and compliance with overall goals and objectives, not allowing "warring fiefdoms" to emerge within the LC. This is where having physical, digital, human, and social resource teams in an advisory oversight role can still be useful in creating a "matrix management" approach. As shown in Figure 8.10, operational authority can flow top-down, while oversight for continuity and compliancy during and after implementation can flow left-right. The Coordinator of Information Services, for example, will clearly have authority for determining the content of the Information Service Center's Web page. But the Digital Resources Team can still assume an oversight role in ensuring that the Information Service Center's Web page maintains the same navigational components and meets the same usability criteria as the Digital Media Center's Web page and the Data Analysis Center's Web page.

In ICs or LCs that have multiple service centers it becomes important to distinguish between implementation oversight and operational authority. A self-managed team may exercise both. The following discussion assumes the formation of the four self-managed resource teams and describes some of the areas of focus and concentration for each. Whether operating in an advisory or supervisory role, each team would work with IC/LC managers and/or internal unit coordinators. In certain cases, teams may need to operate jointly or in close partnership for resolution of key issues.

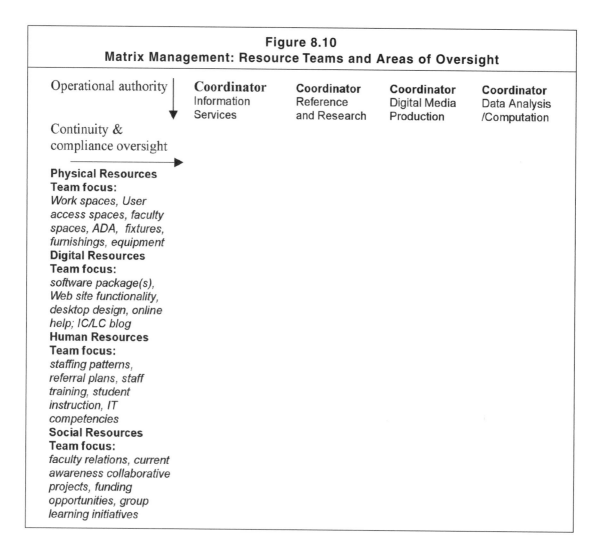

Figure 8.10
Matrix Management: Resource Teams and Areas of Oversight

Operational authority →

	Coordinator Information Services	**Coordinator** Reference and Research	**Coordinator** Digital Media Production	**Coordinator** Data Analysis /Computation

Continuity & compliance oversight →

Physical Resources Team focus:
Work spaces, User access spaces, faculty spaces, ADA, fixtures, furnishings, equipment

Digital Resources Team focus:
software package(s), Web site functionality, desktop design, online help; IC/LC blog

Human Resources Team focus:
staffing patterns, referral plans, staff training, student instruction, IT competencies

Social Resources Team focus:
faculty relations, current awareness collaborative projects, funding opportunities, group learning initiatives

Physical Resources Team

Figure 8.11 lists some sample special areas of focus for the Physical Resources Team. It is assumed that by this point that architectural plans have long since been finalized and the construction or renovation may have already begun. The original IC Planning Team may have approved an overall layout and design with detail work and F,F&E (fixtures, furnishings, and equipment) delegated to this Physical Resources Team. Or, the original IC Planning Group may have carried out decisions to an exacting level of detail and left to the Physical Resources Team the job of simply ensuring their implementation. This team would work in collaboration with (or include representatives from) the campus/library physical facilities office, procurement staff, and architecture and design consultants. On selection of equipment and furnishings specifically involved in IT, local managers need to determine the most effective delegation of authority; the Physical Resources Team could, for example, work in collaboration with (through joint meetings) the Digital Resources Team. Or, to avoid confusion, both hardware and software decisions might be left to the library Head of Systems, who would meet jointly with the two resource teams.

Figure 8.11
Special Areas of Focus for the Physical Resources Team

Layout implementation—fixtures, furnishings, and equipment

Traffic flow; swoopable vs. bookable workstation areas

IT hardware, multimedia platforms, DisplayWall, videoconferencing/AccessGrid, special technologies; adaptive technologies; general ergonomics

Special spaces—presentation rehearsal spaces, gaming/virtual reality studios, multimedia work areas, data manipulation/statistics/GIS work areas

Group study areas; smart classroom(s); faculty studios

Noise issues policy resolution; food issues policy resolution

---

Joanne Henning notes in her "Gleanings" the variety of ways institutions have dealt with queuing and/or monitoring workstations and printers: (1) posters showing workstation locations; (2) an electronic status board where individual workstations "light up" when someone logs on, allowing students to find unoccupied workstations at a glance; (3) a master workstation displaying what machines are in use superimposed upon a software-generated floor plan, and which allows students to reserve a machine by clicking an icon; (4) online reporting of malfunctioning equipment, where students and IT assistants can log equipment problems and see information regarding disposition; (5) printer status software allowing staff to monitor paper and toner levels in real time.[5]

A Physical Resources Team might also be authorized to exercise detailed oversight of the office move into the IC work areas. Figure 8.12 gives an example of a breakout Microsoft

---

Figure 8.12
Microsoft Project Office Relocation Template Adaptation

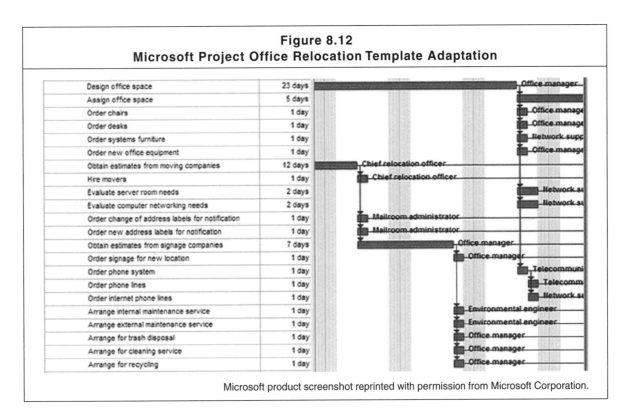

Microsoft product screenshot reprinted with permission from Microsoft Corporation.

Project time line for such a move, here adapted from an office relocation template that can be downloaded from the Office support site:[6]

Digital Resources Team

The Digital Resources Team, with areas of special concern shown in Figure 8.13, would work wherever necessary with the Head of Library Systems, Academic Computing, key IT support specialists within academic departments, key IT support specialists within administrative units, and in some cases, representative faculty with special software interests and needs. This team would coordinate with the Physical Resources Team in the provision of infrastructure, furnishings, and associated workspaces, and with the Human Resources Team in the development of instructional programs, skill support, and IT competency Web pages.

Figure 8.13
Special Areas of Focus for the Digital Resources Team

Network extension & IT infrastructure (coll. with Physical Resources Team)

Network security; firewall; antivirus

Productivity software selection (MSOffice, etc.)

Academic software selection (SAS, SPSS, GIS, discipline-specific software)

Data manipulation special needs; IC/LC blog-space

Library Reference Database access & authentication

Desktop organization & Web site interface "look & feel"

Course management system access & interfacing

Multimedia utilities: production, conversion, distribution

Desktop "webinars" and/or AccessGrid digital conferencing

Gaming infrastructure, related user access & policy issues resolution

Faculty/research project(s) special needs

The resolution of desktop organization and Web site look and feel can be especially thorny, and this is one reason for sharing the breakout oversight responsibility for continuity and compliance among all digital resources across service areas such as *Reference and Research* and *Digital Media Production*. There are real advantages to students and faculty for IC/LC service areas to maintain a "branded" desktop and Web site look and feel across internal units. If all implementation authority is broken out totally to a Coordinator for Reference and Research, for example, with that coordinator and staff having across-the-board responsibility for all resource presentation pertaining to that unit, and similar authority for the Coordinator Digital Media Production unit, then one runs the greater risk of "warring fiefdoms" at a time during implementation when such friction can be least afforded.

Desktop design usability is an issue that may have been taken up during the planning template's focus group stage, or even during Projecting the future commons exercises. Yet, specificity of software choices may not have been possible at those early stages. The existence of a Digital Resources Team can also provide an effective means to conduct final stage usability

Figure 8.14
Building-block Diagram for LC Desktop Implementation

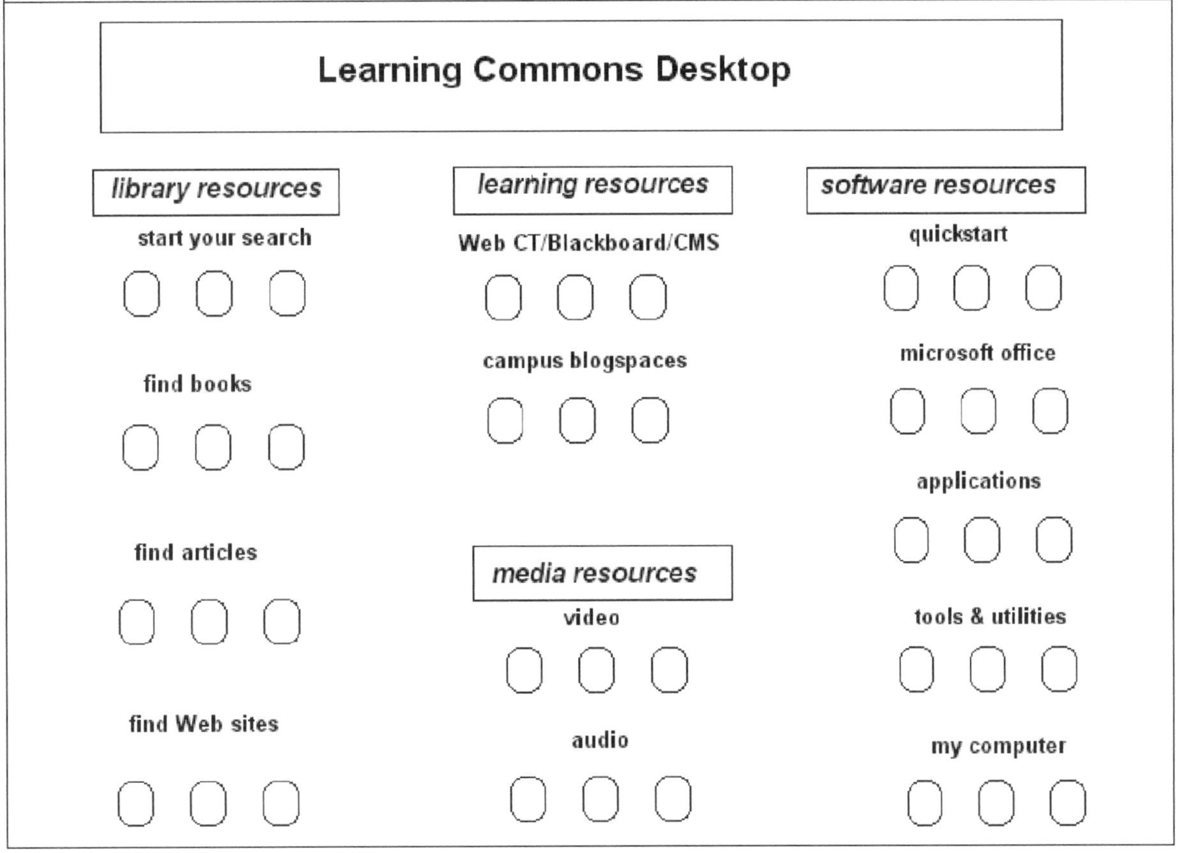

Learning Commons Desktop

library resources

start your search

◯ ◯ ◯

find books

◯ ◯ ◯

find articles

◯ ◯ ◯

find Web sites

◯ ◯ ◯

learning resources

Web CT/Blackboard/CMS

◯ ◯ ◯

campus blogspaces

◯ ◯ ◯

media resources

video

◯ ◯ ◯

audio

◯ ◯ ◯

software resources

quickstart

◯ ◯ ◯

microsoft office

◯ ◯ ◯

applications

◯ ◯ ◯

tools & utilities

◯ ◯ ◯

my computer

◯ ◯ ◯

comparisons even as the calendar is moving toward completion. A building-block exercise similar to that shown for floor plans can be an effective tool; the diagram in Figure 8.14 is loosely adapted from a University of Georgia example used in the Information Commons PowerPoint presentation by the IC planning team at the University of Maryland.[7]

The Digital Resource Team may also hold rollout authority for scheduling actual deployment of servers, workstations, imaging, security profiles, and so forth. Figure 8.15 gives the look and feel for a breakout project time line for desktop deployment, adapted from a free downloadable template from the Office support site.[8]

Human Resources Team

The Human Resources Team would play a vital long-term role in the development of instructional programs, skill support, and IT competency Web pages (see Figure 8.16). Its main area of initial focus during implementation would be on staff training, on setting forth the workflow expectations for any multifunctional service desk(s), and especially on any internal referral procedures (and follow-up assessment) for helping users navigate the entire continuum of the ICT literacy matrix from *identification and retrieval*, through *processing and manipulation*, to *packaging, presentation, and publication*.

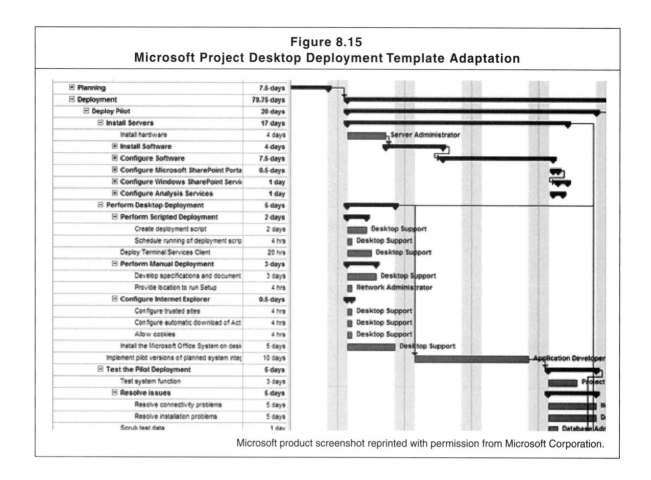

Figure 8.15
Microsoft Project Desktop Deployment Template Adaptation

Microsoft product screenshot reprinted with permission from Microsoft Corporation.

Figure 8.16
Special Areas of Focus for the Human Resources Team

Staff training

Staffing patterns/schedules & rotations

Service desk(s) workflow arrangements; spheres of responsibility

IT competencies

Information Literacy instructional coordination/adaptation

Referral patterns (referral consultancy, walk-through consultancy, case manager)

User orientation & instructional Web sites; materials

Skills support coaching & tutorial arrangements

Liaison to appropriate public service units of traditional library

Collaboration with social resources team on soft/hard IC opening agenda

---

Cowgill, Beam, and Weiss stress this aspect of their IC implementation experience at Colorado State University:

Reference Services staff recognized they would have to answer questions...about e-mail, hardware and software problems, and Microsoft Office.... A series of seven in-house minimal competency-training classes was organized.... Knowledgeable Library staff from LTS and Reference Services conducted the 90-minute classes, held multiple times to accommodate varying work schedules.[9]

Many outlines and listings of staff technology competencies are available. As a representative example, the tables in Figures 8.17 and 8.18 include competencies developed by the State Library of North Carolina. We find them a useful touchstone because they present a matrix divided both by levels of vertical expertise (Levels I and II) and on Level II further divided horizontally by functional focus: Public Services and Technology Management. Level I technology competency would basically represent work-study desk coverage staff at minimal use periods. Level II—Public Services lists technology competencies fundamental to any library technology assistant working successfully in a normally demanding IC environment. Level II—Technology management includes competencies where one would reasonably expect a problem referral from an IC librarian to a Tech Specialist-On-Duty or On-Call. However, while we feel the matrix arrangement is well suited to IC application, the details would need to be customized and negotiated.

Figure 8.17:
Level I Technology Competencies Example

Level I Competencies
Terminology—an understanding of:
  Boot/ CPU/Monitor/Memory/Hard drive/Diskette/CD Rom/Server/
  Web site/Web page/Link/URL

Hardware Knowledge
- Turn a computer on and off correctly
- Use mouse, keyboard, and function keys
- Recognize importance of backing up files
- Printer—add paper, change ribbon/ink-cartridge/toner, clear
  paper jam

PC Security Knowledge—familiar with Internet security risks (e.g., e-mail viruses, spyware) and the security precautions currently implemented in their library (e.g., firewall).

E-mail Skills
- Know e-mail address
- Compose, send, open, read, reply to, forward messages
- Store and retrieve e-mail messages
- Sort messages by date, subject, sender
- Attach a file and open an attachment

PC Troubleshooting Skills
- Use the Task Manager to delete nonresponsive programs
- Reboot the workstation
- Understand cables, power cords, on-off switches on all equipment

---

Cowgill, Beam, and Weiss list the following "minimum" competencies offered in their training sessions for "all Reference Services staff." It basically represent the Level II—Public Service tech competencies plus further operating system and print management skills, along with good functional grounding in MSOffice applications. Sample documents and photographs of the Colorado State University IC can be found on the CD that accompanies this book, and Figure 8.19 lists the Minimum Competencies.

Figure 8.18 **Level II Technology Competencies Example**	

Public Services
 	
Internet
Knowledge of local Internet use policy
Knowledge of netiquette
Interpret URLs
Use navigational buttons: back, home, go, refresh,
  history
Enter URL by typing or pasting
Knowledge of search engines
Access the WWW
Scroll up and down in Web page
Search for text in a Web page
Print all or part of a Web page
Add and use bookmarks, favorites
Move/file bookmarks, favorites
Change bookmark names
Change the default home page
Clear temporary Internet files and clear
History
 	
Search Strategies
Search the WWW
Knowledge of basic search concepts
Knowledge Boolean, proximity search concepts
Knowledge of topic specific searching
Evaluate WWW and electronic database
Results
Proficient in searching various databases in NC LIVE
 	
Electronic mailing list (listserv)
Subscribe and unsubscribe
Post message
Access archived messages
	Technology Management
	
	Hardware
	Install a PC workstation
	Add/install a printer
	Install peripherals such as scanner,
	DVD burner, etc.
	Install software
	
	Operating Systems
	Understand Windows 2000, Windows XP or current
	  platform
	File and memory management
	Resource allocation, optimization, and
	Configuration
	Copy or move a file
	Recover saved files
	
	Networking
	Networking administration
	TCP/IP
	Domain Name service
	
	Specialized System Applications
	Print management
	Workstation management systems
	Server applications
	
	Security
	Internet and workstation security
	Securing user accounts and access to files
	Authentication protocol
	Firewalls
	Proxy servers
	Remote access

Allison Cowgill further noted that the CSU training effort included tutorial pages posted on the staff pages of the library's Web site, and a Tip Sheets Web page with links to explanatory text on applications. Additional class sessions would be scheduled and Web site content revised to track technology changes.

As another good source for competency standards, we also recommend reviewing UCLA's Digital Reference Competencies.[10] When such competencies have been established, the Human Resource Team may want to establish the training initiative as a spinoff Microsoft Project time line and calendar. Figure 8.20 adapts and illustrates a training initiative template that can be downloaded from the Office support site:[11]

Along with managing the staff training and cross-training initiative, this team will need to resolve or negotiate opening-day expectations for handling referrals among and between information desk greeters and rovers, reference subject specialists, IT technical assistants, and media specialists. Perhaps the best way to describe the referral options is to create a scenario where a faculty member comes looking to retrieve data from a reference database, manipulate the data in a statistical package, and "publish" the results to a Web site, CD, or PowerPoint

---

Figure 8.19
Colorado State University Minimum IT Competencies

Windows NT/Windows 2000
Start Button function
Taskbar function
Explorer
Managing Windows (moving, resizing, minimizing, maximizing, and closing)
Familiarity with accessories (Word Pad, Imaging, Paint, etc.)
Rebooting
Log in
Mouse functions (left and right click)
Task manager
Keyboard shortcuts

File Management: Part I
Using "My Computer"
Selecting files/folders
Changing views
Opening files
Cut, copy, and paste functions
Creating new folders
Moving and copying files/folders
Backup files/folders to floppy disk
Renaming files/folders
Deleting files/folders
Restoring files/folders
Recycle bin

File Management: Part II
Formatting floppy disks (Windows 98/NT)
Printing preferences (font size, margins, page orientation, default printer selection, canceling jobs, adding networked printers, etc.)
File extensions, associated applications, useful Web sites (types: .doc, .ppt, .xls, .mdb, .pdf, .gif, .jpg, .bmp, .tip, .html, .txt, .rtf .zip)
Zip drive

Troubleshooting and Maintenance
Printers—UnipriNT and staff station (toner cartridges, paper loading, and maintenance)
UnipriNT system (remote manager, back-up procedures), UnipriNT Troubleshooting Guide
Virus scanning
Thin client (refreshing desktop icons, rebooting), Thin Client Troubleshooting Guide
Internet status testing (ping and trace, test addresses)

Applications: Viewers/Plugins
Adobe Acrobat Reader
Netscape and Internet Explorer
Shockwave/Authorware
QuickTime
Real Player

Applications: Utilities
EnZip
File Transfer Protocol (FTP)
PrintKey 2000
Splitter
Telnet

Electronic Services: General
Proxy server function (basic)
Electronic reserves
Interlibrary Loan (Zap, Webview)
Campus Services (WebCT, RAMWeb, FAFSA)
E-mail (basic knowledge of campus-based lamar or holly, WebMail, independent services, managing attachments)

---

presentation. We can visualize different service pattern responses, including what we call Walk-through Consultancy; Referral Consultancy; and Case Manager (Figures 8.21, 8.22, and 8.23). These headings represent three possible approaches to service delivery within an IC or LC; as always, you can use these as representative options:

Social Resources Team

The need for a Social Resources Team, and the breadth of its responsibility, would depend greatly upon the project goal and scope of Information Commons or Learning Commons. If the former, there may be no need for a breakout Social Resources Team, and any constituent areas of focus might be handled by the Human Resources Team, or other key staff. However, our orientation throughout this book has been to not limit discussion

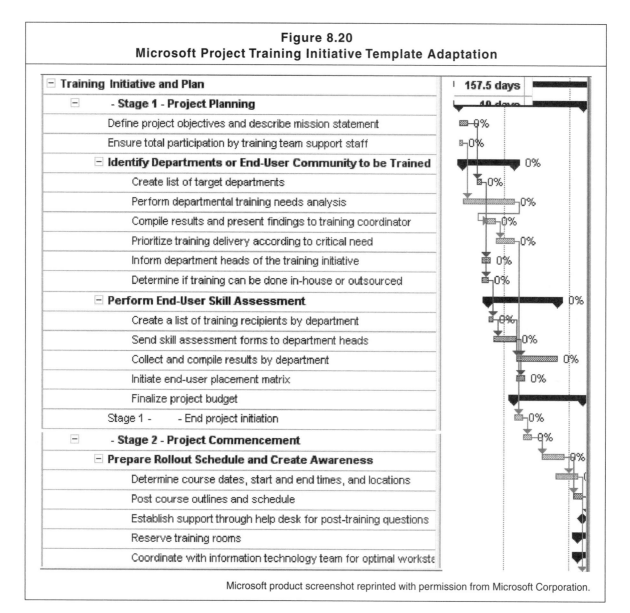

Figure 8.20
Microsoft Project Training Initiative Template Adaptation

Microsoft product screenshot reprinted with permission from Microsoft Corporation.

Figure 8.21
Walk-through Consultancy

The IC librarian identifies the necessary data by discussing the ultimate end use and helps the patron access whatever format is most appropriate for processing and production needs. The same staff member then (at that point or in a later appointment) walks the patron to the processing lab and tutors the patron in the appropriate application [spreadsheet/ database/GIS]. When this is complete, the same staff member then walks the patron to the media production lab and tutors the patron in presentation and production [Power Point[Website/CD-ROM]. The one-person Walk-through Consultancy has the potential to be highly rewarding to the patron in terms of being a satisfying experience, but is also highly demanding of staff in that each staff consultant must receive extensive training in every dimension of the range of needs. The risk is that the Walk-through Consultancy model may not be sustainable from a staff training and scheduling perspective.

Figure 8.22
Referral Consultancy

The librarian identifies the necessary data by discussing its ultimate end use and provides it to the patron in whatever format is most appropriate for processing and production needs. Unlike the traditional reference librarian, the information consultant is familiar enough with processing and production options to make educated guesses and offer initial suggestions. She is familiar enough with relative staff expertise in the processing and production labs (because they all work in the Information Commons and interact frequently) to arrange referral appointments with the database specialist in the processing lab, and the Web site specialist in the production lab. This service pattern projects target internal referrals rather than blind external referrals. Both specialists and their respective labs are alerted to the incoming patron. But also in this referral model, the initial reference librarian then leaves the picture; her responsibility is done. Other specialists become responsible for successful processing and production transactions. This service pattern is more sustainable from a staff training perspective because staff members receive primary training in their respective dimensions while requiring only ongoing orientation and communication across the horizontal. However, an element of the patron experience is at risk because the baton has been passed through successive referrals. There is a risk that follow-through and assessment are likely to be sketchy and anecdotal, because no one has taken full responsibility for the entire sequence of transactions.

Figure 8.23
Case Manager

This model is similar to the Referral Consultancy, except that the initial staff contact (or some designated person) assumes "ownership" of the entire transaction, and becomes a Case Manager for the patron's sequential experience, thus assuming responsibility for systematic follow-through and evaluation. With certain complex or unusual requests, instead of making targeted referral appointments, the Case Manager may need to summon processing and production specialists to a meeting in a Commons conference room to do a small group reference interview with the patron, or a brainstorming session without the patron. In any case, the specialist's responsibilities would not end until they have reported back to the Case Manager in some fashion after their work with the patron is done, and the Case Manager's responsibility would not end until some overall outcome assessment is complete.

to the initial creation of an Information Commons, but to explore organizational structures and processes that can also serve in the phased evolution from an Information Commons to a Learning Commons, or the initial development of an LC from the starting gate. In the case of either LC initiation, or LC evolution, some subgroup like our Social Resources Team may well prove invaluable, even if this "team" is only one key individual with one or two full-time or part-time assistants. Such a team, however designated, may have even greater utility for campus politics than the other resource teams. For example, managers could consider handing this team some responsibility for grant-writing involvement; thereby perhaps attracting the involvement of some key staff member from another unit with special grantsmanship skills. This team could also give potential collaborating partners a single team-point-of-contact for development of special grant-funded proposals that might guide or facilitate the evolution from IC to LC. The team's special areas of focus are shown in Figure 8.24.

Figure 8.24
Special Areas of Focus for the Social Resources Team

May provide oversight for projects with possible collaborating units, such as
    Center for Teaching & Learning
    Writing Center
    Academic Resource/Tutorial/Skills Center
    Curriculum Center
Regular liaison to academic schools, departments, divisions
Liaison to Thematic Learning Communities initiatives
Oversight of interdepartmental & multidisciplinary projects
Oversight of other group learning initiatives
Coordinates IC/LC campus awareness; PR
Grants administration for specialized fund-raising
Coordinates or facilitates rights management oversight
Coll. with Human Resources Team on soft/hard IC opening agenda

---

This team may become involved in oversight and tracking of multiple projects before, during, and after LC implementation, and we strongly recommend a standardized set of online tracking, scheduling, and project update formats based either on custom internally-designed templates, or the sort of adaptations we have used as illustrations and download-able from the Office Web site. This may seem self-evident, but collaborative academic projects frequently are based on, or lead into, some type of grant-based funding arrangement, and require careful documentation of project rollout details, personnel assignments, and work-schedule summations for determining in-kind funding. Figure 8.25 offers a further example adapted from free downloadable templates.

Figure 8.25
Multiple Project Tracking Template Illustration

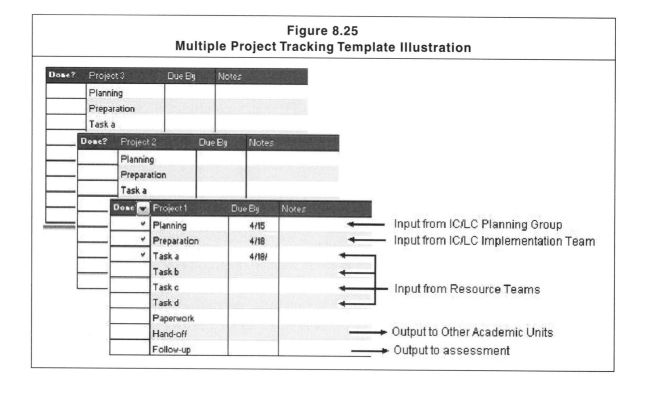

Some managers might object that this entire structure of resource teams as presented here is too cumbersome. Obviously, a good deal depends upon the size of the library or other academic organization that plans and implements the IC/LC. However, the array of ideas here may be viewed as a smorgasbord from which individual ideas, or idea-clusters, may be picked and chosen. But keep in mind that it is likely that the manager who decides to improvise and implement by a seat-of-the-pants approach will ultimately find the rollout and start-up more stressful and risk-laden than the manager who spends the initial time and effort to ground the entire process in a team-based structure that enables staff to steer critical aspects of implementation appropriate to their areas of expertise. The brief narrative in Figure 8.26 brings the generic Implementation Team overview to summation.

Figure 8.26
IC Implementation Team, Overview, Part 3

The breakout team meetings allowed all participants in the implementation to ask questions and submit ideas about the range of topics that would need to be addressed. The first meeting provided context and a great deal of useful information; however, the most important outcome of the first meeting was the establishment of a regular schedule of agenda-driven meetings throughout the process.

After that initial meeting, the full implementation group met on a regular basis, with intervals no longer than a week between meetings. Each meeting followed an agenda, which then became the framework for tracking tasks and completion milestones. Minutes of each meeting were taken in sufficient detail to serve as a history of what was done and record the agreements that were made on priorities, time lines, coding, milestones, and other decisions. Frequent references were made to the minutes throughout the implementation.

As the meetings progressed, the agendas became more detailed, and the focus of each working group's progress better defined. This led the full implementation team to meet monthly, with smaller work groups now meeting weekly, and sometimes meeting in joint session to resolve issues that crossed unit boundaries. Their work was reported in the full group meetings on milestones completed, conflicts resolved, and on any uncertainties that surfaced and required the full implementation team's attention.

The meetings became excellent venues to exchange information and for each office or department within the full implementation team to study the issues from each other's perspective. Interesting balances had to be struck in this project including how to define the project parameters and enhance the final package of resources and services, while at the same time meeting the project go-live date. The team was tempted to refine and to try to perfect every aspect prior to IC opening; however, the project was also on a tight calendar, and many tasks necessary for implementation had to be completed.

In this chapter, we have discussed using the ideas and methods of *project management*, with a few brief references to aspects of something called program management. But with the implementation of a Learning Commons, and especially with the transition from implementation to ongoing operations management, we recommend that the manager consider carefully the full range of ideas and methods of *program management*. Martinelli and Waddell define program management as: "The coordinated management of interdependent projects over a finite period of time in order to achieve a set of business objectives."[12] In another article, they add: "Program management is strategic in nature, while project management is tactical in nature.... Program management is entirely cross-functional, while project

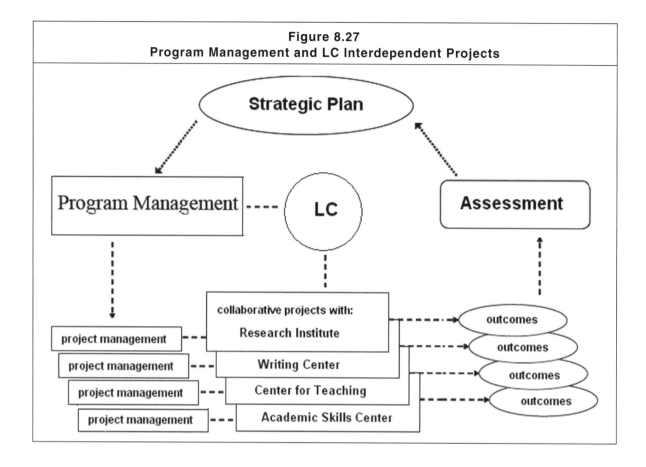

Figure 8.27
Program Management and LC Interdependent Projects

management focuses on a single function..."[13] Martinelli and Waddell have authored a series of papers that can help lay the groundwork for pushing the envelope of a project management mind-set to the more complex and demanding roles of program management. Figure 8.27 loosely adapts a diagram from Martinelli and Waddell to illustrate the relevance of the concept to LC implementation and operations; it shows interdependent LC projects, in collaboration with a Research Institute, Writing Center, Academic Skills Center, and a Center for Teaching. Each is individually managed at an initial oversight level by project management, but because they are interdependent, they are collectively under a higher level of program management, which allows coordinated application of resources, and coordinated assessment of outcomes.

By our definition, an LC targeting far-reaching or transformational change is no longer a single project but an interdependent set of projects, and the problem of guiding each project in a coordinated way to maintain proper alignment with strategic goals and objectives becomes critical. This is precisely what the tools and methodologies of program management are designed to address. This does not guarantee that library managers will be the individuals or group designated as program managers. The university administration may view the LC per se as one of the several connected subsidiary projects to be program managed, and therefore the responsibility for ensuring overall alignment and coordination may rest with an individual or group super-ordinate to LC or library managers. In such a case, the LC manager may essentially be one of several project managers under the general guidance of a program manager.

However, in the loosely coupled world of higher education, the type of collaborative initiative we are envisioning here often comes to fruition without that level of central administrative oversight, and it may fall to the LC or library manager to fill the role of de facto program manager. We see real-world cases where ICs and LCs come to be viewed as innovative and essential collaborative partners across campus simply because their managers took the initiative to play the role of de facto program managers, or similar roles perhaps better described as facilitators or coordinators.

Marketing: The Information Commons and Divergence Branding

In discussing "publicity and marketing of the new commons" the novelty and utility of an IC/LC may seem self-evident, and it may be tempting to settle for the usual methodologies of writing press releases, giving tours, and utilizing normal current awareness techniques. In fact, these are entirely appropriate steps. But they should be utilized in full awareness of the fact that the IC/LC phenomenon offers the library community an extraordinary opportunity to move beyond the usual prescriptions and "launch a new brand," using the concepts and ideas of brand divergence advanced by Al and Laura Ries, in their book *The Origin of Brands*. The inaugural issue of *NextSpace* (formerly the *OCLC Newsletter*) featured an interview with Al and Laura Reis. They commented: "Divergence means to create a new category, have a new name and perform a single function.... Our studies show that virtually every successful new brand was created by divergence of an existing category."[14] If the traditional library "brand" has been viewed categorically as a place to find information in books and a place to learn from books, then the IC becomes an opportunity to fork off a divergent brand that will be presented to students as a new type of place to find information and learn from the multiplying array of knowledge media and online resources. In marketing more specifically to faculty and academic administration, it can be also further branded as a mechanism that empowers users to engage the full scope of the virtual commons and the cultural commons, as well as the array of advanced literacies identified by Shapiro and Hughes.

The irony, of course, is that from a library management and operations point of view, the Information Commons seems an example of *convergence*, bringing together print, digital, and media resources and providing a continuum of service while extending the traditional library. But even when administered with this in mind, this may not be the core motivation behind the IC user's experience or perception. A key point of divergence in IC facilities lies in their differentiated identities to users, in not being "reference room computer labs," or "library database centers," but new types of spaces and places that diverge from the library's set and long-established identity, as represented in startup terminology such as *Information Commons*, *Information Arcade*, *Media Union*, *Media Cloisters*, and *Virtual Village*. Some librarians reacted to such naming with initial skepticism, but in fact such names were an early recognition, whether intuitive or analytical, of the urgent need and unique opportunity for brand divergence presented by the physical commons. Those who insist that ICs should simply be branded as "computer labs in libraries" are perhaps swimming upstream against a massive historical current that Al and Laura Reis have already identified. When asked about the "worst branding mistakes," they simply reply, "Without a doubt, product or service line extension. Instead of launching new brands, companies and organizations try to cover diverging categories by line extending their brand names."[15]

Does this argue for the University of Texas "displaced library" approach, where the former undergraduate library "becomes" the IC, rather than the University of Missouri-Kansas City approach, where the IC is viewed as a space that *extends* the library? The Ries approach does not necessarily imply a need to physically displace the entire library in order to achieve brand divergence for the IC. Contemporary libraries are serving a generation of mall-walking young consumers who have become sophisticated at perceiving multiple branded storefronts within generalized physical enclosures. But if the IC remains physically within the library or conjoined to the library, it does argue for strongly defined visual and semantic "storefront" differentiation of the IC from the rest of the library. A possible model might be seen in Kinko's, which began as a photocopy storefront. When computer workstations and printers were added, they were situated in a highly defined physical subspace. Even though computer printing and digital photocopying have been on a path of technological convergence, Kinko's management wisely realized that for customers, photocopying and computer access and printing represented well-differentiated activities. More recently, the corporate convergence between Kinko's and FedEx has led to packaging and mailing counters that are not only physically differentiated from other Kinko's functional areas, but prominently branded as FedEx counters.

To paraphrase the comments quoted earlier from UMKC managers, this author would argue that it is still feasible for library managers to understand the IC as a place of service convergence that extends the library's traditional services in new directions, so long as it is positioned and branded as a divergent entity within the library's generalized physical enclosure. As Tom Storey points out in his *NextSpace* article preceding the Reis interview, "The data point out a disconnect between the resources of today's libraries and the perceptions held by users. While many libraries provide rich offerings in electronic content and create virtual real-time access via the Web, most library users are unaware of these services."[16] Why has public perception not caught up with reality? Quite frankly, it is far more efficient and effective to repackage those rich offerings as an IC brand that diverges from the traditional library brand, than to flail against an entrenched definition of the library brand as purveyors of books, which has centuries of social momentum behind it. The newsletter article quotes one survey responder as stating the following viewpoint about libraries: "... stacks of books, tables filled with books, people holding books, people checking out books. Libraries are all about books. That is what I think and that is what I will always think."

If the titular leaders of the library community had collectively gathered in the year 1995 to invent out of whole cloth an opportunity for large-scale brand divergence, they could hardly have devised a more perfect candidate than the Information Commons or Learning Commons. This has been reflected, in fact, in the extraordinary door-count figures amassed at some early IC adopters, especially Leavey Library at the University of Southern California. To echo Tom Storey, there is not only a current disconnect between the resources of today's libraries and the perceptions held by users, but we see a striking disconnect between the remarkable use levels at Leavey Library and the continuing appearance of negative articles in the mainstream academic press that pronounce libraries as a dead issue or an endangered species.[17]

For the individual library manager, the question becomes how best to exploit the concept of brand divergence. The Ries approach actually blends well with Library IC needs for reasons beyond divergent branding. The Ries's entire premise is that advertising and marketing may not be as effective at building a new brand as public relations. "Marketing doesn't deal with products. Marketing deals with perceptions," they note, adding, "Publicity or PR is a more effective way [than advertising] to deal with those perceptions."[18] Advertising normally costs money, of course, and scarcity of funds has long directed library managers toward public relations programs in lieu of advertising. What may seem unusual to the library profession is the whole notion of viewing *branding* as an outgrowth of public relations rather than of advertising. In another article, the Ries's note: "Just because a heavy dose of advertising is associated with most major brands doesn't necessarily mean that advertising built the brands in the first place. The birth of a brand is usually accomplished with publicity, not advertising ... starting with your core group and then rolling out the story."[19]

Divergence branding does not mean making the library "go away" or turning it invisible. But it may mean putting the IC "out front," virtually as well as physically. A good exemplar can be found on the current awareness Web page for the Pace University Learning Commons Initiative.[20] The design elements of the Pace University example are shown in Figure 8.28. It

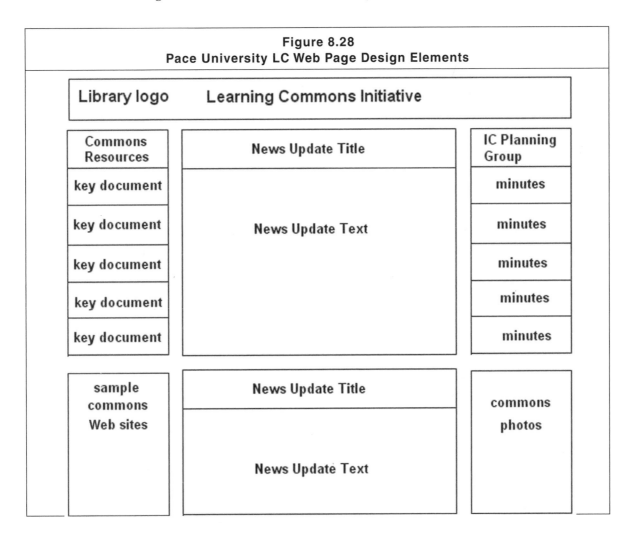

**Figure 8.28
Pace University LC Web Page Design Elements**

Library logo	Learning Commons Initiative	
Commons Resources	**News Update Title**	**IC Planning Group**
key document		minutes
key document	**News Update Text**	minutes
key document		minutes
key document		minutes
key document		minutes
sample commons Web sites	**News Update Title**	commons photos
	News Update Text	

carries the library logo as an element of continuity (and resides within the library's Web space) but otherwise the LC has been given divergent branding even at an early stage of initiative planning, being brought online before the actual LC rollout. The page components are reduced to abstract elements in Figure 8.26 to show how the key components can be abstracted out for usability analysis. Usability analysis can serve the overt formative purpose of testing alternative Web site designs, but also as a summative tracking of the success of divergent branding of the LC initiative.

According to the survey summarized in ARL's SPEC Kit on the Information Commons, the library Web site was the most common channel used for IC publicity, followed by posters and press releases.[21] Speeches, e-mail, and media stories followed in preference, all tied for fourth. This generally accords with the findings of OCLC's *Perceptions of Libraries and Information Resources*, where college students indicated that they learned about library digital services primarily through physical walk-in visits followed closely by visits to the library Web site.[22]

Thus visually differentiating or "framing" the physical IC from the rest of the library along with maintaining its distinctive Web page identity seem to project a two-pronged branding strategy that accords quite well with the Ries concept. What may be missing, surprisingly, is the effective leveraging of a benefit-related or service-related word or phrase. In yet another article, the Ries's commented: "No matter how complicated the product, no matter how complicated the needs of [the user], it's always better to focus on one word or benefit rather than two or three.... Words come in different varieties. They can benefit related (cavity prevention), service related (home delivery), audience related (younger people)..."[23] Because of its nebulous etymology, it is unclear whether "Information Commons" works better in propelling brand divergence based on an association with *service*, *benefit*, or *audience*. Perhaps, one might speculate, its relative force in the literature reflects a simultaneous association with benefit, service, and audience! However, the Ries's also note the importance of a "halo effect," where one readily identified benefit may imply or entail still others. Since libraries were already given higher marks than search engines for credibility and reliability in the OCLC *Perceptions* study, it may be possible to extend that halo around the Information Commons even while branding it as a divergent service unit. One neglected area of potential word emphasis may lie in the naming of online catalogs. Trade names for these products tend to be "techie," yet do not seem to associate readily with the underlying semantics of words such as "credibility," "reliability," or "accuracy." (If an auto company had not already taken "Acura," it might have made an advantageous brand name for a library OPAC). And the naming of statewide consortial portals also seems more related to convenient acronyms composed for internal consumption by library peers rather than focused attempts to project brand identities.

In brief, the use levels and doorcount figures of existing ICs may reflect a serendipitous combination of visual IC storefront distinctiveness within library buildings, an easily comprehensible name that is both service-related and benefit-related, and the fortuitous use of public relations techniques in lieu of advertising. Opportunities may still exist to reinforce this divergent brand with OPAC naming and signage that appeals to benefits of credibility, accuracy, and reliability already associated with libraries. Beyond these typical methodologies, there also exists great potential to offer IC/LC programming that can "build the brand" through audience enlistment. A fine example of this potential was realized in the "Faculty Showcase" program held annually at UNC-Charlotte in the years overlapping the opening of the Information Commons. Conceptualized by then Head of Media Services Beverly Mitzel, the Faculty Showcase became an outstanding success on several levels. On one level, it offered a summer-long learning environment for faculty to master and develop new IT and multimedia tools in pursuit of proposed instructional and research projects. Second, it then provided a forum shortly after the start of the fall term for faculty members to demonstrate their completed projects for interested colleagues. On a third level, it functioned indirectly as a sort of Media Services "open house" that showcased benefits and services and staff expertise in the best possible context. Particularly for a Learning Commons, the Faculty Showcase model offers many intrinsic advantages to faculty while also functioning as a subtly powerful public relations tool.

Scanning the Horizon

A related operational priority appropriate for an IC/LC would involve ongoing "scanning-the-horizon" current awareness functions to keep abreast of the rapid innovations in academic technology, pedagogical practice, and educational methodology initiatives. This can be a periodic renewal of the earlier scenario-building focus group exercises from the planning template, perhaps with representatives from each resource team, and/or unit coordinators. As a programming function, it can also propel "brand divergence," as it positions the LC as preparing for and oriented toward the future, whereas the library is sometimes perceived (with or without justification) as oriented toward preservation of the past. As we noted in our earlier discussion of Hypercard and the Web, new technologies such as iPod emerge and proliferate in a quasi-underground cultural milieu. They can fly under the radar screen for a time, until they burst out into wider acceptance and awareness. If the LC is to meet its potential within its loosely coupled organizational schema as a sensory mechanism for coping with rapid change, this type of regular scanning-the-horizon exercise can be a vital part of organizational culture. (To see one example of how a "Harman fan" might be used to explore various possible futures for colleges and universities, we recommend a PowerPoint presentation by Ruud van der Helm from a class exercise during the Futures Research Methods II graduate seminar from the Summer 2002 program at the University of Houston-Clear Lake.[24] However, some of the particulars of this 2002 example are already outdated, thus reinforcing the importance of continual horizon-scanning activities.)

Horizon-scanning programs can be an extension of current awareness staff development activities already under way in many libraries. One example, shown in Figure 8.29, is a "watch list" fairly typical of lists maintained by the IS departments on several campuses, described in one instance as a list of emerging areas monitored each year through attending conference presentations and holding team discussions. This list is only a representative sampling.

Following are several horizon-scanning topics that may have special potential for IC/LC programming use while also serving to "build the divergent brand."

Figure 8.29
"IS Watch List" at Connecticut College

Information Resources
Copyright
Cost of Information
Electronic Databases & Information Access products
Open Access Publishing
Stack and Storage Space

Instructional Technology
Digital Spatial Data and Maps
Electronic Classroom and Lab Security
Emerging Technologies in Teaching
Remote Collaborations and Conferencing

Research Support and Instruction
Virtual Reference
Online Plagiarism
Information Literacy
Reference Service

Special Collections and Archives
Institutional Digital Repository
Preservation and Conservation

Technical Support
Campus Data Wiring Infrastructure
Content Management
E-Commerce
Identity and Access Management
Internet2
Microsoft Operating Systems and Applications
Mobile Computing
Network Security
Open Source Software
Peer-to-Peer File Sharing
Privacy
Remote Application Hosting
Web Convergence and Self-Service

Horizon 1: Social Learning in Massive Multiplayer Online Games

Researchers are devoting increasing attention to the social implications of the MMOG (Massive Multiplayer Online Game), as John Kirriemuir describes:

> ...online games have evolved into...the MMOG (Massive Multiplayer Online Game)....thousands of players to simultaneously interact...in an online, multiplayer-only persistent world. Some are played on a mobile device, typically a phone...In a Role-Playing Game, a pre-configured avatar [is] controlled by the player,...encountering other characters, communicating, trading and fighting.[25]

These games have a far more widespread social impact and cultural level of engagement than many in the general population may realize. The LC may follow the Georgia Tech example and hosts gaming nights; and a more embedded cross-disciplinary approach to game-related learning theory and social group analysis may flow from relatively modest beginnings. One purpose of scanning-the-horizon programs and activities is to repeatedly "troll the river" of social and technological change to see what new previously unsuspected connections, initiatives, and relationships may emerge.

Horizon 2: Internet2, Web 2.0, the Semantic Web

Various initiatives for enhancing the bandwidth, infrastructure, middleware, "intelligence," and scope of the Internet and WWW have significant implications for the future of higher education, libraries, and knowledge itself. LC staff in collaboration with campus IT specialists and key academics not only have a significant stake in such developments, but in the context of Learning Commons implementation, have significant opportunities to host scanning-the-horizon focus groups and seminars on their ongoing developments as a service to colleagues across campus. The range of related innovation, from enhanced active desktop utilities, to "MyLibrary" personalized Web-client interfaces, to "semantic Web" deep structure are too vast, of course, to be dealt with here. Stephen Abram, Vice President for Innovation at SirsiDynix, summarizes key features:

- RSS (really simple syndication)
- Wikis
- New and revised programming methods like AJAX and APIs
- Blogs and blogging
- Commentary and comments functionality
- Personalization and "My Profile" features
- Personal media such as Podcasting and MP3 files
- Streaming media audio and video formats
- Reviews and user driven ratings
- Personalized Alerts
- Web Services
- Instant messaging and virtual reference including co-browsing
- Folksonomies, Tagging, and tag clouds
- Photos (e.g., Flickr, Picasa)
- Social networking software
- Open Access, Open Source, Open Content
- Socially driven content
- Social bookmarking (such as Delic.io.us)[26]

These innovations bring with them the potential to achieve and go beyond the type of hypermedia shell or learning management system that was envisioned in the original Learning Commons proposal at Jackson Community College in the late 1980s. The development of small, personalized handheld devices, from Blackberry to iPods, enhances the possibility that such a hypermedia shell could be transportable in small physical packages, as well as conveyable across wireless Webspace.

Horizon 3: The IC Copyright-Free Zone

Some, myself included, would like to see LC-based discussions around the possibility of creating an IC-networked *copyright-free zone* for purely academic purposes. The ideas would be loosely based on the concept of a *free trade zone*, which the Wikipedia defines as: "A free trade zone or export processing zone is a part or parts of a country where tariffs and quotas are eliminated and bureaucratic requirements lowered to attract companies to raise the incentives of doing business there."[27] In a copyright-free zone, a network of campus-based physical ICs and LCs, nationally or internationally, would establish a "closed circuit network" operating in parallel to the normal open Internet infrastructure. This network would only be accessible from workstations and data access points *physically located* in campus-based ICs and LCs. No commercial development would be permitted within the zone, and embedded metadata and other security provisions would prevent export of Zone content to the open Internet, or access to Zone content from any workstation beyond a properly designated campus-based IC/LC. Content could be imported, but once within the Zone, it could be accessed and manipulated and copied only by faculty and students within the Zone and without concern for copyright. However, proper citation and crediting would still be required; plagiarism would not be tolerated. Many librarians and academics are concerned about erosion of academic fair-use exceptions and provisions in copyright law, and see a dampening effect upon free inquiry and creative innovation. The initiative known as the Creative Commons already offers creators a way to define "...the spectrum of possibilities between full copyright—*all rights reserved*—and the public domain—*no rights reserved*."[28] However, we believe a copyright-free zone would still be a useful way to strongly assert academic fair use provisions for all content created and licensed in any context. In the virtual commons, or across the Web, embedded rights-management metadata can function only as a proximate control on use of content files. An IC-based cross-institutional *extranet*, synchronized with rights-management metadata, offers the potential for a tangible locus of control, much like the physical, tangible boundaries of a free-trade zone, and a closed circuit network would allow faculty and students at multiple ICs to pool ideas and online creative content in ways that protect the tradition of academic fair use, while still allowing creators to market and profit from content creation and replication beyond the physical and virtual boundaries of the Zone.

Horizon 4: Serendipity, Metabrowsing, and Subject Visualization

The announcement of Google Print, an effort to digitize large research collections in cooperation with major research libraries, has led to some predictions that physical collections will eventually be warehoused and user access to their content will take place almost exclusively through full-text keyword searching across the aggregate virtual commons. In this scenario, it would be logical to assume that the entire range of traditional library print resource utilization would then take place within the rubric of the Information Commons, representing a "beaming up" of content en masse from the physical to virtual levels. However, some scholars and researchers have raised an important flag of caution. Thomas Mann comments: "Researchers in this country have long been accustomed to having direct access to large book collections shelved in subject-classified stacks.... Classified shelving enables researchers to recognize sources whose keywords they could never specify in advance."[29] Nor is this concern strictly limited to advanced academic researchers. Mann's concern echoes the unnamed student at the University of Texas who commented on the undergraduate library being physically displaced by the Information Commons: "When I do research, I like to go to a section of the library where I might stumble on another book that's useful."

In fact, such "serendipitous browsing" represents a vital aspect of physical libraries that has long been under-recognized, under-appreciated, and insufficiently leveraged by librarians in both instructional and public awareness settings. One wonders whether the lack of serious attention to this issue might partly stem from the word "serendipity" itself, which sounds vaguely like something from the film *Mary Poppins*. In fact, serendipity refers to the end result of a process that is only approximated by the word "browsing," which again implies a rather offhand excursion through assembled books. In fact, the sort of highly directed and purposeful browsing through subject-classified bookstacks described by Thomas Mann might better be characterized by the term "metabrowsing."

However, while Mann has done a real service by again bringing this issue to the fore, he has not broached the possibility that metabrowsing could, and probably should, be enabled in digital contexts. This was, in fact, the goal of a research project at Belmont Abbey College, called *Scholastica*. *Scholastica* gathered the records from a library OPAC into an XML-based visualization database called VisualNet. Surrogates representing print books, ebooks, and Web sites were displayed as clickable targets arrayed across angular diagrams representing LC classes and nested diagrams representing LC subclasses. Student focus group results indicate that students who engaged in metabrowsing across such visual diagrams (tagged and indexed by LC subclass captions) diplayed expanded search strategies and enriched search vocabularies.[30] This result of expanded vocabularies specifically addresses the issue raised by Mann in noting that proper keywords for directed searches could not always be specified in advance. Other subject visualization products, such as Aquabrowser and Grokker, have also begun making appearances in the library marketplace. The entire issue of metabrowsing, visualization, and serendipity would make an excellent "scanning the horizon" topic for a Learning Commons program, and beyond that, a research collaboratory. Figure 8.30 presents the start screen for Scholastica, where LC-classed collections are represented by colored blocks that dynamically resize themselves over time as books in their their respective collections are added and withdrawn. Figure 8.31 presents a typical schematic of an LC subclass (GF-75 Human influences on the environment) together with targets representing titles that would normally be shelved within that subclass. In this diagram, of course, the targets representing print books, e-books, and digital resources are all interfiled to encourage metabrowsing.

Horizon 5: New Shamanism, New Scholasticism

Lastly, we offer the thought that the new realities of the physical, virtual, and cultural commons offer interesting (and sometimes unexpected) avenues for very old ways of learning and understanding to reemerge in modern technological society. In tribal cultures, shamans played the role of guides and initiators, leading their students and acolytes through various levels of reality, meaning, and perception, while articulating the notion of the global interrelatedness of all phenomena. In certain ways, the student may be introduced to and guided through the manifestations of knowledge in the physical, virtual, and cultural levels of the Information Commons in ways that seem oddly reminiscent of the shamanic method.

Figure 8.30
Home Page for the Scholastica Visualization Project

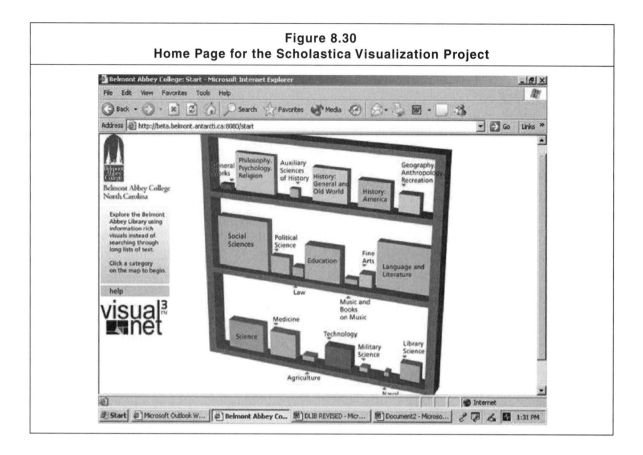

Figure 8.31
Sample LC Subclass Diagram: Scholastica Visualization Project

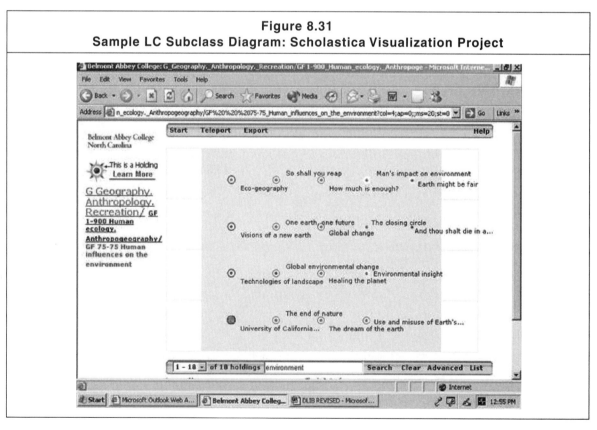

This parallelism would make for an interesting topic for a scanning-the-horizon LC seminar. Similarly, the internal rhetoric of online monologue, dialogue and discourse in blogging and other hypertext online venues, like the "closed worlds" of online gaming, recall in certain ways the self-referential rhetorical structures of medieval scholasticism. The potential advantages and possible pitfalls of the growth of an online scholasticism also seems a topic of significant future relevance.

Endnotes

[1] Lowrey, Charles B. "The Vision of a Team-Based Learning Organization" *Working Paper #1 on Team Management. University of Maryland.* (2000). Available: http://www.lib.umd.edu/PUB/team_management.html

[2] Stoffle, Carla, and Shelley Phipps, 2003. "Creating a Culture of Assessment: The University of Arizona Experience." *ARL Bimonthly Report.* 230/231(October/December). Available: http://www.arl.org/newsltr/230/cultureaz.html

[3] Lakos, Amos A. "Implementing a 'Culture of Assessment' Within the Information Commons." Presentation for Information Commons Symposium, University of Southern California (September 2004). Available: http://www.usc.edu/isd/libraries/locations/leavey/news/conference/presentations/presentations_9-16/Assessment/UCLA_Lakos.ppt#1

[4] Ibid.

[5] Henning, Joanne. 2005. "Information Commons Study Leave: October 2, 2004–March 31, 2005." University of British Columbia. Available: http://jhenning.law.uvic.ca/

[6] "Microsoft Office Online: Templates:" Available: http://office.microsoft.com/en-us/templates/default.asp

[7] "Information Commons Committee: Vision." University of Maryland Libraries. The IC Committee Web page is available at: http://www.lib.umd.edu/groups/infocommons/home.html. The PowerPoint slides are available at http://www.lib.umd.edu/groups/infocommons/presentation.ppt

[8] "Microsoft Office Online: Templates:" Available: http://office.microsoft.com/en-us/templates/default.asp

[9] Cowgill, Allison, Joan Beam, and Lindsey Wess. 2001. "Implementing an Information Commons in a University Library." *Journal of Academic Librarianship.* 27 no. 6 (November).

[10] "Digital Reference Competencies." UCLA Library. University of California at Los Angeles. Available: http://www.library.ucla.edu/digref/competencies.htm

[11] "Microsoft Office Online: Templates:" Available: http://office.microsoft.com/en-us/templates/default.asp

[12] Martinelli, Russ, and Jim Waddell. 2005. "Aligning Program Management to Business Strategy." *PMForum Featured Papers.* Available: http://www.pmforum.org/library/papers/2005/AligningPMBusiness%20Strategy.pdf

[13] Martinelli, Russ, and Jim Waddell. 2004. "Program and Project Management: Understanding the Differences." *PMForum Featured Papers.* Available: http://www.pmforum.org/library/papers/2004/ProgramandProjectMgmt.pdf

[14] Storey, Tom. 2006. "Q&A: Launch a New Brand." *NextSpace: The OCLC Newsletter.* 1: 10.

[15] Ibid.

[16] Storey, Tom. 2006. "Extreme Makeover: Library Edition." *NextSpace: The OCLC Newsletter.* 1: 7.

[17] Gandel, Paul B. 2005. "Libraries: Standing at the Wrong Platform, Waiting for the Wrong Train?" *EDUCAUSE Review.* (November/December). Available: http://www.educause.edu/ir/library/pdf/erm05610.pdf

[18] Budd Jr., John. 2004. "How Not to Get the Word Out." *Across the Board.* 39 no. 5 (September).

[19] Ries, Al, and Laura Ries. 1999. "First Do Some Great Publicity." *Advertising Age.* 70. no. 6 (February 8).

[20] "Learning Commons Initiative." Pace University. (2006). Available: http://libtech.typepad.com/commons/

[21] Haas, Leslie, and Jan Robertson, 2004. *SPEC Kit 281: The Information Commons.* Washington, D.C.: Association of Research Libraries. 42.

[22] "Part 2: Using the Library—In Person and Online." *Perceptions of Libraries and Information Resources OCLC.* (2005). Available: http://www.oclc.org/reports/pdfs/Percept_pt2.pdf

[23] Ries, Al, and Laura Ries. 1998. "Checking the Brandbook." *Brandweek.* 39 no. 42 (November 9).

[24] "The Future of Universities: An Example of the Harman Fan Scenario Approach." Available: http://www.infinitefutures.com/tools/sbharman.ppt

[25] Kirriemuir, John. "Parallel Worlds: Online Games and Digital Information Services." *D-Lib Magazine.* Vol. 11 No. 12. (December 2005). Available: http://www.dlib.org/dlib/december05/kirriemuir/12kirriemuir.html

26 Abram, Stephen. "Web 2.0, Library 2.0, and Librarian 2.0: Preparing for the 2.0 World." *SirsiDynix OneSource*. January 2006. Available: http://www.imakenews.com/sirsi/e_article000505688.cfm?x=b6ySQnR,b3B5r7pL

27 "Free-trade zones." *Wikipedia, the free encyclopedia*. Available: http://en.wikipedia.org/wiki/Free_trade_zone

28 "Learn More About Creative Commons." Available: http://creativecommons.org/learnmore

29 Mann, Thomas. "Google Print vs. Onsite Collections." *American Libraries*. August 2005. p. 45.

30 Beagle, Donald. "Visualizing Keyword Distribution Across Multidisciplinary C-Space." *D-Lib Magazine*. Vol. 9 No. 6 (June 2003). Available: http://www.dlib.org/dlib/june03/beagle/06beagle.html

9

Assessing Success to Enhance Space and Improve Service

by Donald Russell Bailey

Assessment Defined

Since it is ever more common to assess or evaluate services to ensure accountability, it is appropriate and justifiable that Information Commons services be viewed with such scrutiny. Assessment is certainly not new to library services of all kinds, but it is particularly important for the Information Commons model of integrated services, which is focused and based on the notion of better and more effectively meeting patron needs.

First, IC service providers need to know how effective the services are, how they might be improved, and even whether there is demonstrable evidence that they should be continued. Second, patrons need to know in order to decide whether to use these services and which ones are worth the expenditure of time, money, etc. Third, funding agents (administration, government, etc.) need to know to determine whether to provide funding support and how much to provide. Each of the three groups seeks and in some way makes an assessment of the services in terms of value, effectiveness, and basis for funding or continuation of funding.

Compared with Evaluation

The term assessment is variously used to refer to a sort of single-photo determination of how things are going, how someone is performing, how effective a service is. This more common single-photo view is what is termed summative evaluation: how things look at an end-point. The discussion on assessment of Information Commons services that follows uses the more precise types of *evaluation*, since the term *assessment* is the broader evaluative umbrella and is less helpful in assessing the value of IC services and resources.

Summative and Formative Evaluation

Summative evaluation of library and information services for patrons usually indicates, on an annual or multiannual basis, whether the library is providing adequate, super-, or sub-adequate services as reflected subjectively by patron opinion or perceptions (Likert scale responses, multiple choice, comments): i.e., patron satisfaction. Summative evaluation may also be objective, empirical, and quantitative in terms of desk service statistics, gate-count, circulation transactions and the like: more/fewer desk service queries were answered, gate-count was up/down, circulation transactions increased/decreased. Assessment is usually synonymous with summative evaluation. While summative evaluation has value, especially in the larger picture and over time (especially to upper administration and to funding agencies), it provides minimal information about the day-to-day flow of service provision and impact and is less useful in ongoing service management and improvement. It would then indicate whether a new service model like that of the IC has proven to be a more effective model after a year, two years, etc., of implementation; it does not, however, provide finer, more granular data for careful refinement and improvement. Formative evaluation serves that purpose much more effectively.

Formative evaluation consists of multiple snapshots (more like moving pictures) of more subjective patron perceptions and of empirical evaluative data (desk service statistics, etc.). The primary difference between summative and formative is intent and use: formative evaluation informs decision-making, refinement, improvement, and reform in an ongoing manner. For example, if one discovers that there are too many or too few staff at a particular desk for the number and type of queries coming to the desk, then fewer or more staff will be scheduled appropriately. Another example: if we learn (as we have) that sitting behind a service desk is less inviting and elicits fewer patron queries than "roving" or "lurking," then we encourage staff to alter their location and move out from behind the desk.

Much greater value accrues to service quality (creating and maintaining it) from evaluative data that are used formatively rather than summatively. Critical, evaluative scrutiny needs to be used to inform and reform our decisions on which services librarians provide and how they go about providing them.

Formal and Informal Evaluation

While most evaluation and commentary on evaluation is formal, informal evaluation is at least as valuable. Formal evaluation can take numerous forms, e.g., surveys, focus groups, usability studies, virtual pop-up/drop-down questionnaires, comment forms/cards, etc. Some types of formal evaluation (virtual pop-up/drop-down questionnaires and comment forms/cards) or less formal, are simply made available "just in case" the patron is interested in commenting or willing to provide feedback. Formal evaluation usually entails greater investment of time and resources for development over a longer period of time (e.g., widely-used assessment instruments such as LibQUAL+™ and SAILS) and more time and resources in processing and analyzing the data into meaningful results.

Informal evaluation, while very common, is often considered less important and reliable than formal evaluation. Informal evaluation is information contained in, e.g., (1) observations or anecdotal statements from patrons, staff, or administration, as well as patron comments on surveys or comment-boxes, or (2) changes or variations in activities, such as gate-/head-count, number of patrons reserving and using IC group study rooms and specialty labs, numbers and types of queries at IC desks, authenticated and other user logons, etc.

An example of number 1 would be an administrator's comment to an IC supervisor, that she/he sees "too many staff" at a desk, or "the staff doesn't appear to be busy," or "the staff doesn't make eye contact with patrons." This could then result in a review of the desk staff scheduling or staff training. An example of number 2 would be increased gate-/head-count, logons and use of group study rooms and specialty labs when an IC is implemented (a very comment observation), which would serve as informal evaluative documentation that patrons perceive by their actions that the service is effective.

While formal evaluation is preferred and more often used in institutional reports, informal evaluation should be seen as at least equally valuable. The comment section of LibQUAL+™ has yielded helpful insight into patrons' perceptions. Informal reviews of the comments as well as more rigorous theme-analysis provide interesting insight.

Quantitative and Qualitative

While most evaluation and commentary on evaluation emphasize quantitative evaluation, qualitative evaluation should be considered of equal importance. Institutional reports lend more credence to quantitative data; thus we are asked or even urged to include and emphasize quantitative data in reports (even scholarly impact reports rely on the quantity of citations in publications considered qualitatively more scholarly).

The most common and easily available quantitative evaluative data are carefully gathered service desk statistics, IC group study room and specialty lab usage data, and gate-/head-count. Greater value accrues to these data as they are gathered, reported, and analyzed longitudinally over time. Examples from the University of North Carolina at Charlotte's IC for the three-year period 2001–2004 are shown in Figures 9.1 and 9.2. Statistics gathering was systematic at all the IC service desks, using standard categories (e.g., directional, reference, reference-referral, etc.). Where possible these statistics were reviewed regularly (e.g., at weekly or monthly area meetings) and graphed to determine patterns. All statistics were reviewed at least annually by the Public Service Committee (representing all areas of the library) for patterns and trends. Weekly, monthly, and annual discussions and analyses of these data helped inform staff changes, staff-training, and cross-training needs and changes, focus on problems and solutions, and, in general, provided extremely valuable insight into services provision in the IC and other areas of the library.

Additional, incidental value of the data gathering accrued from the many discussions of methods and significance of the statistical data gathered. This value was the shared understanding and insight into the workings of the library, the individual desks, and the individual staff members. An increased pool of human resource capital accrued—goodwill, cooperation, and an informal but very valuable exchange of knowledge, insights, and skills.

Qualitative evaluation is more subjective, less empirical, and often considered less reliable for institutional reporting. Nevertheless, there is tremendous value in qualitative evaluation, especially when used together with quantitative data. Common types of qualitative data are anecdotal observation, surveys with open-ended questions, surveys of perceptions (LibQUAL+™), usability studies, and focus groups. The last three will be discussed below, with special attention being given to LibQUAL+™.

Figure 9.1
Statistical Cumulations UNC Charlotte IC: Part 1

I. University of North Carolina Charlotte IC Public Services Statistics.

IC Public Services Statistics—UNC Charlotte Atkins Library

Area:		Activity:	2003–2004	2002–2003	2001–2002
Information Desk		**Directory & directions**	**10,042**	**9,814**	**9,799**
	Referrals -	Reference referral	3,504	2,967	2,356
		Pres. Support referral	1,296	1,185	926
		Circulation referral	3,618	3,838	5,880
		Collections/2nd-floor ref.	1,605	1,579	1,270
		Spec. Coll. Referral	88	133	59
		VTS/Xerox referral	1,136	1,062	—
		Other referrals	8,701	1,175	—
		Total referrals	**14,948**	**6,526**	**4,848**
	Assistance -	Jasmine/catalog	2,293	1,909	1,334
		Password/proxy	374	461	222
		Gate alarms	1,833	1,148	947
		Grp. Std. Rms.	12,633	9,527	5,683
		No Grp. Std. Rms.	2,056	1,145	—
		Phone	6,620	4,892	1,698
		E-mail/Novell/49erExpr.	1,549	935	—
		Machine trouble	1,223	1,033	427
		Retrieve books	222	180	—
		Reference	442	544	—
		Presentation Supp.	763	778	—
		Total assistance	**30,008**	**22,552**	**10,311**
		Total desk questions	**54,998**	**50,831**	**35,459**
		Group study rooms	**12,633**	**10,343**	**7,174**
		GSR patrons	**43,498**	**34,989**	**20,530**
Instruction		**Sessions**	**453**	**311**	**301**
		Students	**8,729**	**7,153**	**7,151**
Presentation Support		Login/e-mail -	1,850	2,016	—
		Printer support -	912	1,041	—
		Directional -	707	723	—
		FacCntrTeaching referrals	50	48	—
		Reference referrals	235	179	—
		Scanning support	912	528	—
		Software support	1,459	1,229	—
		Other/general	1,244	1,224	—
		Remote access	331	—	—
		VTS (copy card)	222	—	—
		49er Express	291	—	—
		Total	**8,213**	**7,078**	—
		Scanning lab users	**1,529**	**1,457**	—
		Multimedia lab users	**559**	**542**	—

Figure 9.2
Statistical Cumulations UNC Charlotte IC: Part 2

Reference	Ref under 5 min.	14,030	—	—
	Ref over 5 min.	2,964	—	—
	Phone—proxy/pwrd.	1,873	—	—
	Phone—other	1,518	—	—
	Technical - proxy/pwrd.	351	—	—
	Printer	1,233	—	—
	Technical—other	484	—	—
	Documents—fed/local	346	—	—
	Documents—state	136	—	—
	Referrals—desk	531	—	—
	Referrals—person	104	—	—
	Directional	3,655	—	—
	Ready Ref—Circ.	774	—	—
	Total questions	**27,998**	**32,136**	**30,650**
Virtual Reference	**Questions**	**326**	—	—
Research Data Srvics	SDC/Census	88	193	—
	Data files	48	122	—
	General reference	90	174	—
	Marketing	38	95	—
	Maps	28	98	—
	Other	210	298	—
	SAS/SPSS	44	41	—
	Systems	33	39	—
	Liaison	104	213	—
	Total	**739**	**1,273**	—
Circulation Desk			Jan.–June, 2003 only	
	Desk specific	24,571	3,805	—
	Reference	7,324	793	—
	Directional	4,914	1,359	—
	Technical & Equipment	4,143	1,891	—
	Total	**40,952**	**7,848**	—
Collections/2nd Fl. Desk			Jan.–June, 2003 only	
	Desk specific	8,596	4,002	—
	Reference	3,441	1,776	—
	Directional	6,215	2,872	—
	Technical	1,114	779	—
	Equipment	—	—	—
	Software	298	—	—
	Total	**19,664**	**9,429**	—
Archit.Rec.Cntr Desk			Jan.–June, 2003 only	
	Desk specific	—	569	—
	Reference	—	410	—
	Directional	—	187	—
	Technical	—	159	—
	Equipment	—	847	—
	Total	**4,718**	**2,172**	—
Circulation	**Check-out**	**154,788**	**162,738**	**175,125**
	Renewal	**32,033**	**51,380**	**42,229**
Gate count		**835,270**	**797,844**	**893,506**
Web site page views		**3,421,728**	—	—
Web site distinct hosts served		**69,404**	—	—
Logins (sessions) to networked electronic resources		**482,122**	—	—
Queries (searches) in networked electronic resources		**1,167,153**	—	—
Items requested (downloads) in networked electronic resources		**1,244,226**	—	—

Needs Assessment

It is common for libraries to conduct some form of needs assessment as part of strategic planning cycles (every two to five years). Assessment of needs provides helpful insight into changing needs and expectations of patrons, how well your library is currently meeting the needs of your community, and what other types of resources and services it can provide in the future. A needs assessment can help determine, e.g., who uses the library and ways to reach nonusers; how effective are staffing patterns, hours of operation, library services, facilities, and resources; and how these can be improved based on patron needs.

Conceptualizing, designing and implementing the needs assessment influence the value of the assessment. One must determine:

- a clear purpose for the study with intent to use the results;
- who will conduct the assessment;
- what method(s) and instrument(s) will be used and how it will be administered;
- what data will be gathered; and
- how the information will be used.

The clearer these issues are at the outset, the more valuable are the results and the more likely they will be used.

As mentioned previously, additional value to such an undertaking is the incidental understanding, teamwork, and synergistic goodwill of the process. Such informal and incidental by-products of collaborative and cooperative efforts can often be more valuable than the reported results.

Most IC implementations are preceded by a needs assessment either in-house or as an environmental scan. As Information Commons facilities and services become more widely established (almost de rigueur in the library world), the need for their assessment becomes more acute, and this understanding is already emerging in environmental scans (note especially recent OCLC and ACRL environmental scans and EDUCAUSE's *Education the Net Generation*). For many library planners and administrators, the needs assessment already exists and need not be repeated by them.[1] Rather they need to bring it to the attention of their funding administrators, their peers, and their staff.

Usability Studies and Focus Groups

Both usability studies and focus groups offer opportunities to formatively evaluate Information Commons services. They are often used together, but focus groups should be designed and run first, since they are more formative in nature, while a usability study documents usability at a point in time. Both must be carried out with the goal in mind of increasing usability and effectiveness of services for targeted patron groups.

Assessment focus groups are guided discussions of resources, services, etc., to elicit users' and patrons' preferences, opinions, perceptions, and expectations, and to determine how well based these are in patron needs. The focus group needs to be designed (for validity) and run/administered (for reliability) by someone other than those responsible for the resources, services, etc., in order for it to be objective and thus reliable and valid. In other words, IC staff should neither design nor run the focus group(s). Focus groups should be demographically representative of the patron population. The discussions are often recorded, and the recorded discussions (or transcripts) are analyzed for themes and trends. For example, one focus group indicated:

- the need for additional software (with specifics) on public service computers; i.e., they preferred ubiquity of resources on institutional computers;
- the need for longer hours of operation, i.e., they preferred that more resources be available at time of need, perhaps that resources be made better and more easily accessible remotely;
- the desire to access refreshments somewhere in the library, i.e., they preferred a full-service library;
- the desire for staff to be "nicer" and more willing to respond to technology questions, i.e., they preferred better affect of service based on patron needs; and
- a clear purpose for the study with intent to use the results.

Each of these needs/desires suggests that services often provided in an Information Commons environment would are desirable.

A usability study is an assessment of resources, services, etc., to determine how usable they are: which aspects are more or less usable by patrons. The usability study needs to be designed (for validity) and administered (for reliability) by someone other than those responsible for the resources, services, etc., in order for it to be objective and thus reliable and valid. Again, IC staff should neither design nor administer the usability study. Participants should be demographically representative of the patron population. Participants are usually given an articulated series of real-world application tasks, observed (from an objective distance and perhaps videotaped), with the details of their efforts to perform the tasks carefully noted. These observations are then analyzed (together with videotapes) for themes and trends. For example: one usability study indicated:

- patrons had difficulty saving informational files, which they had located, onto a disk (or other storage device) to be transported to productivity machines, i.e., they preferred productivity software on research computers; and
- patrons became frustrated and confused.

While data from focus groups can be relatively subjective, they can nevertheless be extremely beneficial in determining patron preferences, opinions, perceptions, expectations, and needs, as one looks to refine, improve, or restructure services. Data from usability studies are usually more objective than those from focus groups and often indicate minor or major concerns for usability of services for patrons. These evaluative data should be used together with other assessment tools and methods to understand the value of services to patrons and productively adjust and refine services for greater effectiveness.

Explicit and Implicit Assessment

Few assessment or evaluation methods or instruments focus directly or explicitly on the effectiveness of Information Commons services. While some explicit evaluative instruments have been developed in the past few years, most deal implicitly or indirectly with the effectiveness of Information Commons services.

Implicit

There are three well-known and one new evaluative instruments, which constitute implicit assessment of library and Information Commons effects on student learning and engagement. The first is the National Survey of Student Engagement. While several of the survey questions broach collaborative research, the integration of various information resources, and the use of technology resources common to ICs, there is no explicit reference to the library or IC-type facility.

The second is LibQUAL+™ (http://www.libqual.org/).[2] The 22 items in the three domains produce a great deal of valid, reliable, and demographically representative data on patron perceptions of library services, facilities, personal control, and access to adequate collections. Of the 22 survey items, 19 overlap extensively with desired aspects of service and resources in most ICs. Those 19 items are:

From LibQUAL+™ 2004

Information Control
- Making electronic resources accessible from my home or office.
- A library Web site enabling me to locate information on my own.
- The electronic information resources I need.
- Modern equipment that lets me easily access needed information.
- Easy-to-use access tools that allow me to find things on my own.
- Making information easily accessible for independent use.

Affect of Service
- Employees who instill confidence in users.
- Giving users individual attention.
- Employees who are consistently courteous.
- Readiness to respond to users' questions.
- Employees who have the knowledge to answer user questions.
- Employees who deal with users in a caring fashion.
- Employees who understand the needs of their users.
- Willingness to help users.
- Dependability in handling users' service problems.

Library as Place
- Library space that inspires study and learning.
- A comfortable and inviting location.
- A getaway for study, learning, or research.
- Community space for group learning and group study.

The use of LibQUAL+™ has numerous advantages:
- It is valid, reliable, and demographically representative.
- It can be repeated over time for longitudinal perspective.

- It is full-market and offers broad comparative dimensions.
- It allows supplemental questions tailored to the library's specific concerns.

Still, as an IC evaluative instrument, it is more implicit than explicit and should be complemented by more explicit evaluative activities.

The third instrument is the Standardized Assessment of Information Literacy Skills (SAILS, http://sails.lms.kent.edu/index.html). SAILS was inspired by Wisconsin Ohio Reference Evaluation Project (WOREP) and based on ACRL's information literacy standards, competencies, and objectives. While the SAILS instrument is not as settled as LibQUAL+™, the bank of questions and selection for each participant are grounded in information literacy research (with high validity, reliability, and demographic representativeness), the questions are mapped to ACRL's information literacy materials, and the resulting data overlap significantly with desired aspects of skills and competencies which are desired outcomes for services and resources in most ICs. One might view the Information Commons as the framework of services and resources in which information literacy is the curriculum. As such, patron success in the information literacy curriculum implies effectiveness of the IC framework of services and resources. Still, like LibQUAL+™, SAILS should be complemented with other explicit IC evaluative activities.

Finally, there is Information & Communication Technology Literacy, or ICTL, developed by ETS (www.ets.org/ictliteracy/ and http://www.ictliteracy.info/). On ETS's ICTL Web site, ICTL proficiency is defined as "...the ability to use digital technology, communication tools and/or networks appropriately to solve information problems in order to function in an information society. This includes the ability to use technology as a tool to research, organize, evaluate, and communicate information, and the possession of a fundamental understanding of the ethical/legal issues surrounding the access and use of information." The proficiency certainly overlaps implicitly with that of many ICs, but it is too early to characterize the instrument's validity, reliability, or demographic representativeness. Early reports suggest that the instrument emphasizes NetGen facility with IM and e-mail without articulated connection to or integration with more complex aspects of the activities emphasized in most ICs.

Explicit

There are several examples of explicit evaluative programs for the Information Commons. There are four programs that will be looked at here, since they serve as good illustrations and models.

At the University of Southern California's Leavey Library, the Information Commons staff developed and administered an instrument that focuses explicitly on the effectiveness of their Information Commons services (see Figure 9.3).

They have made it available for use and adaptation to other IC practitioners, and the staff at the University of North Carolina Charlotte modified it for their use; other ICs are in the process of adapting it to their IC. The University of Southern California IC administered the survey instrument in 2004 and used the results to refine and adjust IC services, as they expanded and created an additional IC area. The questions focused on patron demographic data, use patterns, and satisfaction levels. One interesting discovery was that half of their IC

Figure 9.3
USC Leavey Library IC Survey

Leavey Information Commons Survey

We will appreciate your taking a few minutes to help us learn more about the interests and satisfaction level of the students using the **Information Commons** (the combination of computing and reference services, collection, and studying facilities in the Lower and Upper Commons).

1. What is your status?

    ____Freshman   ____Sophomore   ____Junior   ____Senior   ____Masters   ____PhD

    ____Faculty   ____Staff   ____Other

2. What is your Major/School? _____

3. How often do you use the Information Commons in Leavey Library?

    ____Daily   ____Several times a week   ____Several times a month

    ____Several times a semester   ____Once a semester   ____First time user

4. Which of the following tools and services do you usually use while in the Information Commons? (Check all that apply)

    ____PC Workstation   ____Public i-Macs (USCInfo Kiosk)   ____Collaborative Workrooms

    ____Mac Workstation   ____Print Center   ____Reference Books

    ____Photocopy Machines   ____Handouts and brochures   ____Other:_____

    ____Computing/Research Staff

5. How much time do you usually spend in the Information Commons per visit?

    ____Less than an hour   ____1 to 3 hours   ____3 to 5 hours   ____More than 5 hours

    ____Other: (Please indicate) _____

6. How much time do you usually spend in the Collaborative Workrooms per visit?

    ____Less than 30 minutes   ____1 to 2 hours   ____4 to 6 hours   ____Not applicable

    ____30 to 60 minutes   ____2 to 4 hours   ____ over 6 hours

7. While in the Information Commons have you ever asked for assistance? ____Yes ____No

    If yes, did you request help with: (mark all that apply)   ____Software   ____Equipment

    ____Printing   ____Research/Information

8. Do you usually work: ____Alone ____Part of a group: What size? ____ ____Both

9. Do you own your own computer? ____Yes ____No

10. Why do you use the Information Commons? (Mark all that apply)

    ____Availability of software   ____Get technical assistance   ____Class related activities

    ____Personal/recreational computer usage   ____Study with a group or another student

    ____Use computer between classes   ____Consult reference librarians; get research assistance

    ____Fast connection   ____Other:_____

11. While on a workstation, which of the following types of applications do you usually use? (Mark all that apply)

    ____Web browser   ____E-mail   ____TOTALe (Blackboard)

    ____Word processing   ____Spreadsheet   ____Presentation

    ____Graphics   ____Web publishing   ____Statistics

    ____Review class lectures (Web cast) ____CAD

    ____Class applications: (please indicate title) _____

    ____Other: (please specify) _____

    ____Not applicable

(cont'd.)

Figure 9.3
USC Leavey Library IC Survey (Continued)

12. How often do you visit the Help desk in the Information Commons?

____Daily ____Several times a week ____Several times a month ____Several times a semester ____Never

13. While in the Information Commons, how frequently do you look for information or do research for a class assignment?

____Weekly ____Occasionally ____Once a semester ____Never ____Other: (indicate) _____

14. Which of the following do you (frequently or typically) use? (Mark all that apply)

____Internet search engines (e.g., Google, Yahoo)

____Homer, Library online catalog

____E-resource Data-base: ____Lexis/Nexis   ____ProQuest   ____Expanded Academic

____Other: (specify) _____

____E-Journals ____   E-Reserves   ____E-Books   ____Not applicable

15. How satisfied are you with the Information Commons computing resources?

____Extremely ____Very   ____Somewhat   ____Not very   ____Not at all   ____ Not applicable

16. How satisfied are you with the assistance you have received at the Information Commons' desks?

____Extremely ____Very   ____Somewhat   ____Not very   ____Not at all   ____ Not applicable

17. How satisfied are you with the Print Center services?

____Extremely ____Very   ____Somewhat   ____Not very   ____Not at all   ____ Not applicable

18. How satisfied are you with the Collaborative Workroom facilities?

____Extremely ____Very   ____Somewhat   ____Not very   ____Not at all   ____ Not applicable

19. How satisfied are you with the Collaborative Workroom reservation process?

____Extremely ____Very   ____Somewhat   ____Not very   ____Not at all   ____ Not applicable

20. What do you like **most** about the Information Commons?

21. What do you like **least** about the Information Commons?

22. Do you have any suggestions or comments regarding the Information Commons' equipment or services?

If you would like to be considered for a follow-up focus group, please indicate your contact information:

Name: _____   E-Mail Address:_____

Thank you for providing your input. Your answers will be used to shape future services and may be quoted in reports and published studies of the Information Commons.

---

patrons were graduate students and faculty, even though the Leavey Library IC is in USC's undergraduate library; this led to the creation of a second IC in Leavey Library with greater focus on graduate student and faculty use. This corroborates earlier notions that the IC model is functional for patrons at various levels of need and research sophistication, and that it is imminently scalable. Thus, the notion that it serves a limited, less sophisticated group of patrons is called into question. Shahla Bahavar and Linda Weber provided analyses and overviews of assessment efforts at USC during the 2004 USC IC Conference.[3]

The University of Calgary created an online IC feedback survey (see Figure 9.4) and has used it since 2001 as formative evaluation. Clearly, the advantage of the online survey is that

---

Figure 9.4
University of Calgary IC Survey Form

Information Commons Feedback
To Susan Beatty, Head, Information Commons

The following statements relate to your feelings about the service provided at the Information Commons. For each statement, please show the extent to which you believe this facility has the feature or service described by the statement.

- Choosing a **1** means that you **strongly disagree** that the Information Commons has that feature or provided that service.
- Choosing a **7** means that you **strongly agree**.
- You may choose any of the numbers in between to show how strong your feeling is.

There are no right or wrong answers. We are only interested in the numbers that best show your perceptions regarding the quality of the Information Commons service.

1. I did not have to wait more than 20 minutes for a computer.
   ___1 (strongly disagree) ___2 ___3 ___4 ___5 ___6 ___7 (strongly agree)

2. I was able to book a collaborative workroom when I needed it.
   ___1 (strongly disagree) ___2 ___3 ___4 ___5 ___6 ___7 (strongly agree)

3. Staff at the Service Desk are helpful and friendly.
   ___1 (strongly disagree) ___2 ___3 ___4 ___5 ___6 ___7 (strongly agree)

4. Staff at the Service Desk are able to answer my questions.
   ___1 (strongly disagree) ___2 ___3 ___4 ___5 ___6 ___7 (strongly agree)

5. The facility is welcoming, safe and clean.
   ___1 (strongly disagree) ___2 ___3 ___4 ___5 ___6 ___7 (strongly agree)

6. Signs within the Information Commons are clear.
   ___1 (strongly disagree) ___2 ___3 ___4 ___5 ___6 ___7 (strongly agree)

7. How long did you have to wait for a computer?
   ___10 minutes or less   ___30 to 45 minutes
   ___10 to 20 minutes   ___more than 45 minutes
   ___20 to 30 minutes

8. Please choose one of the following categories:
   ___Undergraduate Student   ___Staff
   ___Graduate Student   ___Alumni
   ___Faculty   ___Community Reader

9. Please provide more details about your experience in the Information Commons. Please comment on the atmosphere, the staff and the service.

---

it provides ready feedback and an opportunity for dynamic ongoing conversations with users. These are probably the most valuable sort of evaluative data. The University of Calgary survey focuses on access to resources, affect and usefulness of service, and patron type, and provides data from more than 10 terms since early 2001. Darlene Warren included detailed analysis of their findings over time at the 2004 USC IC Conference.[4]

The University of Arizona survey (see Figures 9.5, 9.6, and 9.7) focuses on "action" rather than "satisfaction." It covers types of research and production assistance, which patrons

---

Figure 9.5
University of Arizona Survey Form, Page 1

Mark up to *five* things you feel are *Most Important*

☐ Help identifying articles and/or books for your research topic

☐ Help finding if we own the articles and/or books you have already identified

☐ Help providing alternative access to missing or checked out items, or items we don't own

☐ Help with physically locating items in the building

☐ Help with questions about campus information and/or services

☐ Explaining our policies

☐ Help with computer hardware and software problems or questions

☐ Help with other equipment (e.g., printers, card readers, copiers, etc.) problems or questions

☐ Help finding a computer when it is busy

☐ Providing accurate answers for factual questions

☐ Providing information that helps you answer your question

☐ Making sure we understand your question

☐ Explaining the search process/showing how we got the answer

☐ Teaching you how to solve your problem or get the answer yourself

☐ Providing brochures, on-line help, and signage

☐ Showing an interest in assisting you and treating you with courtesy

☐ Length of time you have to wait to ask your question

☐ Spending an appropriate amount of time to answer your question(s)

☐ Providing all the information you need

☐ Checking to ensure your need was met

☐ Referring you to the correct person or place if we can't answer your question

☐ The specialist we refer you to responds quickly to set up an appointment when you contact her/him

☐ Providing service at the times you need it

☐ Publicizing our services

---

need, and rates these based on those that are "most important, those which the IC "does best," and those where the IC "needs improvement." Bracke's presentation reveals a well-designed, carefully administered, and useful review of valid data on patron needs and how the UA IC was meeting these needs.[5]

At UCLA, as at the University of Arizona, the Information Commons staff has decided to focus on action rather than satisfaction. They collect and use data on patron demographics, needs, learning styles, type and time of patron needs, and how successful patrons are in the IC work. UCLA emphasizes assessment as formative evaluation.[6]

Beyond Assessment: Transcending the "Tragedies of the Commons"

The Information and Learning Commons have enjoyed a growing presence and profound impact on the quantity, quality, and variety of effective informational services and opportunities provided to patrons over the last fifteen years. Yet the volume of qualitative and critical validation also corroborates that the potential of the Information and Learning

---

Figure 9.6
University of Arizona Survey Form, Page 2

Mark up to *five* things you feel we *Do Best*

☐ Help identifying articles and/or books for your research topic

☐ Help finding if we own the articles and/or books you have already identified

☐ Help providing alternative access to missing or checked out items, or items we don't own

☐ Help with physically locating items in the building

☐ Help with questions about campus information and/or services

☐ Explaining our policies

☐ Help with computer hardware and software problems or questions

☐ Help with other equipment (e.g., printers, card readers, copiers, etc.) problems or questions

☐ Help finding a computer when it is busy

☐ Providing accurate answers for factual questions

☐ Providing information that helps you answer your question

☐ Making sure we understand your question

☐ Explaining the search process/showing how we got the answer

☐ Teaching you how to solve your problem or get the answer yourself

☐ Providing brochures, on-line help, and signage

☐ Showing an interest in assisting you and treating you with courtesy

☐ Length of time you have to wait to ask your question

☐ Spending an appropriate amount of time to answer your question(s)

☐ Providing all the information you need

☐ Checking to ensure your need was met

☐ Referring you to the correct person or place if we can't answer your question

☐ The specialist we refer you to responds quickly to set up an appointment when you contact her/him

☐ Providing service at the times you need it

☐ Publicizing our services

Commons models can be threatened by certain tendencies in human nature and society. These are related to issues raised in Garrett Hardin's article and subsequent commentary, which brought the notion of a "Tragedy of the Commons" into widely held intellectual parlance.[7] The most consistent and obvious threats (or "Tragedies") are:

1. Resource depletion, degradation, and dilution. Lessig describes this as resulting from "rivalrous" tendencies in the Commons, competing for apparently finite resources.[8] We know from experience that

> [left] unmonitored some patrons would abuse resources to the point that they were *depleted*, . . . and made insufficient for patron needs. One can take certain steps to monitor and apply resources in an appropriate and efficient manner. . . . One implements "pay-for-print" to stem the flood of patron printing. One can lock down access to computer profiles and segments of the drives and network and can implement self-re-ghosting (re-creating the computer's image) or use self-cleansing software (e.g., Fortress' Clean Slate [DeepFreeze]) to prevent downloading of software (resource pollution), purge unwanted files, etc., as a means of ensuring the most efficient and equitable use of resources. Only certain patrons (institution's students, faculty, and staff) are authenticated to

---

Figure 9.7
University of Arizona Survey Form, Page 3

Mark up to _five_ things you feel _Need to Improve_

☐ Help identifying articles and/or books for your research topic

☐ Help finding if we own the articles and/or books you have already identified

☐ Help providing alternative access to missing or checked out items, or items we don't own

☐ Help with physically locating items in the building

☐ Help with questions about campus information and/or services

☐ Explaining our policies

☐ Help with computer hardware and software problems or questions

☐ Help with other equipment (e.g., printers, card readers, copiers, etc.) problems or questions

☐ Help finding a computer when it is busy

☐ Providing accurate answers for factual questions

☐ Providing information that helps you answer your question

☐ Making sure we understand your question

☐ Explaining the search process/showing how we got the answer

☐ Teaching you how to solve your problem or get the answer yourself

☐ Providing brochures, on-line help, and signage

☐ Showing an interest in assisting you and treating you with courtesy

☐ Length of time you have to wait to ask your question

☐ Spending an appropriate amount of time to answer your question(s)

☐ Providing all the information you need

☐ Checking to ensure your need was met

☐ Referring you to the correct person or place if we can't answer your question

☐ The specialist we refer you to responds quickly to set up an appointment when you contact her/him

☐ Providing service at the times you need it

☐ Publicizing our services

☐ I am an: Undergraduate○ Graduate○ Student○ Faculty○ Staff○ Other○

---

use proprietary databases. These are common steps to transcend this particular tragedy in the Commons' information environment.[9]

For example, staff might encourage patrons to use the most appropriate form for saving and moving work (floppy disk, zip disk, readable CD, or e-mail attachment) instead of printing. This approach saves paper, toner, and other printing resources. These steps should be part of an articulated program of consistent, ongoing training and education of staff and patrons. Formal education, training, and cross-training sessions for all (sometimes required, sometimes voluntary), as well as informal, peer-to-peer (student-to-student, student-to-staff, staff-to-student, staff-to-staff), incidental education and training: at the teachable moment. Often the education and training are _upward:_ student assistants are the "experts" teaching full-time staff, or paraprofessionals are the "experts" teaching professional staff. Web-based education/training modules have been proven effective in many Commons environments—the University of Arizona has implemented Web-based education/training modules in a well-articulated and effective manner.[10]

2. Resistance (to change, etc.). It is far too common for an individual or group to proscribe participation in the provision of a service, which is "not in my job description." An example of this *tragedy of resistance* is when a technology/software support staff in the Commons responds to a basic reference question by saying "I don't do that—that's a library question." If this staff were educated and trained to provide basic-level reference assistance, this staff could instead take time to "interview" the patron, respond immediately, or research a helpful response, or refer the question to someone more expert. It weakens and at times debilitates the effectiveness of the Commons concept when services are segregated in terms of responsibility or authority. Some resistant staff can be lured informally or incidentally into other areas of new responsibility outside of their "official job responsibility," into sometimes refreshing and energizing areas of activity. Education and training can defuse resistance and transform the impasse into possibility. The use of self-managed teams for operations and/or assessment, as described earlier in this book, can also help move some staff beyond the stage of resistance by introducing a new level of peer interaction and motivation.

3. Chauvinism. The chauvinist culture of expertise can sometimes emerge among "professional" staff, who feel that only they and their similarly credentialed "peers" can provide the particular service at a quality level; all other provision of the service is "diluted" or "dumbed-down." An example is when a high-end graphic specialist (or a chemistry reference librarian) wants *all* queries related to graphics (or to chemistry) sent to her/him to avoid *diluted, dumbed-down* or *wrong* responses. The successful implementation of tiered services (e.g., levels 1 through 10, from lesser to greater complexity) reveals that it is neither sufficient in meeting patron needs nor cost-effective to require the most *expert* (and usually most expensive) service provider for all levels of complexity in queries. Many institutions train and use student assistants (freshmen to graduate students) to provide "peer assistance": information, technology, and reference. Paraprofessional/classified staff are often very successful when trained and cross-trained to provide service in virtually all areas, often at relatively high levels of complexity. It is regrettable that often the "chauvinist experts" are the slowest and least willing to relinquish control and welcome paraprofessional and student colleagues onto the service team.

> The idea that only an expert should be allowed to respond to any query in her/his area has been questioned and at times countered in practice and studies of computer labs, libraries and schools (peer tutoring and counseling) for some years.... Concepts such as cross-training to provide first-response and to clarify the valuable role of informed referrals to areas or staff with expertise (be it for chemistry databases, PhotoShop capabilities or accurate rendering of diacritics from another language) can be very helpful in transcending this tragedy of chauvinism, when these concepts are integrated into the Commons culture.[11]

At times ironically, it is budget cuts and restricted resources that *force* chauvinist experts to relinquish control and accept productive collaboration. Education, training, and cross-training provide opportunities to soften or transform inveterate chauvinism.

4. Success—punished for success. In 1999, Steve Gilbert, then president of the TLT Group, the Teaching, Learning, and Technology affiliate of the American Association for Higher Education, published a short series on the "support services crisis," which he referred to as the providers being "punished for success."[12] Technology resources had become so popular and widespread in higher education, and their use had become so successful, that requests for more and better resources and support escalated at an unsustainable rate: IT resource and support providers were being "punished for success." This is the case as well in the IC environment. Cross-training of professional, paraprofessional, and student staff has proven to be effective in helping alleviate this problem. As Gilbert points out, the greatest, most constant supply of savvy IT support is that of student assistants:

> These students can recruit, train, supervise, and evaluate other students; although it is essential to provide skilled professional management overseeing the full complement of student assistants. These student assistants can help their peers and the faculty and every category of support professionals (library, faculty development, disabilities, etc.) As students gain the knowledge and skills needed for these more varied roles, they have more opportunities to become more active in shaping their own education.[13]

5. Either/Or. Many of the more traditional service providers argue that high-touch, paper-print service is superior and deserves most if not all resources. Others, the more technology-savvy and expert service providers, emphasize a preference for high-tech, remote-accessible, asynchronous services. In fact, the greatest successes and effectiveness are not Either/Or, but rather Both/And. High-touch and high-tech are mutually inclusive, and various amalgams of the two are selected, as appropriate to the task at hand. The same is true for the false dichotomy of patron needs vs. staff needs: while patron needs are certainly central to IC work, effective provision of value-added services to meet patron needs simultaneously allows great value to accrue to the staff, not the least of which are job security, job satisfaction, and greater assurance of resource funding. What proves to be good, valuable and effective for the patron is *also* good, valuable, and rewarding for the staff. Education and training help soften the simplistic Either/Or dilemma.

6. Dogmatism. While libraries and librarians have developed and long employed extensive and complex structures, rules, and regulations for organizing, cataloging, placing, providing authority control for, and safeguarding information and informational resources, there is a point of diminishing returns when librarians prescribe the correct ways and proscribe the incorrect ways. Librarians have seen patrons indicate their opinions and *vote* with their time and money to abandon the library and go elsewhere for their informational needs, to those providers who study and understand customer and patron needs and preferences. As noted previously, it has become ever clearer since the late 1980s that the nexus of technologies, increased variety and speed of access, resultant learning styles, and preferences all demand nondogmatic approaches to library information and technology resources and support to meet these demands. If and when you do not evolve to meet these demands, someone else will. As with the tragedy of chauvinism, it is sometimes budget cuts and restricted resources that *force* the dogmatists to relinquish control and accept productive collaboration. Here as well, education, training, and cross-training provide opportunities to soften or transform inveterate attitudes.

7. Professional identity. Librarians as professionals, who demonstrate self-respect and respect for professional behavior in paraprofessionals, engender respect and create a culture of respect and professionalism. However, this means recognizing and appreciating real professional competence, behavior, and relative expertise wherever it is demonstrated, irrespective of degree (Ph.D., MLS, college degree or not), age, or other characteristic. Professional identity based on anything other than these valid criteria only enervates and squanders potential and prevents the potential for professional growth and the creation of a true and inclusive culture of professionalism. This is a long-term concern in schools of library and information science and can best be dealt with in the graduate curriculum.

8. Symbiosis. Creating a culture of dependence (vs. personal control). A tendency among library staff is to serve as the keeper and protector of information and knowledge, to create among patrons a sense of dependence on the expertise of library staff to provide access to the best information, the "correct" information. While an expert, a sage-on-the-stage, has clearly unique value, study after study (e.g., LibQUAL+ and the OCLC Environmental Scan 2003) has revealed that our patrons want to be and to feel independent and self-reliant. Self-control/informational control is consistently perceived as the most important service domain by our patrons. They reject service providers who tend to create patron dependence on their expertise, especially if the patrons sense that such dependence serves a symbiotic need. As with the tragedies of chauvinism, dogmatism, and professional identity, counterproductive symbiosis is best mitigated or resolved through education and training—here based on our knowledge that *information control* (not dependence) is of utmost importance to the patron. We can also help by teaching staff to respond simply: "No, I'm sorry, that is not something I can help you with," then refer patrons to a more appropriate office or simply remind them that some problems (e.g., computer incompatibilities, ISP difficulties, etc.) are not the responsibility of the commons staff.

In his writings Garrett Hardin reviews options for resolving and transcending tragic problems in the Information Commons. Among the strategies reviewed, he discounts internal self-monitoring, self-control (conscience-control) as being unrealistic and unworkable. To the extent that Hardin's view is valid, the most effective strategy may be to use, in addition to conscience, a framework of external locus of control—simply *education*, and what has often been called staff development, within a framework of opportunities and incentives along with guidance and mentoring. In the Information and Learning Commons environment, user education and staff development can be designed and implemented as a sort of "Curriculum": a set of parameters and guidelines (rules and regulations, technological systems and fixes, and, at its most extreme, disincentives for breach of the common good). The effort will be most effective if it is implemented and pursued in an ongoing way, rather than as a onetime, one-session, one-lesson phenomenon. This educational curriculum has a *cognitive* component, with prescriptions and proscriptions based on logical reasoning, and an *affective* component aimed at developing an awareness that maintenance of the common good requires and needs communal attitudes and behaviors infused with goodwill and humor from all staff and patrons.

Conclusion

The Information Commons model is a planfully ambitious framework integrating traditional library services, the broad array of high-technology resources, and informational resources of the digital commons, in aesthetically pleasing and learner-friendly spaces for individual and group learning, research, and information manipulation. It is intended as a dynamic, integrated, and articulated continuum of resources and services based on patron needs and preferences, while retaining the greatest flexibility for ongoing change. With the complexity of such a framework, evaluating and assessing quality and effectiveness would necessarily be a complex undertaking.

This section has broached important issues differentiating formative and summative, quantitative and qualitative, formal and informal, implicit and explicit, action- and satisfaction-based assessment. Together these constitute what Peggy Maki refers to as a *culture of evidence*.[14] It is clear that the 150+ IC implementations have enjoyed relative to phenomenal success in attracting patrons over the last decade; thus, the conceptual direction has proven valid. As with all integrated combinations of facilities, resources, and activities dedicated to teaching, learning, and research, effective planning and ongoing evaluative assessment are essential, if one hopes and intends for the Information Commons to retain its dynamism, vitality, and effectiveness. The newer generation of Information Commons emphasize the evolution to greater integration into the institutional mission and transformative change. Instruments, methods, and programs to assess and evaluate the quality and effectiveness of these newer IC generations must also evolve while retaining proven assessment programs and instruments from the past.

Endnotes

[1] Danielson, Ron. "Santa Clara University's Information Commons Needs Assessment Survey and Results." (December 24, 2005). Available: http://www.scu.edu/newlibrary/

[2] Heath, Fred M., et al., eds. 2004. *Libraries Act on Their LibQUAL+™ Findings. From Data to Action.* Binghamton, N.Y.: Haworth Information Press.

[3] Bahavar, Shahla. "Information Commons User Assessment: Perspectives from the USC Leavey Library." USC Leavey Library 2004 Conference. Information Commons: Learning Space Beyond the Classroom. (September 16–17, 2004). Available: http://www.usc.edu/isd/libraries/locations/leavey/news/conference/presentations/

[4] Warren, Darlene. "Information Commons at the University of Calgary." USC Leavey Library 2004 Conference. Information Commons: Learning Space Beyond the Classroom. (September 16–17, 2004). Available: http://www.usc.edu/isd/libraries/locations/leavey/news/conference/presentations/

[5] Bracke, Marianne Stowell. "Culture of Assessment in the Information Commons: Listening to Customers." USC Leavey Library 2004 Conference. Information Commons: Learning Space Beyond the Classroom, (September 16–17, 2004). Available: http://www.usc.edu/isd/libraries/locations/leavey/news/conference/presentations/

[6] Lakos, Amos A. "Implementing a 'Culture of Assessment' Within the Information Commons." USC Leavey Library 2004 Conference. Information Commons: Learning Space Beyond the Classroom. (September 16–17, 2004). Available: http://www.usc.edu/isd/libraries/locations/leavey/news/conference/presentations/

[7] Hardin, Garrett. 1968. "The Tragedy of the Commons," *Science.* 161 no. 3859 (December), 1243-1248; and follow-up publications: Beryl Crowe. "The Tragedy of the Commons Revisited," *Science.* 166 (3909), November 1969, 1103–1l04; Garrett Hardin and John Baden. *Managing the Commons.* (San Francisco: W.H. Freeman, 1977); Garrett Hardin. "Extensions of 'The Tragedy of the Commons'," *Science.* 280 (5364) May 1998, 682–683; Lawrence Lessig. *The Future of Ideas. The Fate of the Commons in a Connected World* (New York: Random House, 2001); Elinor Ostrom, et al., eds. *The Drama of the Commons.* (Washington, D.C.: National Academy Press, 2002).

[8] Available: http://dizzy.library.arizona.edu/library/teams/ust/ICTraining/online/index.html and http://www.library.arizona.edu/ic/infocommons-guides.html (Dec. 24, 2005).

[9] Bailey, Russell, and Barbara Tierney. 2002. "Information Commons Redux: Concept, Evolution and Transcending the Tragedy of the Commons," *Journal of Academic Librarianship.* 25, (September) 283.

[10] Bailey and Tierney, pp. 283f.

[11] Available: http://www.edutech-int.com/documents/Punished%20For%20Success.htm (Dec. 24, 2005).

[12] Ibid.

[13] Weber, Linda. "Customizing Information Commons Environments to Address Learning and Research Differences Between the Disciplines." USC Leavey Library 2004 Conference. Information Commons: Learning Space Beyond the Classroom. (September 16–17, 2004). Available: http://www.usc.edu/isd/libraries/locations/leavey/news/conference/presentations/

[14] Maki, Peggy L. 2004. *Assessing for Learning: Building a Sustainable Commitment across the Institution.* Sterling, Va.: Stylus. See also: Harvey Varnet and Martha Rice Sanders, Asking Better Questions. Small-scale assessment measures that inform ongoing work. *CR&L News* 66 (5). June, 2005. 461–465.

10

Balancing User Community Needs with Intellectual Property Rights to Create Practical Public Policies

Community-Building and Ethnographic Research

In his article "The User Community as a Responsibility and Resource," David Seaman describes how the user community of the Electronic Text Initiative at the University of Virginia became a "shaping force" that has helped managers guide the ongoing development of the initiative. Interestingly, Seaman views this user community, and its channels of communication with library staff, has having grown out of early *user training* sessions.

> Well-crafted training sessions, coupled with *ad hoc* user support given to walk-in clients...provides the 'primordial soup' from which rises both a general literacy in the use of on-line resources, and...a growing suite of individual research and teaching projects....A stable, local user community, once created, becomes a great asset...[1]

Seaman places focus on faculty as the core of a stable local user community. We will include comments pertaining to user community-building for both faculty and students. For students, opportunities exist for IC user community-building at four points: (1) in group process settings for initial information literacy instruction; (2) in group process assessment settings for evaluating those sessions; (3) in reference interviews or project-development consultations; and (4) in programming activities such as "horizon scanning." This chapter discusses how both staff and faculty can gain a better understanding of the user community through ethnographic research, then goes on to discuss how multiple or aggregate academic user communities in ICs and LCs across the United States might collectively become a shaping force in key public policy issues, such as copyright, public domain, and intellectual property—topics that loom large in future formulations of the cultural commons.

In Chapter 3, the idea of information literacy sessions for the IC was framed within the eight dimensions as described by Shapiro and Hughes. In this chapter, you will see how such an information literacy program can be deliberately fashioned to promote IC user community-building. Perhaps the most direct way to promote a user community through instructional sessions is to employ group-process techniques similar to those discussed in Chapter 3, including a mixture of online embedded interactive resources and peer interaction through both in-person sessions and virtual communications such as blogging.

A user community is not a "yes/no" "present/absent" phenomenon. All ICs have users, and all users network into various types of communities, so that any IC projects an identity into multiple slices of extended user communities. But the degree of community involvement revolving around the IC itself obviously varies. Is the IC central to any recognizable user community, or is it peripheral to multiple communities, or both? We want to find ways to encourage constructive, creative user involvement and feedback, and that implies moving the IC from peripheral to central status within one or more communities. Obviously, community-building through information literacy instruction or skills training may be easier to implement in a semester-long format. But even in one-shot instructional sessions for students in First Year Seminar, some of the following techniques may be useful.

The Classroom Flip and User Communities

In Chapter 3, we discussed the classroom flip as a technique employed by faculty through which library staff might explore enhanced collaboration. Here, you have it as a technique to be employed directly by library instructional staff, regardless of general academic faculty initiatives. By putting the lecture component of information literacy online and pulling that lecture component out of instructional sessions, time can then be spent on project-based interaction and discussion, with the important side effect of welcoming participating students into the IC's user community. This could be utilized for an entire program structured around the Shapiro-Hughes model, or you could try a two-tier approach (see Figure 10.1).

In a two-tiered approach, the first four dimensions in the Shapiro-Hughes framework could be presented as foundational literacies in traditional instructional sessions by IC staff for lower division students, especially First Year Seminar.

Then, the remaining four dimensions could be presented to upper-division students in a more innovative classroom-flip approach, where the detailed instructional content is presented out-of-session using screencasting software like Macromedia Captivate. Actual session time could then be used for problem-solving and research strategy demonstrations that would serve the corollary purpose of user community-building (see Figure 10.2).

This approach also allows IC staff to explore potential relationships between these second-level literacies and the "horizon-scanning" programming advocated for brand divergence. One can see a natural synergy between user training sessions in research, publishing, new technologies, and online communities, and current awareness programs that discuss new trends in those very areas. Students who complete second-level instructional programs might be enlisted to collaborate with IC staff in organizing and presenting horizon-scanning sessions in their areas of special interest. Just as general faculty use the classroom flip to extend discussion beyond class through techniques such as threaded discussion, so too IC staff can extend peer interaction (and community-building) through blogging and social networking sites.

Figure 10.1
Foundational Dimensions for Initial Instruction

 **Physical**   **Human**

Tool Literacy   Critical Literacy

Foundational literacies
presented in FYS & lower
division instructional sessions...

Resource Literacy   Social-structural Literacy

 Digital   **Social**

Figure 10.2
Second-Level Dimensions for User Community-Building

 **Physical**   **Human**

Second-level literacies presented to upper division students...

Emerging Technology Literacy

Research Literacy

Publishing Literacy

Online Community Literacy

with interactive screencasting software like Macromedia Captivate.

 Digital   **Social**

Blogs, Linkfests, and Blog Carnivals

IC instructional staff can establish one or more blogs that deal with information literacy issues and course-related research skills. A single omnibus information literacy blog might suffice, or you could try multiple blogs that place focus on research within disciplines or subject majors. Students would be asked to post their own research experiences, positive or negative, or reactions to searches attempted, or ratings of databases, and could be invited to continue posting after the end of the formal information literacy session or course. This is an especially useful technique where information literacy is constrained to one-shot sessions for entering freshmen.

As postings accumulate, you can explore "linkfests" and "blog carnivals." A linkfest is a blog post containing links to posts from other blogs (as well as links to resources such as course syllabi and faculty subject sites). A blog carnival is a series of such linkfests. The links can be chosen by the owner of the blog, but also are submitted as entries by the student authors of blog posts or by faculty. By initiating and perpetuating this cycle of personal involvement and investment among the student peer group, the effectiveness and cohesiveness of the IC user community can be enhanced. The idea is certainly not limited to research skills as a topic; blogs could also provide pooling of experiences and insights for multimedia development, courseware innovations, and other creative applications of technology.

Social Networking Sites

The appearance of sites such as MySpace.com offers a new level of online resource that librarians have only recently begun to explore. Brooklyn College Library has set up a presence on MySpace with a page that provides library contact links, service snapshots, collection factoids, a blog entry point, and space for postings from students and other library friends.[2] Anecdotal comments are also surfacing from individual librarians who are profiling their professional personas, including instructional librarians who are casting for new ways to reach students needing help in information access and research. The close application of such sites to the dimensions of social-structural literacy and online community literacy are clear. And the relation of social networks to library realms of discourse is also unexpectedly apropos; a page in MySpace becomes a personal surrogate in an "online catalog" of socially networked individuals, equivalent to a cataloging record as a surrogate for a book in an OPAC.

Assessment Focus Groups

In fashioning user training in "tool literacy," for example, we want students to acquire "the ability to understand and use the practical and conceptual tools of current information technology, including software, hardware, and multimedia," as described by Shapiro and Hughes. Such sessions need to be followed by an assessment or feedback loop that not only gauges the levels of tool literacy achieved, but also gauges whether the particular tools we provide in the IC are the optimal set of tools really needed by students. In fact, as shown in Figure 10.3, a comprehensive assessment rubric for instructional activities may be said to encompass three levels: assessment of students, sessions, and tools.

Figure 10.3 Example Levels of Assessment for Tool Literacy	
Tool Literacy	"the ability to understand and use the practical and conceptual tools of current information technology, including software, hardware and multimedia."
Assessment part A: student assessment	Measurement of students' ability to use the tools
Assessment part B: session assessment	Measurement of training program effectiveness
Assessment part C: tool assessment	Measurement of tool adequacy; and feedback about what tools are needed or desired, but not currently provided

This type of feedback can be gained by survey instruments, of course, and in Chapter 4, the case was made that surveys may be best for ascertaining use of and need for physical and digital resources, while focus groups might be a better arena for ascertaining use of and need for human and social resources. However, if one also has a goal of using the assessment process to enhance user community-building, one may wish to utilize focus groups across the board for instructional assessment to take advantage of the peer interactions they permit. It may also be easier to convene students in focus groups and conduct real-time interpersonal exchanges that touch on all three areas of skills, instruction, and tools, than to try to design a survey instrument that effectively parses out these requisite assessment levels. Obviously, one-shot efforts may not suffice for meaningful assessment of student skills or tool adequacy, and follow-up focus groups at semester intervals can provide longitudinal data, and along the way, reinforcement of the community-building enterprise.

Ethnographics

On the level discussed here, ethnographic research can be described as an effort to develop better services by developing a better understanding of users. This can include a spectrum of inquisitive activities, ranging from an informal personal conversation where a scholar is simply asked to describe the research strategy used in a particular project, or visual inventories of books and media collected in a researcher's study carrel, to more sophisticated real-time tools such as portable cams that record a student's physical movements within the IC space, and screen-captures that record Web surfing, search-engine querying, and data-gathering. The spectrum can range from a quick or "innocent" ethnographic study to provide an introductory overview of a facility or activity. Formal or "informed" ethnographic methods are often more characteristic of research meant to inform concurrent system design and development. Evaluative ethnographic study can then be used to validate or critique design decisions after implementation.

Generally, informed enthnography, rather than innocent ethnography, would be well suited to the sort of systems design and development effort that moves an IC toward an LC, because it entails techniques that we might best describe as naturalistic, persistent, behavioral, and contextual.

1. Naturalistic: The study should not rest on assumptions or simulations, but should feature real users seeking real information in real settings. The relevant features of a setting will not be known in advance. The ethnographer, whether staff or consultant, will need to relate key features of the setting to system design. Simulated environments cannot possibly capture all of the relevant features.

2. Persistent: The study should be longer than an isolated snapshot of information gathering activity, and should if possible extend across the full scope of a project. The IC's continuum of service presents an ideal venue for persistent ethnographic techniques, because the ethnographer can gather data on the scholar's full experience with identification and retrieval, processing and interpretation, and through packaging and presentation.

3. Behavioral: Understanding must be based in the user's point of view, and provide understanding about how students and faculty employ particular strategies and why they rely on particular resources. When viewed collectively, as a series of studies covering multiple subjects, this level of behavioral understanding allows the ethnographer to separate out those elements of each project that present idiosyncratic aspects, from other elements that have broad implications and potential application across the IC's user community.

4. Contextual: Placing the observed research within disciplinary and/or institutional contexts; is the student working on a project for a major-field course or an elective? Is the faculty member writing a book, presenting at a conference, or chairing a fact-finding task force? Is this a relatively new topic for the student or faculty member, or the latest iteration of a long-standing disciplinary focus?

A full-scale ethnographic study to support design or redesign of IC/LC facilities might well make use of techniques that encompass setting(s), person(s), object(s), and task(s) as shown in Figure 10.4:

Figure 10.4 Scope of Formal Ethnographic Research for IC/LC Development		
Orientation	**Methodology**	**Outcome**
Setting	Camera positioned to cover as activity in a physical space	To see how people move around within their space(s) to complete tasks.
Person	Recording equipment moves with person being recorded	To understand the work from a particular person's point of view.
Object	Tracks particular technology or artifact	To see how various people interact with a particular technology or artifact and what types of tasks they use it to perform.
Task	Tracks individuals working toward a group objective.	To see the interactions required between individuals to achieve a common goal.

For further information, see the work of Nancy Freid Foster, Anthropologist, and Susan Gibbons, Associate Dean of River Campus Libraries at the University of Rochester. In their presentation for ACRL's New England chapter, Foster and Gibbons describe use of ethnography in three projects, including an "Undergraduate Research Project," where librarians and staff go to student locations and employ "user-centered design methodology" to gain insights into how students actually use systems and facilities.[3] They describe one outgrowth of their ethnographic research as "facilitating student and staff participation in renovation of a learning center in the library."

The IC User Community, Intellectual Property, and Public Policy

In one very fundamental sense, the ultimate form of the Information Commons is *human language*. Language is the base mode of human information exchange, and in itself a body of shared knowledge—lexical, syntactical, and cultural—that lays the foundation for almost all other forms of knowledge. Interestingly, language also has three levels: its physical manifestation as patterns of sound; its virtual structure as abtract syntax or rules of grammar; and its cultural level of pragmatic meaning among interacting social groups. One might speculate that these three levels or characteristics of human language have become extended or elaborated into the physical, virtual, and cultural levels of the Information Commons discussed previously.

In early cultures, the layering of accumulated knowledge on top of the substrate of language first took shape as the oral tradition. Rich and deep folk literatures developed that carried cultural memory and accumulated wisdom across generations. The role of the oral tradition as a conveyor of knowledge has sometimes been belittled since the development of writing and print literacy. But impressive examples of knowledge preservation and transmission across centuries and continents through oral literatures abound. The Bantu-speaking southern African tribe called the Lemba preserved through generations their seemingly incredible tribal legend of an ancient Jewish ancestry, an oral knowledge-transmission recently validated by DNA testing which has revealed genetic markers common to the Lemba and Middle Eastern Judaic subpopulations.[4] News stories about this discovery have placed focus on the marvel of modern genetic testing, but equally remarkable is what it reveals about an ancient oral tradition that preserved cultural memory through a human migration across thousands of miles for thousands of years.

The folk tales of oral traditions survived for centuries, in part, because they worked on a virtual level of memory and cognition. It was their very ephemeral physical nature, as sound patterns passing through air among native speakers, from storytellers to listeners, from parents to children, that ironically made them almost impervious to physical destruction. And they worked equally on a cultural level; the Lembas' tribal memory persisted because it was held as a common resource among all members of the tribe, as a type of cultural commons. The type of Information Commons that existed in the oral tradition resisted the development of normal marketplace or even barter economics; it was often viewed as *price-less* and *in-valuable*. Some cultures developed socially shared spaces within villages as arenas for the storytelling, an early instance of the physical commons, and forerunner of the speechmaking political arena of the Greek acropolis.

Language is also a Learning Commons, for each human child must individually acquire the complex rules of phonology and morphology for word formation, and semantics and syntax for sentence construction. This learning substrate is still not well understood, although significant strides were made by linguists such as Noam Chomsky, who helped to develop the concept of *generative grammar*, presenting language as a fundamentally creative act. The famous interchange between Chomsky and behavioral psychologist B. F. Skinner dramatized Chomsky's pivotal insight that children do not acquire language by rote parroting of all sentences word for word in a pure stimulus-response model.[5] While they certainly employ repetition in the learning process, children quickly show the ability to use the words they have learned in novel ways to generate new sentences in highly creative constructs, including sentences unique to each child that have never been uttered before. In fact, this feature of linguistic creativity actually rests at the heart of the underlying premise for copyright law. David R. Koepsell comments in *The Ontology of Cyberspace*: "The extent of copyright protection afforded to authors is based upon an assumption that no two authors will express the same idea in exactly the same way."[6]

Why has language developed as an inherently creative process, giving each child the ability to almost immediately construct novel sentences that have never been constructed before? Perhaps the ability to generate new sentences never previously uttered provides human beings the ability to cope with novelty and change, to interpret situations never previously encountered. As human populations grew and scattered across the globe, the accumulated store of human knowledge also grew, and revealed the most serious shortcoming of the oral tradition: the limitations that attention span and biological memory place on information storage and transmission capacity. The technologies of writing and printing were developed to accommodate the need for banking the ever increasing store of written information and knowledge. And as words such as "banking" and "store" imply, these technologies also began to permit physical enclosures such as books and bookstores that enabled commodification, and the assignment of exchange value, to chunks of information and knowledge. The same technologies permitted assignment of value to media that capture the inherent novelty of information passing across the world, in the commodification of "news" and "newspapers." This created an immediate line of tension between the *price-less* and *in-valuable* information commons of traditional culture, and the modern price-tagged marketplace of ideas, news, and expression. That line of tension was even reflected in the quote from John Drury (ca. 1650) at the head of Chapter 2: "Librarie-keepers ought to become Agents for the advancement of universal Learning...his work then is to bee a Factor and Trader for helps to Learning..." That quote dramatized the long-standing role of librarians in furthering *learning*, and not just information access. But in repeating it here, one should note how the words "factor" and "trader" place marketplace involvement central to the librarian's job description.

The full extent of this historical overview is obviously beyond the scope of this book; you may wish to study books such as Peter Burke's *A Social History of Knowledge*, and Brown and Duguid's *The Social Life of Information*. But it is important to recall here the very earliest and most basic forms of the levels of information commons as levels of language and culture, because the line of tension between commons and marketplace has, in some quarters, begun to look like a linguistic and cultural battleground. The issue goes beyond political ideology because technology, as a tool, remains in itself ideologically neutral. It created new types of enclosures for commodification and pricing of information, but it has also shaped the new digital continuum of the Web, where the concept of commons finds renewed possibilities. And in so doing, it has generated the need for a new look at public policy.

In a report prepared under the auspices of the Free Expression Policy Project at the Brennan Center for Justice, Nancy Kranich studied the challenges facing the concepts of public domain and maintenance of the public good in the face of threats posed by vested economic and political interests that seem to be eroding these long-standing traditions of what we are calling the cultural information commons.[7]

> In the last decade, mass media companies have developed methods of control that undermine the public's traditional rights to use, share, and reproduce information and ideas. These technologies, combined with dramatic consolidation in the media industry and new laws that increase its control over intellectual products, threaten to undermine the political discourse, free speech, and creativity needed for a healthy democracy.

Kranich concluded her report with a position statement that advocates a set of "Policy Recommendations and Strategies." Figure 10.5 presents this statement in full, as reprinted

---

**Figure 10.5
"Policy Recommendations and Strategies"**

Create a movement similar to environmentalism promoting the information commons:
- Focus on what we are fighting for, not just against.
- Emphasize the public interest in information access.
- Highlight successes; document problems and chilling effects of enclosure; identify examples of harm caused by technological controls and digital rights management.
- Educate concerned individuals and groups, the press, and the public.
- Organize coalitions based on common interests among disparate groups that cut across traditional alliances.
- Encourage the development of robust information communities.
- Seek funding for demonstration projects and ongoing support.

Apply common property resource models to the information sphere:
- Spell out common property resource economic models that elevate the value of shared access.
- Involve information communities in the design, creation, governance, and management of information resources.

Support legislation that encourages information sharing and oppose legislative, regulatory, and judicial actions that undermine opportunities to participate in the information society:
- Promote legislation that ensures public access to public research.
- Oppose new copyright laws and regulations that limit the public's access rights.

Develop, make available, and adopt open source software, content, standards, and best practices:
- Publish in open access publications.
- Sign only those licenses and contracts that enable open access and guarantee user rights such as fair use and "first sale" sharing of copyrighted works.
- Encourage peer production of information.

Apply open access, digital repository, and other practices developed by scholars more widely.

Value the public domain:
- Protect it as a sanctuary against enclosure.
- Develop advocacy programs, governance structures, and new laws that ensure it is well preserved, governed, managed, and valued.
- Resist attempts to apply technological measures that control access to ideas.

from "The Information Commons: A Public Policy Report" by Nancy Kranich (Free Expression Policy Project, Brennan Center for Justice), Available at: http://www.fepproject.org/policyreports/InformationCommons.pdf.

The idea of a "copyright free zone" was suggested previously as a possible strong assertion of academic fair use and open access within the context of a tangible locus of control among multiple physical ICs. Unlike the contiguous physical footprint of a "free trade zone," the copyright free zone would project an array of "fingerprints" on campuses across a map of the United States. The fingerprints, while physically disassociated, would be invisibly coordinated by an electronic network that would reflect the underlying reality of a virtual social network. The purpose here is to make the added case that the development of the physical Information Commons as an anchor of access and focus of expertise can help generate and sustain an aggregate IC user community whose collective interest appears to coincide with the Kranich statement. The purpose is not to serve a particular political ideology, left or right, but to inform and empower an aggregate IC user community in pursuit of the public good. To understand how the electronic network and the social network might develop in parallel, we need to reconsider intellectual property and copyright issues more closely in the context of a set of ideas loosely known as "Actor-Network Theory" (ANT). A portion of this description is taken from an article that appeared in *portal: Libraries and the Academy*.[8]

ANT is not really a theory in the truest sense of that word, as its own proponents admit. Bruno Latour has come to describe it as "...a method and not a theory."[9] John Law has elaborated: "...[ANT] has converted itself into a range of different practices which have also absorbed and reflected other points of origin: from cultural studies, social geography, and organizational analysis..."[10] It is thus more properly viewed as a conceptual framework linked to a descriptive vocabulary, open to revision and expansion from various interdisciplinary perspectives. ANT makes the claim that our civilization has been increasingly organized around *sociotechnical networks*. These networks are populated by a variety of *actors*. The word "actor" describes those entities whose actions define these networks, and whose interactions frequently involve the playing of one or more *roles*. The most common actors are individual human beings, but actors can also be groups of human beings operating as organizations or corporations. On a broader scale, formal or informal alliances among organizations and corporations may become collective actors. And one of ANT's most important and timely insights is its inclusion of machines and other pieces of technology as actors of equal standing, such as personal computers, operating systems, software packages, and the Internet itself. Because of ANT's symmetrical treatment of human and nonhuman agents, all components of computer networks (workstations, Web sites, search engines, software agents) become potential actors in the sociotechnical networks of scholarly communication.

To understand sociotechnical networks, ANT researchers Michel Callon and Bruno Latour insist that we must *follow the actors*. That is to say, we must identify and analyze their beliefs, motivations, and interests. In the case of nonhuman actors such as workstations or software agents, we must study how their properties and limitations may help shape the network and modify the behavior of its individual and collective actors. The importance of including technological actors becomes clearer when we hear predictions about the future of instructional technology, such as the following by Judith Boettcher: "... isn't it likely that the wireless Web will enable the addition of a ... dialogue between inanimate objects that will support faculty and student needs? Might this dialogue assume the shape of a robot or appliance that responds to a student's request for information by doing a search of available resources? Similar robots, or agents, might also support the faculty work of identifying resources and helping students answer questions. These robots will become powerful, customizable PDAs—personal digital assistants that come to know us, our habits, and our ways of working."[11] The issues potentially presented to us by these robots and agents was wonderfully presaged by Meredith Merritt's 1985 article "Racter the Author."[12] Racter was a computer narrative-generating program that had just authored its first book, *The Policeman's Beard is Half-Constructed*. Merritt interviewed catalogers, philosophers, and English professors to ascertain how authorship should be assigned in a library catalog. In our context, we might equally inquire how copyright would be assigned in today's intellectual property climate. Whether or not Racter can be an author or copyright holder, Racter would definitely (and legitimately) be considered an *actor* in the tenets of Actor-Network theory.

Sociotechnical networks emerge through a process of *enrollment*, as they serve to mediate among divergent or conflicting motivations and beliefs of potential actors. They typically pass through a period of struggle as these divergent beliefs are *translated* and conflicts are negotiated. If successful, the negotiations lead to a state where the network *stabilizes* around a modified set of actors; an open system homeostasis where the activities and behavior of all actors have been modified to the degree necessary to allow network operations to address their common interests in a mutually beneficial way. This process of enrollment, translation, and stabilization typically involves the production of *artifacts*. While this particular term is not consistently used across the ANT literature, artifacts are frequently types of textual documents: vision statements, contracts, feasibility studies, proposals, agreements, mission statements, goals and objectives, etc. These artifacts can be studied to gain insight into the underlying motivations of actors, especially those of collective actors. However, ANT recognizes that such artifacts can also serve at times to mask the underlying reality of motivations.

To illustrate how key concepts of ANT could be applied, consider an artificially simplified and idealized portrayal of an early phase of scholarly communication, the "correspondence model," as mentioned by Brisson and Carter.[13] In this model, knowledge was generated by scholars working independently who voluntarily communicated their findings with one another via written correspondence. This type of network was formed by only one type of actor, the individual scholar, and was characterized by one type of artifact, the written letter. Each actor's participation in the network was most likely prompted by motivations directly related to their motivations for doing scholarship. These may have included intellectual curiosity and thirst for discovery as in pure research, the desire to solve one or more specific problems (e.g., to find a cure for a disease) as in applied research, and the impetus of potential profit or professional notoriety.

It is useful to consider the correspondence model as a loop, with individual scholar-actors anchoring the start and end points of the loop as writers and readers. As the network developed, these actors came to play a number of other embryonic roles related to their activities, though such roles may not have been as fully articulated as their anchor roles of writing and reading. In communicating with one another, the scholars acted as publishers, distributors, and peer reviewers. Those who collected and organized correspondence over time became archivists, indexers, and compilers. Those who worked to extend access to interested third parties may have become editors and translators. Thus, even this abbreviated review of an artificially simplified correspondence model suggests that as many as 8 to 10 discernible roles may have been bundled within the activities of individual actors in the course of maintaining the network. These emergent roles would have occupied various intermediary points around the conceptual loop.

The correspondence model network was dependent upon a very small cluster of technologies gathered in support of writing and correspondence: papermaking, inking, mail conveyance, and so forth. It also depended upon certain shared assumptions about literacy and learning common to the actors, presumably influenced by other social networks promoting scholarship in the age of written correspondence, such as the early academy, the monastic scriptorium, and so forth. These technological and social dependencies created potential niches for intermediation in future expansion of the loop, and hence the opportunity for the emergence of a true sociotechnical network. This emergence would have been influenced by the parallel evolution of those related social networks and the technologies supporting them, such as research universities, and their motivational impact upon scholars through enrollment in systems of academic tenure. Lastly, the loop configuration can be a useful metaphor for comparing network activities to an underlying economic premise of scholarship in support of the public good, which has been described by Okerson as "a circle of gifts."[14]

It is a premise of ANT that as such a network furthers the growth of knowledge, the growth of knowledge should in turn lead to ongoing elaboration of the network model, and to a modification of the roles of its individual actors. The network can grow directly, of course, through the addition of a larger number of individual actors. But the typology of the network can also grow more complex through the appearance of different types of actors. For example, two or more individual scholars may come to collaborate and form a research team. Such collective actors became clusters of shared and mutually modified motivations which would have overlaid (or even occasionally contradicted) the motivations of individuals. These layered motivations impacted the network model in ways that must be differentiated (see Figure 10.6).

Over time various individual and collaborative actors who shared interest in a subject would have organized themselves into another type of collective actor, the learned society. If the learned society or professional association came to enroll all actors from an original network, it's own workings may have represented a destabilization of the correspondence model and a restabilization around a modified set of actors. The membership of a learned society may exhibit collective motivations and behaviors to be distinguished from individuals and partnerships. For example, a major advantage frequently enjoyed by collective actors involves access to new and relatively expensive technologies. To whatever extent access to the technologies of printing became a significant motivational factor in the enrollment of scholars in early learned societies, it marked the appearance of a true sociotechnical network.

Actor roles	Model 1	Model 2	Model 3	Model 4	Model 5
Figure 10.6 **Successive Network Models for Scholarly Communication**					
author	scholars	scholars	scholars	scholars	scholars
reviewer	scholars	Learn. societies	Learn. societies	Learn. societies	Univ/priv press
editor	scholars	Learn. societies	Learn. societies	Univ/priv press	Univ/priv press
publisher	scholars	Learn. societies	Learn. societies	Univ/priv press	Univ/priv press
aggregator	scholars	Learn. societies	libraries	libraries	vendors
indexer	scholars	Learn. societies	libraries	libraries	vendors
preserver	scholars	Learn. societies	libraries	libraries	vendors
Reader	Scholars	Scholars	Scholars	Scholars	scholars

Figure 10.6 represents successive network models for this unfolding process. Each model represents a loop anchored at one end by the scholar-as-writer and at the other end by the scholar-as-reader. The other roles become unbundled and distributed out at intermediate points around the loop among an increasing diversity of actor-types. Column 2 shows a model where learned societies, empowered by printing technology, have taken all intermediary roles other than the anchor points. Column 3 marks the appearance of libraries, empowered by self-description, as actors taking over the intermediary roles of aggregator, indexer, and preserver. In Column 4, the learned societies have been replaced in the role of managing increasingly sophisticated printing technologies by private or university presses. Finally, Column 5 represents a potential future model in which control of digital technology has permitted private vendors to assert themselves in the roles of electronic aggregation, indexing, and preservation, thereby potentially eliminating any role whatsoever for academic libraries.

This simplified matrix makes it appear that the successive emergence of models 2 through 4 obliterated the correspondence model, but of course this was never truly the case. Correspondence among scholars continued, and was itself transformed by further technologies such as e-mail, Listservs, and blogs. More precisely, models 2 through 4 created new levels of specialization based on appropriate technologies that essentially subdivided the scholarly communications network into interrelated subnetworks for correspondence, peer review, publishing, distribution, aggregation, and so forth. The precise details by which new actors have taken over differentiated roles in these subnetworks is less important at this point than to understand the processes of enrollment, translation, and mediation of interests that allowed the process to unfold. While financial gain presumably played some role in the motivations of certain individual scholars throughout, the appearance of private publishers in the model 4 loop clearly introduced a new degree of entanglement between public interest and private enterprise, as actor-network intermediaries were replaced by economic middlemen whose roles in the network shifted from facilitation to commodification.

This was possible because the subnetworks were still loosely coupled even while they were interrelated, allowing commercial parties to exploit intermediate niches. It was only in the mid-twentieth century, when a significant percentage of the publishing of academic journals was being transferred from university presses and learned societies to the commercial sector, that prices of journals began to climb at an accelerated rate. Chodorow explained this as being rooted "...in the way the nineteenth-century revolution in higher education divided the responsibility for the production of knowledge from the authority to carry on the work." Universities, he said, consume vast quantities of information but are divided from the faculties which "...carry on the business of making knowledge and teaching the arts of knowledge-making."[15] As a result, colleges and universities fell into a scholarly publishing crisis, meaning that their libraries cannot afford to purchase the material needed to support teaching and research in support of the public good.

ANT interpretation of marketplace forces further suggests how commercial interests were able to exploit this loose coupling. In the early correspondence model there would have been a reasonably close correlation between the morphology of data streams at the forefront of research and the resulting exchange of written correspondence among researchers. It was an information flow intrinsically resistant to commodification. But as the scholarly communications network incorporated printing technologies, an elaborate subnetwork devoted to formal publishing evolved. Publishing as a process required that subsets of data streams be detached and extracted to form discrete entities or artifacts. The morphology of knowledge representation became formalized and further removed from the underlying processes of knowledge growth.

Similar processes of detachment and extraction form the very underpinning of the ANT interpretation of transactional economics, though they may carry different labels. As Michel Callon wrote: "To construct a market transaction, that is to say to transform something into a commodity, it is necessary to cut the ties between this thing and other objects or human beings one by one. It must be decontextualized, dissociated and detached....it is only if this can be achieved that the calculation can be looped; that the buyer and the seller, once the transaction has been concluded, can be quits."[16] But while printing technologies facilitated the detachment and eventual commodification of scholarly writings, the layered motivations of actors in the network prevented a rational calculation of marketplace value. This is because while the artifacts produced by these actors could be detached and extracted, the actors themselves could not become disentangled from their network motivations to become effective calculative agents. As Callon added: "The market as a method of coordination implies the existence of agents capable of calculation";[17] and "...if calculations are to be performed and completed, the agents and goods involved in these calculations must be disentangled and framed."[18] But many of these actors were already enrolled in academic networks that independently placed great reward value on their record of publications. The disentanglement and framing necessary for rational pricing was not possible on the part of these actors. Thus the publishers came to occupy a niche where they enjoyed a perpetual buyer's market in the acquisition of raw material and a perpetual sellers market in the provision of subscriptions to finished goods.

If this ANT analysis is accurate, then any strategy for reasserting the importance of the public good narrowly based on economic incentives or technological innovation is not likely to succeed, because it would fail to acknowledge and address the conflicting and divergent motivations of the entrenched intermediary actors. Instead, an ANT analysis would argue for a strategy acknowledging and addressing the motivations of as many constituent actors in this sociotechnical network as possible, through concerted techniques of enrollment, translation, and mediation. Three researches have applied ANT in ways that may cast light on the social and electronic networks of IC user communities.

Hilgartner and Brandt-Rauf used ANT to examine the development and exchange of scientific knowledge in the field of molecular biology.[19] In work for the National Science Foundation, the authors developed what they refer to as the *data stream perspective*. This framework conceptualizes scientific data not as isolated objects, but as entities embedded in complex assemblages that weave together many elements used by scientists during the process of research. Such assemblages are transformed and manipulated as work proceeds, producing evolving streams of products. For example, streams of inscriptions will evolve as the output of instruments, to be manipulated mathematically and incorporated into tables, diagrams, and graphs that in turn are explicated and discussed in written texts. To provide general insights into how data are shared or otherwise exchanged among scientists, the authors use the data-stream perspective to frame two central questions: What portions of a given data stream typically are distributed to whom and under what terms and conditions? How are these portions bounded? In other words, the authors attempt to describe how discrete entities are extracted from the continuously evolving streams of scientific production and entered into exchange relations.

Because data do not arrive on the scene in neatly packaged units that are naturally ready to be disseminated, each scientific field must develop conventions about what constitutes a publishable paper and an interesting result. However, these conventions are neither identical across fields nor entirely stable. The importance of open publication in academic reward structures is a given, but there are many other means of distributing data. Data are sometimes given to colleagues, they are patented, they are transferred when visitors come to the laboratory to learn new techniques, they are bought and sold, they are privately released to corporate sponsors, and they are retained in the laboratory pending future decisions or observations. They also become bargaining chips in the formation of collaborations. A common feature of scientific collaboration is the merging of portions of data streams into new data streams that span the boundaries of individual laboratories. In such situations, complex and protracted negotiations can arise, especially when actors possess relatively equal resources and there is no clear hierarchy governing the relationship.

At the research front, data streams contain elements that vary greatly in perceived credibility, and thus in potential transactional value. Some entities are considered to be well established when researchers have great confidence in the accuracy of a particular instrument or the reliability of a given observation. Others are of questionable validity. Perceived credibility often fluctuates throughout the process of scientific production. Much of the research process in science involves the progression of judgments toward definitive resolution, and thus toward a maximization of value. Some data are rejected and others deemed reliable, but the temporal nature of the evaluation process—with the shifting perceptions that often accompany it—adds complexity to data streams.

The value of scientific data in exchange markets was also the focus of an essay by Strathern, whose ANT analysis concerned the use of intellectual property rights (IPR) to control knowledge after it had left the laboratory and entered the wider political arena.[20] Strathern's conceptual definition of IPR would resonate with librarians: "Using knowledge to gain knowledge would not qualify for IPR protection; using knowledge to produce a commodity would. For the problem is how to make knowledge socially effective, how to make it transactable—knowledge must be turned into something else with its own independent value. The process of transformation may be attributed to the author of a work ready for consumption (copyright). However, it may instead be embedded in a tool, which becomes part of the capital needed to exploit other resources. Any tool thought of as making knowledge useful acquires the attribute of 'technology,' the term points to the human resources contained within it. The more widely available the technology becomes, the more evident the continuing usefulness of knowledge.... At the point of invention, then, an after-life is given to the application of knowledge (patent). Patents are regarded as crucial to technology development—for technology is both a product and produces products..."[21]

Strathern's central example contrasted the social knowledge of medicinal flora in tribal societies with the ethnobotanical data gathered and formalized by scientists, noting that the scientists are actors in sociotechnical networks whose power and governance are typically privileged in the application of IPR artifacts. Copyrights and patents are premised on the specific need to give a secondary social effect to "works" and "technologies" that are already in themselves social effects. People first author or invent a device and then lay claims to its anticipated social utility. They have to mobilize society to lay such claims. Society figures not only in commerce but also in the procedures, such as legislation and contract, which govern access and control. The question to be asked on behalf of tribal cultures is whether IPR could offer appropriate procedures for aligning social interests with new resources. Because IPR is constructed around the figure of the solitary author or corporate inventor, it is likely to work against people for whom knowledge and the determination of resources are collective and intergenerational.

Strathern also observed the rise of a particular type of sociotechnical network in the political arena, an alliance of empowerment between "knowledge organizations" and the state. This arrangement translates knowledge held by certain actors, such as legal knowledge of IPR, into a power-holding competence which acquires the capacity to effect further translations through *self-description*. Self-description is the chosen instrument that, in Strathern's view, allows these social actors to obtain influence and proliferate. The motivating factor in the self-description is a definition of competence, the description of the particular arena of specialized knowledge the actor can deliver, and what it can empower others to do.

These organizations are self-determining, to the extent that the state becomes dependent upon them for detailed and specialized information, while having to recognize their decentralizing effect. The state gains access to the knowledge and skills at these organizations' disposal. They in turn gain influence over the state's policy-making apparatus, while also gaining the chance to reproduce themselves in numerous fields of expertise. Such group-actors produce similar artifacts, speak a common metalanguage across their boundaries of specialization, and thus communicate with one another as mutually recognized experts.

What enables them to multiply is, among other things, the generative language of self-description in a network constituted by entities communicating their descriptions to one another. The self-description becomes a kind of currency circulating in the network, creating a new type of knowledge economy. Strathern suggested that self-referential networking among "knowledge actors" becomes necessary for the overall policy-making system to deal with the increasing complexity of the many technologies now impacting society.

Swan, Langford, Watson, and Varey applied ANT to the study of corporations connecting themselves into larger *knowledge networks*, which they describe as being characterized by recurring exchange relationships among a limited number of organizations that retain residual control of their individual (knowledge) resources yet periodically jointly decide over their use.[22] The authors used several techniques frequently seen in the ANT literature: first, they reinterpreted core ANT methodology from other interdisciplinary perspectives, in this case supply chain management, transactional economics, and soft systems methodology. Second, the authors contrasted two types of frameworks for knowledge exchange: the tightly bounded transactions between buyers and sellers in a strictly defined economic market, and the more loosely defined exchanges among actors in a knowledge network. The former are characterized by unilateral decision control over property rights, discrete resource transactions, narrow information flow confined to contractual terms of exchange, and mutual coordination through bargaining and competition. The latter are characterized by joint decision making among transaction partners, opportunities for resource pooling, wide information flow including contractually unspecified reciprocal obligations, and mutual coordination through negotiation and concurrence.

The authors' analysis leads to a clearer view of the roles of intermediaries in knowledge networks. The notion of an intermediary in a network can be described as that of an actor providing the "knowledge bandwidth" for transactions to take place and facilitating information flows, as opposed to a "middleman" in an economic market who may wish to restrict or commodify information flow. The intermediary can also effect network consolidation and the development of new links between member organizations. This coordination role of the intermediary can allow the member organizations to focus their resources in the pursuit of knowledge and generate "club-goods." The intermediary provides a focal point and can lever the development of knowledge by the network where an individual organization may not be prepared to invest.

ANT analysis can further our understanding of current debates in the public policy arena, such as the pressing issue of "Network Neutrality." The Public Knowledge site hosts a blog by Gigi Sohn, who describes the focus of network neutrality. "...net neutrality is not about regulating the Internet. The networks, applications and services that make up the Internet are unregulated.... Net neutrality is about regulating the on-ramps to the Internet, and, up until about a year ago, the government regulated the on-ramps to our communications system."[23] The recently introduced Internet Freedom Preservation Act would presumably ensure that all content, applications, and services are treated equally and fairly on the Internet by prohibiting broadband network operators from blocking, degrading, or prioritizing service on their networks. Advocates of net neutrality have expressed concern about the potential for broadband service providers to choose who can or cannot get priority service or content delivery to the broadband subscriber, a discriminatory practice that could erode equal access on the Internet. The blog includes a posting from Art Brodsky, who states: "Consumers have an expectation that all Web sites and services will work equally well when they access the Internet . . . but network operators have become increasingly interested in acting as gatekeepers on the Internet and providing faster delivery for only certain information of their choosing."[24] Or, to use the terminology of ANT, network operators who control the on-ramps to the Internet have the clear potential to act as middlemen instead of intermediaries.

The assertion here is that IC user communities in the aggregate, working from the base of academic fair use and, potentially, from the enclave of a copyright free zone, could use analytical tools such as ANT to bring analysis and understanding to such issues very much in need of open informed discussion. Discussions framed only in political ideology tend to collapse into interchanges of "sound bites," such as a blanket assertion that "deregulation is good." One need only recall the *Depository Institutions Deregulation and Monetary Control Act of 1980*, otherwise popularly remembered as the Savings & Loan Deregulation Act, to recognize that such simplistic, blanket assertions as "deregulation is always good" can become a starry-eyed road of good intentions that lead to unintended consequences.

Because knowledge networks encompass both commercial and public interests, individual and collective actors, human and technological elements, it is not necessary or wise to posit an inherent opposition or incompatability between an IC user community and a free market of capitalist economics. The Founding Founders recognized an inherent line of tension between private and public interests. They sought to balance the interests of creators in reaping rewards from their creations with the national interest in the cultivation of new ideas and inventions through an intellectual property and copyright framework. This ingenious framework, together with university-based research and private sector investment, has helped to generate the ongoing knowledge explosion and revolution in information technology. The IC user community must continue to act as a shaping force in furthering the public interest in the physical, virtual, and cultural levels of the Information Commons.

Endnotes

[1] Seaman, David. 1997. "The User Community as Responsibility and Resource." *D-Lib Magazine*. 3, no. 7 (July/August). Available: http://www.dlib.org/dlib/july97/07seaman.html

[2] Brooklyn College Library. "BC Library—Here on Your Space!" *MySpace.com*. Available: http://www.myspace.com/brooklyncollegelibrary

[3] Foster, Nancy Fried, and Susan Gibbons. 2006. "Understanding Users to Develop Better Library Services." Presentation for *Leveraging Our Strengths: Alliances, Interdependencies and Developing Services:ACRLNew England Chapter Annual Conference*. Available: http://www.acrlnec.org/springconf06/FosterGibbons.ppt

[4] "The Lemba, The Black Jews of Southern Africa." *NOVA Online*. (November 2000). Available: http://www.pbs.org/wgbh/nova/israel/familylemba.html

[5] Chomsky, Noam. 1959. "A Review of B. F. Skinner's *Verbal Behavior*." In *Language*. 35, no. 1. 26–58. See also: Noam Chomsky, 1967. "Preface" to the 1967 reprint of "A Review of Skinner's *Verbal Behavior*." In *Readings in the Psychology of Language*, ed. Leon A. Jakobovits and Murray S. Miron. Englewood Cliffs, N.J.: Prentice-Hall. 142–143

[6] Koepsell, David R. 2000. *The Ontology of Cyberspace*. Chicago: Open Court. 73.

[7] Krannich, Nancy. 2004. "The Information Commons: A Public Policy Report." Free Expression Policy Project. Available: http://www.fepproject.org/policyreports/infocommons.II.html

8 Beagle, Donald. 2001. "The Sociotechnical Networks of Scholarly Communication." *portal: Libraries and the Academy.* 1, no. 4. 421–443.

9 Latour, Bruno . 1999. "On Recalling ANT." *Actor Network Theory and After*, ed. John Law and John Hassard, Oxford, U.K.: Blackwell. 20.

10 Law, John. 1999. "After ANT: Complexity, Naming, and Topology." *Actor Network Theory and After,* ed. John Law and John Hassard. Oxford, U.K.: Blackwell. 10.

11 Boettcher, Judith. 2001. "Wireless Teaching and Learning: Mobile and Untethered." *Syllabus.* 14, no. 6 (January). 43.

12 Merritt, Meredith. 1985. "Racter the Author." *Library Journal.* 110 no. 18 (November). 160.

13 Brisson, Roger, and Ruth C. Carter. 1999. "Cataloging & Classification Quarterly: A Web site for a professional journal in librarianship." *Serials Librarian.* 35 no. 3. 97.

14 Okerson, Ann. 1992. "The Missing Model: 'A Circle of Gifts,'" *Serials Review.* 18, no. 1–2 (1992). 92–96.

15 Chodorow, Stanley. 1998. "The Faculty, the University, and Intellectual Property." *The Journal of Electronic Publishing.* 3, no. 3 (March). Available: http://www.press.umich.edu/jep

16 Callon, Michel. 1999. "Actor-Network Theory—the Market Test." In *Actor Network Theory and After*, ed. by John Law and John Hassard. Oxford, U.K.: Blackwell. 189.

17 Callon. p. 183.

18 Callon. p. 186.

19 Hilgartner, Stephen. 1997. "Access to Data and Intellectual Property: Scientific Exchange in Genome Research." In *Intellectual Property Rights and the Dissemination of Research Tools in Molecular Biology.* Washington, D.C.: National Academy Press. 30.

20 Strathern, Marilyn. 1999. "What is Intellectual Property After?" In *Actor Network Theory and After*, ed. by John Law and John Hassard. Oxford, U.K.: Blackwell. 161.

21 Ibid. 161–162.

22 Swan, William, Nigel Langford, Ian Watson, and Richard G. Varey. 2000. "Viewing the Corporate Community as a Knowlede Network." *Corporate Communications: An International Journal.* 5, no. 2. 97–106. Available: http://www.cs.auckland.ac.nz/~ian/papers/corp_comm.pdf

23 Sohn, Gigi. 2006. "The Myth of Internet Regulation." *Public Knowledge* [blog]. Submitted by Gigi Sohn on May 19, 2006—8:11am. Available: http://www.publicknowledge.org/node/367

24 "The Official Word from Snowe and Dorgan." *Public Knowledge* [blog]. Posted by Art Brodsky on May 19, 2006—4:48 pm. Available: http://www.publicknowledge.org/taxonomy/term/62%2C0/all

Selected Bibliography

Selected Web Sites

"Archives of INFOCOMMONS-L@LISTSERVE.BINGHAMTON.EDU," Information Commons
Interest Group. (May 2004 – current)
Available: http://listserv.binghamton.edu/cgi-bin/wa.exe?A0=infocommons-1

Coalition for Networked Information, Collaborative Facilities
[Dartmouth College & Coalition for Networked Info.]
http://www.dartmouth.edu/~collab/

Henning, Joanne. "Information Commons Study Leave"
[Personal Web Site of Joanne Henning, Head, Reference Services, McPherson Library, University of
Victoria, Canada].
http://jhenning.law.uvic.ca. (Notes & images from her IC site visits)

Kate Edger Information Commons Publications
[University of Auckland Library, New Zealand]
www.information-commons.auckland.ac.nz/?page=publications

Murray, David.
[Brookdale Community College, Lincroft, N.J.]
Web site: "Information Commons: A Directory of Innovative Services and Resources in Academic
Libraries." http://www.brookdale.cc.nj.us/library/infocommons/ic_home.html

University of North Carolina at Charlotte, Russ Bailey and Barbara Tierney
Web site: "Information Commons. . . . Conference Documents"
http://library.uncc.edu/infocommons/

Speaker's Documents from ACRL Conferences, Information Commons Programs

"Information Commons Issues and Trends: Voices from the Front-Line—Colorado State University,
Emory University, University of Arizona, University of NC Charlotte, University of Southern
California, Elon University (NC), Brookdale Community College (NJ)." Association of College and
Research Libraries National Conference 2003 (Charlotte, NC).

"Information Commons 101: Nuts and Bolts Planning." Association of College and Research
Libraries Pre-Conference, January 9, 2003 (San Diego, CA).

"Information Commons 101: Nuts and Bolts Planning." Association of College and Research
Libraries Pre-Conference, June 25, 2003 (Orlando, FL).

"From Information Commons to Learning Commons." Association of College and Research Libraries National Conference 2005 (Minneapolis, MN).

Books

Bazillion, Richard J., and Connie Braun. *Academic Libraries as High-Tech Gateways: A Guide to Design and Space Decisions.* Chicago, Illinois. American Library Association, 1995.

Bennett, Scott. *Libraries Designed for Learning.* Washington, D.C.: Council on Library and Information Resources, 2003.
http://www.clir.org/pubs/abstract/pub122abst.html

Building Blocks for Planning Functional Library Space. Lanham, Maryland. American Library Association, Library Administration and Management Association, Buildings and Equipment Sections, Functional Space Requirements Committee. Scarecrow Press, 2001.

Eckel, Peter, et al. *On Change III—Taking Charge of Change: A Primer for Colleges and Universities.* Washington, D.C. American Council on Education (2000).
http://www.acenet.edu/bookstore/pdf/on-change/on-changeIII.pdf

Haas, Leslie, et al. *The Information Commons* [SPEC Kit 281]. Washington, D.C.: Association of Research Libraries, 2004.

Oblinger, Diane, and James L. Oblinger, eds. "Educating the Net Generation." *EDUCAUSE,* 2005. (Online publication) www.educause.edu/educatingthenetgen/

White, Peggy, Susan Beatty, and Darlene Warren. "Information Commons." In *Encyclopedia of Library and Information Science.* New York, NY. Marcel Dekker. Published online: 03/03/2004, pp. 1–7.
http://www.dekker.com/servlet/product/DOI/101081EELIS120020359

Journal Articles

Albanese, Andrew Richard. "Indiana University Builds Another Info Commons." *Library Journal.* 129:18 (November 1, 2004). pp. 22ff.

Albanese, Andrew Richard. "The Future is Now." *Library Journal.* 129:7 (April 15, 2004). pp. 32ff.

Bailey, Russell, and Barbara Tierney. "Information Commons Redux: Concept, Evolution, and Transcending the Tragedy of the Commons." *Journal of Academic Librarianship.* 28:5 (September 2002). pp. 277ff.

Bazillion, Richard J., and Connie Braun. "Academic Library Design: Building Teaching Instrument." *Computers in Libraries.* 14:2 (1994). pp. 12ff.

Beagle, Donald. "Conceptualizing an Information Commons." *Journal of Academic Librarianship.* 25:2 (March 1999). pp. 82ff.

Beagle, Donald. "Extending the Information Commons: From Instructional Testbed to Internet2." *Journal of Academic Librarianship.* 28:5 (September 2002). pp. 287ff.

Bollier, David. "Why We Must Talk About the Information Commons." *Law Library Journal.* 96:2 (Spring 2004). pp. 267ff..

Church, Jennifer. "The Evolving Information Commons." *Library Hi Tech.* 23:1 (2005). pp. 75ff.

Church, Jennifer, Jason Vaughan, Wendy Starkweather, and Katherine Rankin. "The Information Commons at Lied Library (UNLV)." *Library Hi Tech.* 20:1 (2002). pp. 58ff.

Cowgill, Allison, et al. "Implementing an Information Commons in a University Library." *Journal of Academic Librarianship*. 27:6 (November 2001). pp. 432ff.

Crockett, Charlotte, et al. "Integrating Services in the Information Commons—Toward a Holistic Library and Computing Environment." *Library Administration & Management*. 16:4 (Fall 2002). pp. 181ff.

Ehrmann, Stephen C. "Beyond Computer Literacy: Implications of Technology for the Content of a College Education." *Liberal Education*. (Fall 2004). pp. 6ff. http://www.aacu-edu.org/liberaleducation/le-fa04/le-fa04feature1.cfm

"The Fate of the Undergraduate Library: Views of Six Librarians and one Faculty Member." *Library Journal*. 125:18 (November 1, 2000). pp.38ff.

Gardner, Susan, and Susanna Eng. "What Students Want: Generation Y and the Changing Function of the Academic Library." *Libraries & the Academy*. 5:3 (July 2005). pp. 405ff.

Garrett Hardin, "The Tragedy of the Commons," *Science*. 161 (December 1968). pp. 1243ff.

Green, Marybeth, and Daniel V. Eastmond. "The Information Commons: A Public Policy Report." *Quarterly Review of Distance Education*. 6:4 (Winter 2005). pp. 409ff.

Halbert, Martin. "Lessons from the Information Commons Frontier." *Journal of Academic Librarianship*. 25:2 (March 1999). pp. 90ff.

Holmes-Wong, Deborah, et al. "If You Build It, They Will Come: Spaces, Values, and Services in the Digital Era." *Library Administration & Management*. 11:2 (Spring 1997). pp. 81ff.

Hughes, Carol Ann. "Facework: A New Role for the Next Generation of Library-Based Information Technology Centers." *Library Hi Tech*. 16:3-4 (1998). pp. 27ff.

Hughes, Carol Ann. "Information Services for Higher Education, A New Competitive Space." *D-Lib Magazine*. 6:12 (December 2000). (Text version available at http://www.dlib.org/dlib/december00/hughes/12hughes.html#ref29)

Kratz, Charles. "Transforming the Delivery of Service: The Joint-use Library and Information Commons." *College & Research Libraries News*. 64:2 (February 2003). pp. 100ff. http://www.lita.org/Content/NavigationMenu/ACRL/Publications/College_and_Research_Libraries_News/Back_Issues__2003/February1/Transforming_delivery_ofservice.htm

Lippincott, Joan K. "New Library Facilities: Opportunities for Collaboration." *Resource Sharing & Information Networks*. 17:1/2 (2004). p. 147.

Lowry, Anita. "The Information Arcade at the University of Iowa." *Cause/Effect*. 17:3 (Fall 1994). pp. 38ff.

MacWhinnie, Laurie A. "The Information Commons: The Academic Library Of The Future" *portal: Libraries and the Academy*. 3:2, (April 2003). pp. 241ff.

Miller, Michael. "Anticipating the Future: The University of Michigan's Media Union." *Library HiTech*. 16:1 (1998). pp. 71ff.

Oblinger, Diana. "Leading the Transition from Classrooms to Learning Spaces." *EDUCAUSE Quarterly*. 28:1 (2005). pp. 14ff.

Orgeron, Elizabeth."Integrated Academic Student Support Services at Loyola University: The Library as a Resource Clearinghouse." *Journal of Southern Academic and Special Librarianship*. 2:3 (Spring 2001). http://southernlibrarianship.icaap.org/indexv2.html

Pierce, Jennifer Burek. "Next Stop, Information Commons." *American Libraries*. 35:4 (April 2004). p. 87.

Tompkins, Philip. "New Structures for Teaching Libraries." *Library Administration & Management*. 4 (Spring 1990). pp. 77ff.

Presentations

Acker, Stephen R. and Michael D. Miller. "Stewardship of the Information Commons: Cultural, Service, and Operational Issues." Presented at EDUCAUSE Annual Conference, 2004. (ID: EDU0479).

Bailey, Russell. "Information Commons Services for Learners and Researchers: Evolution in Patron Needs, Digital Resources and Scholarly Publishing." Presented at INFORUM 2005, Prague, Czech Republic
http://www.inforum.cz/inforum2005/english/prispevek.php-prispevek=32.htm

Beagle, Donald. "Visions Going Forward." Presented at Triangle Research Libraries Network, 2005. Chapel Hill, NC.
http://www.unc.edu/~pmpittma/InfoCommons/Visions%20Going%20Forward.ppt

Beatty, Susan. "The Information Commons at the University of Calgary: Strategies for Integration." PowerPoint slides from a presentation at the 1st International Conference on IT and Information Literacy in Glasgow, March, 2002.
www.iteu.gla.ac.uk/elit/itilit2002/papers/ppt/06.ppt

Cowgill, Allison. "The Information Commons Challenge." PowerPoint slides from a presentation at the American Library Assoc. MARS Chair's Program in Toronto, June 22, 2003.
www.iub.edu/~librcsd/mars/2003annual/MARS2003Cowgill.ppt

"Elements of an Information Commons. . . ." EDUCAUSE 2005 Workshop Presented at EDUCAUSE in Australasia 2005 Conference, Auckland, Australia.
http://www.educause2005.auckland.ac.nz/interactive/presentations/3%20Elements%20and%20coll aboration.pdf

Gjelten, Daniel R., et al. "The Architecture of an Idea: The Information Commons and the Future of the Academic Library. Presented at EDUCAUSE Annual Conferences, 2004. (ID: EDU4107)

Mountifield, Hester M. "Learning . . . with a Latte. The Kate Edger Information Commons—providing student-centred learning support. Presented at EDUCAUSE in Australasia 2003 Conference, Adelaide, Australia.
http://www.information-commons.auckland.ac.nz/content_files/publications/educause_article.pdf

Stoan, Steve. "The Library as an Instrument for Teaching and Learning." Presented at the 2002 Workshop on the Transformation of the College Library, Council of Independent Colleges Conference (Sept. 19–21, 2002), Columbia, Maryland.
http://www.cic.edu/conferences_events/workshop/library/2002/steve_stoan.asp

Other Publications, Reports, Papers

Freeman, Geoffrey E., et al. "Library as Place: Rethinking Roles, Rethinking Space."
Council on Library and Information Resources (February 2005).
Available: http://www.clir.org/pubs/abstract/pub129abst.html

King, Helen. The Academic Library in the 21st Century—What Need for a Physical Place? *IATUL Proceedings*. ns 10 (2000).
http://www.iatul.org/conference/proceedings/vol10/papers/king_full.html

Leavey Library, University of Southern California, September 16–17, 2004 Conference. "Information Commons: Learning Space Beyond the Classroom."
www.usc.edu/isd/libraries/locations/leavey/news/conference/presentations/ . . . . .
With accompanying papers by Donald Beagle: "Information Commons to Learning Commons" and "Learning Beyond the Classroom."
http://www.usc.edu/isd/libraries/locations/leavey/news/conference/supplemental_info

Rao, Robert, et al. Public Access to Information and the Creation of an 'Information Commons.'" Proceedings of the 76th ASIS&T Annual Meeting, vol. 41 (2004). pp.198ff.

Wilson, Lizabeth A. "Collaborate or Die: Designing Library Space." ARL Bimonthly Report 222 (2002).
http://www.arl.org/newsltr/222/collabwash.html

Index

About the Contributors

Dr. Donald Russell Bailey is currently Library Director at Providence College. He formerly served as Associate University Librarian for Information Commons, University of North Carolina at Charlotte. Dr. Bailey co-authored (with Barbara Tierney) "Information Commons Redux: Concept, Evolution, and Transcending the Tragedy of the Commons." *Journal of Academic Librarianship* 28:5 (Sept. 2002) pp.277ff. He was Contributing Author, *Multicultural Resources on the Internet*, Libraries Unlimited, 1999 and Author, "U.S. Influences on Korean Education..." Fulbright Occasional Papers, 1996.

Dr. Bailey has also organized, convened, and presented at Information Commons and Learning Commons panels and workshops for ACRL/ALA 2003-2006; INFORUM 2005, Prague, Czech Republic. Dr. Bailey received his Ph.D. German Studies (1981, LSU), M.Ed. Gifted Education (1987, LSU), MALIS Academic Librarianship (1995, USF).

Fulbright research, Korea (1990), Japan (1994). He is also composer and artist of two recorded musical ballad collections: *Tossed Ballads* (1984) and *2nd Chants* (1988).

Barbara Tierney is Associate Professor at the J. Murrey Atkins Library, University of North Carolina at Charlotte. She serves as both the Coordinator of the Library's Information Commons Desk and as UNCC Science Reference Librarian. Prior to joining Atkins Library in Feb. 1999, Ms. Tierney served as Senior Librarian for Public Services at San Leandro Public Library (Calif.) and Head of Reference Services for the Monroe County Library System (Mich.). She holds a B.A. Degree in History from Northwestern Univ. and an M.L.S. from the Univ. of Michigan. With Dr. Bailey, she served as co-planner and co-convener of the following IC programs: "Information Commons Issues and Trends: Voices from the Frontline Association of College and Research Libraries, National Conference, April 9, 2003 (Charlotte, N.C.); "Information Commons 101: Nuts and Bolts Planning." Association of College and Research Libraries, Pre-Conference Institute, Jan. 9, 2004 (San Diego, CA)., and "Information Commons 101: Nuts and Bolts Planning." Association of College and Research Libraries, Pre-Conference, June 25, 2004 (Orlando, FL).

About the Author

Donald Beagle joined the faculty of Belmont Abbey College in 2000 as Director of Library Services, having previously served as Head of the Information Commons and as Associate University Librarian at UNC Charlotte. This followed fifteen years in public library management positions, most recently as Regional Branch Head and then Head of Main Library with the Charleston County Public Library in South Carolina. He has also consulted in association with the Himalayan Group (corporate technology consulting) and Informed Strategies (InformedStrategies.com). Beagle did his graduate work at the University of Michigan where he won the Hopwood Writing Award (1977), and was later the first recipient of NCLA's Doralyn J. Hickey Award for his first article about library technology. His research and Web-publication projects have received support from the Benton Foundation, the National Endowment for the Arts, the Apple Library of Tomorrow, and LSTA Digitization grants. Beagle's twenty-four published articles include "Conceptualizing an Information Commons" (1999) which Paul Conway of Duke University has called "... the seminal article that defined the core requirements of an Information Commons." He has presented at state, national, and international conferences.